Museum of Street Art
East Village

June 23, 2017

Created by Benjamin Stein

Designed by Frank Guia

CONTENTS

AREA MAP

*

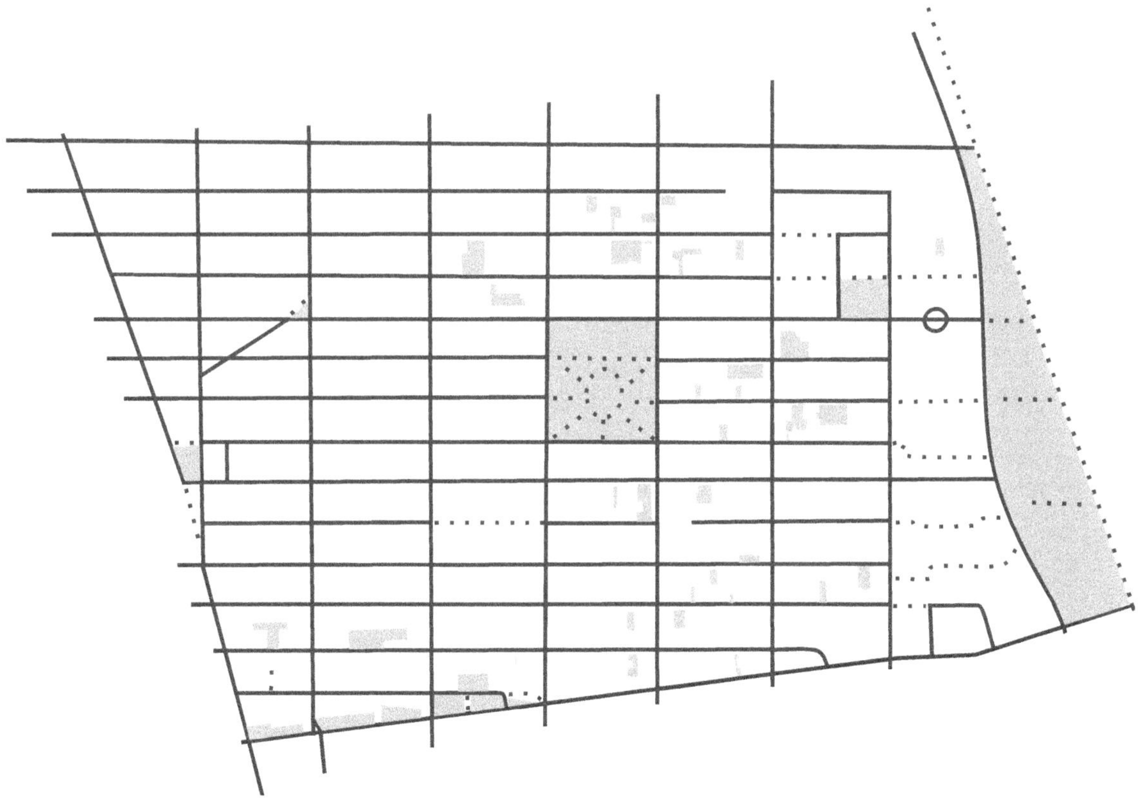

Welcome to the Museum of Street Art (MoSA). One could also say welcome back because there is a chance you have been here before while walking the streets of your city. The MoSA concept is intuitive, but you might not have noticed it unless you were looking for it.

A MoSA is a phenomenon that occurs when you have a high concentration of art and local stakeholder support in a particular outdoor area. This combination creates living, breathing outdoor museums in our cities. Entry is free and daily exhibits are managed by the residents, landlords, local government, visitors, and mother nature. These stakeholders alter the exhibition every day with their competing opinions and priorities, which in turn creates the most dynamic and meritocratic museums in the world. MoSA explores this concept by photographing these museums in their entirety on one particular day, as a record and snapshot in time.

MoSA locations can be found in dozens of cities around the world, but in this edition, we explore the East Village in New York City on June 23, 2017. The East Village has a long history of supporting the arts and showcases a variety of mediums by a host of local and global artists. Read on to see exactly how we captured the exhibit.

METHOD

All photographs were shot sequentially in 14 hours starting at 12 AM midnight on June 23, 2017. The area of interest covers 430 acres known as the East Village, located in Manhattan, New York. Its boundaries from West to East are from Bowery/4th Ave. to East River Park. Its boundaries North to South are from 14th St. to Houston St. The editor systematically canvassed this area by bicycle to capture each piece of art. “The Streets” began at Bowery and Houston and were traversed Northward in ascending order from Houston to 14th St. “The Avenues” began on Avenue D and Houston and were traversed Westward from Avenue D to Bowery/4th Ave.

DOCUMENTATION

Artists are credited if their work can be identified. When the art can not be identified the artist is noted as “Unknown”. Artists are listed in order of their position in the photograph. Artist’s work can be identified from top to bottom, left to right in each photo they are credited. Some artists are credited in quotations. This notation indicates that someone else, besides the artist posted their work in the public domain.

THE STREETS

12:00 AM

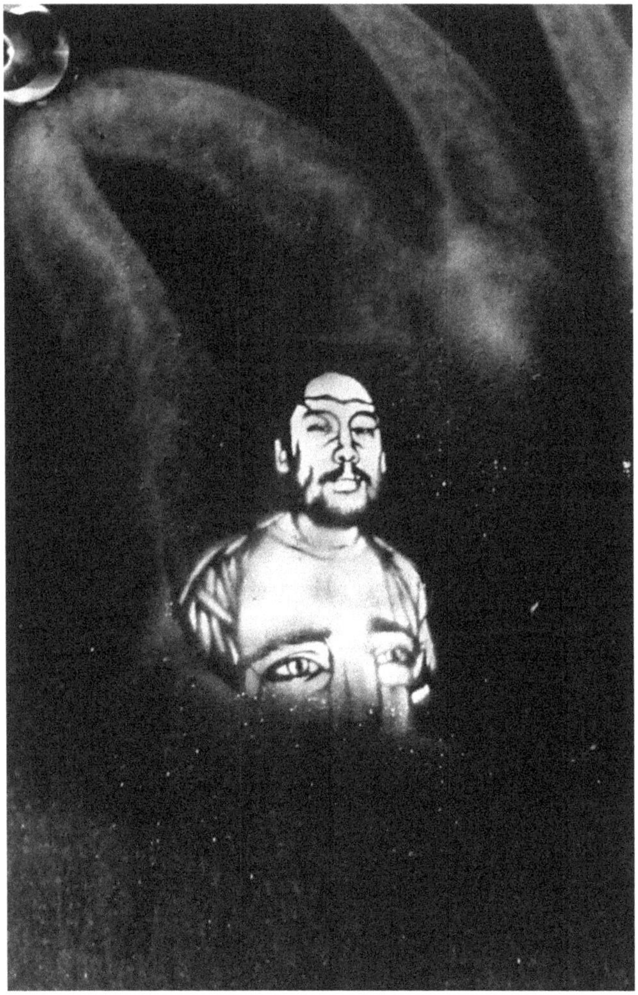

Houston St. & Bowery

Unknown

12:01 AM

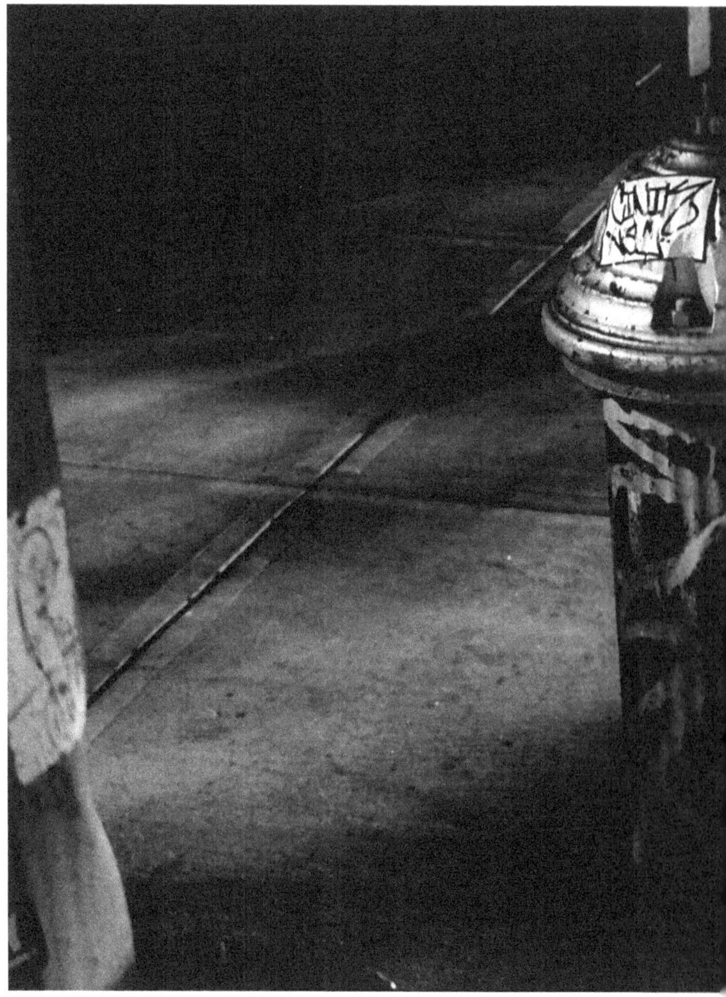

Houston St. & Bowery

Unknown

12:05 AM

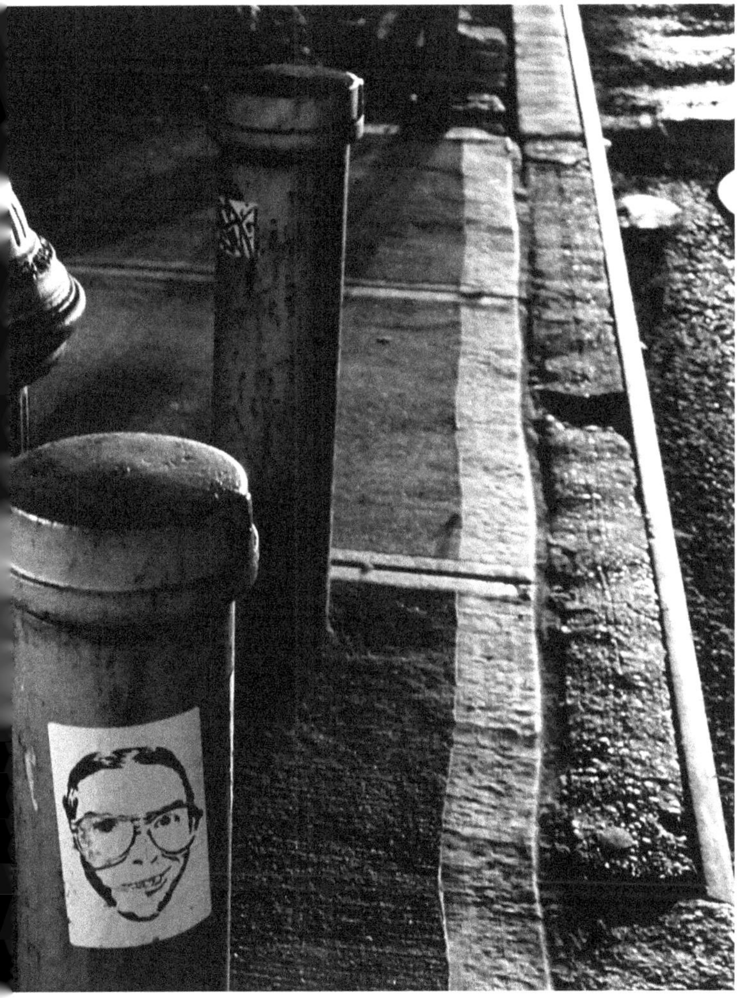

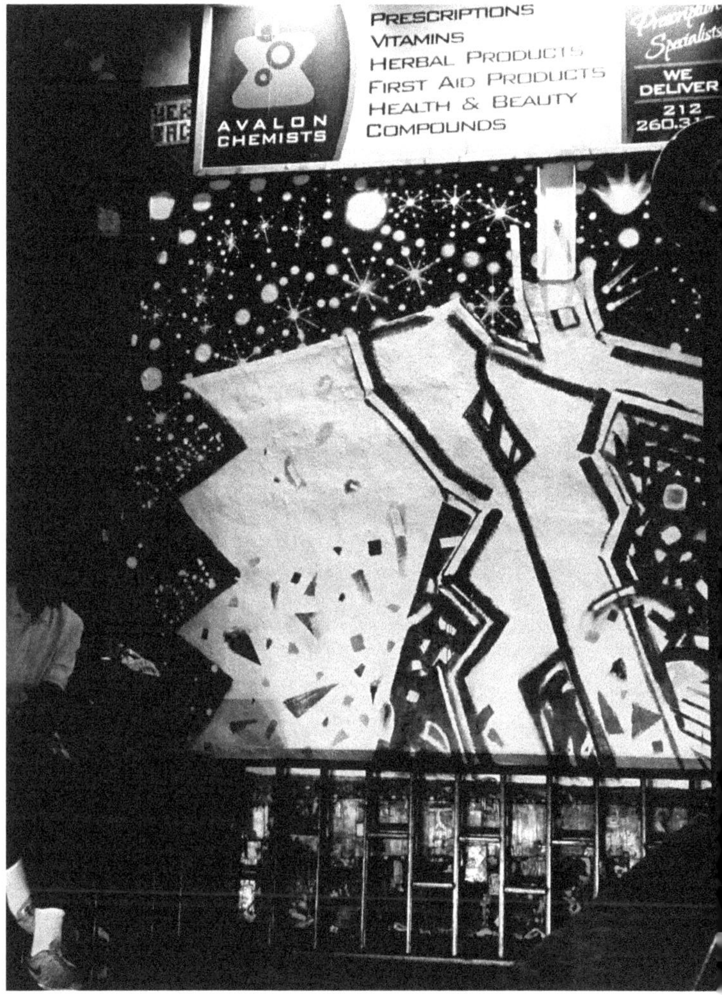

Houston St. & 2nd Ave.

Unknown

12:06 AM

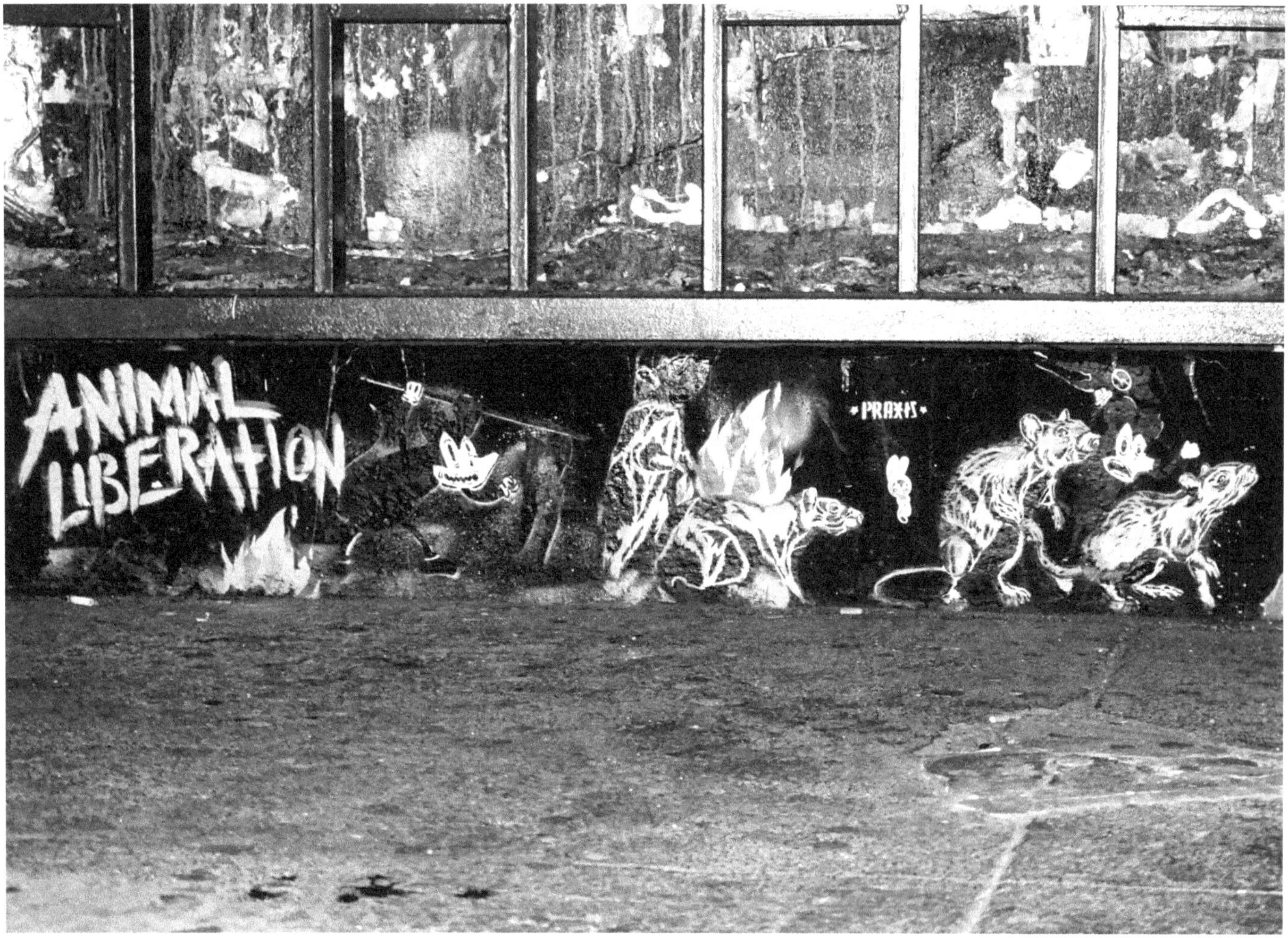

Houston St. & 2nd Ave.

Praxis

12:07 AM

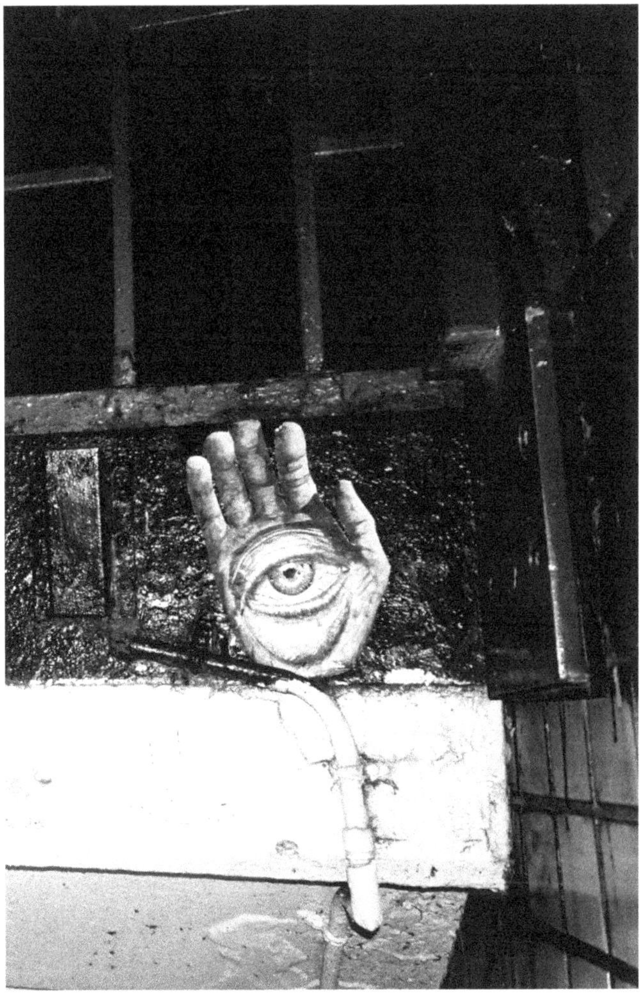

F Train Stairs @ 2nd Ave.

Dr. Scott

12:08 AM

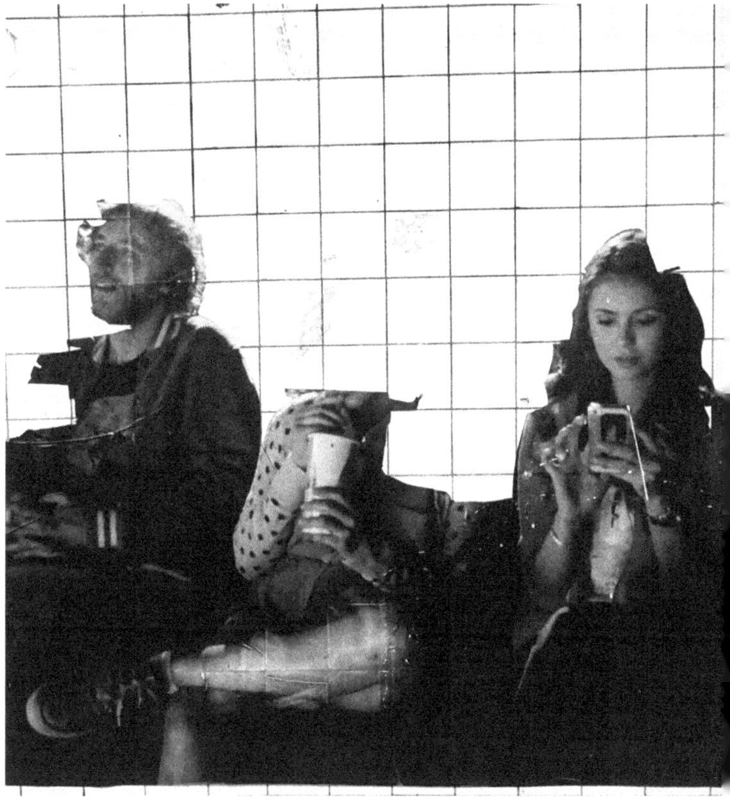

F Train Station @ 2nd Ave.

Unknown

12:12 AM

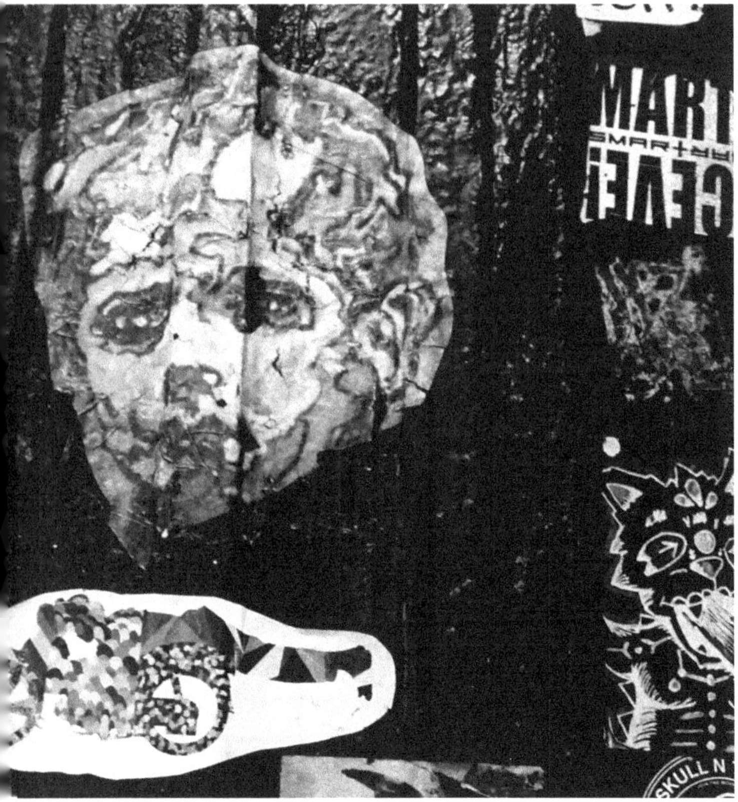

Houston St. & 2nd Ave.

Unknown

12:23 AM

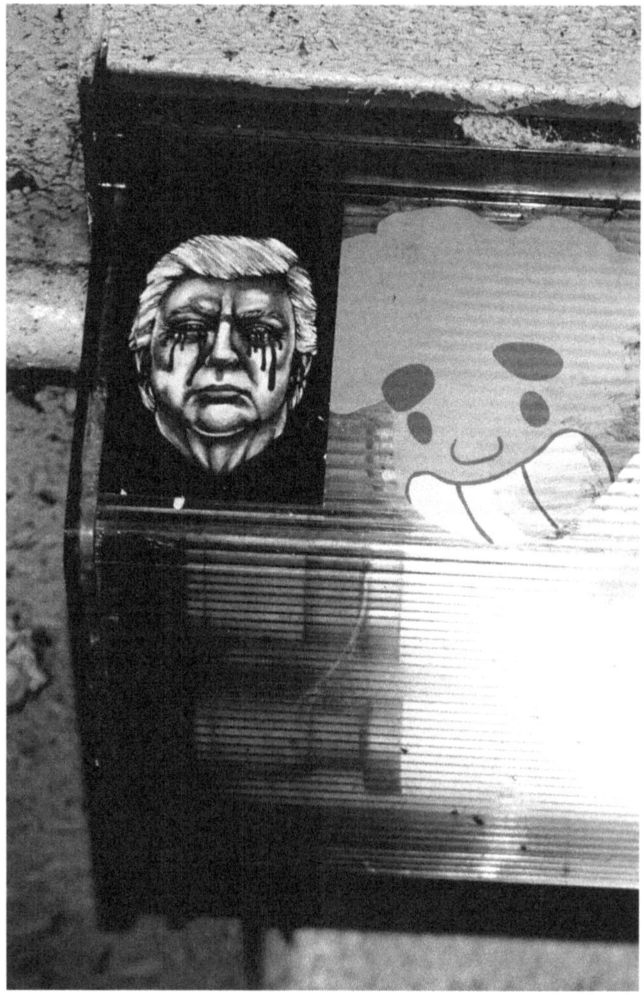

F Train Stairs @ 1st Ave.

Unknown

12:24 AM

F Train Stairs @ 1st Ave.

Unknown

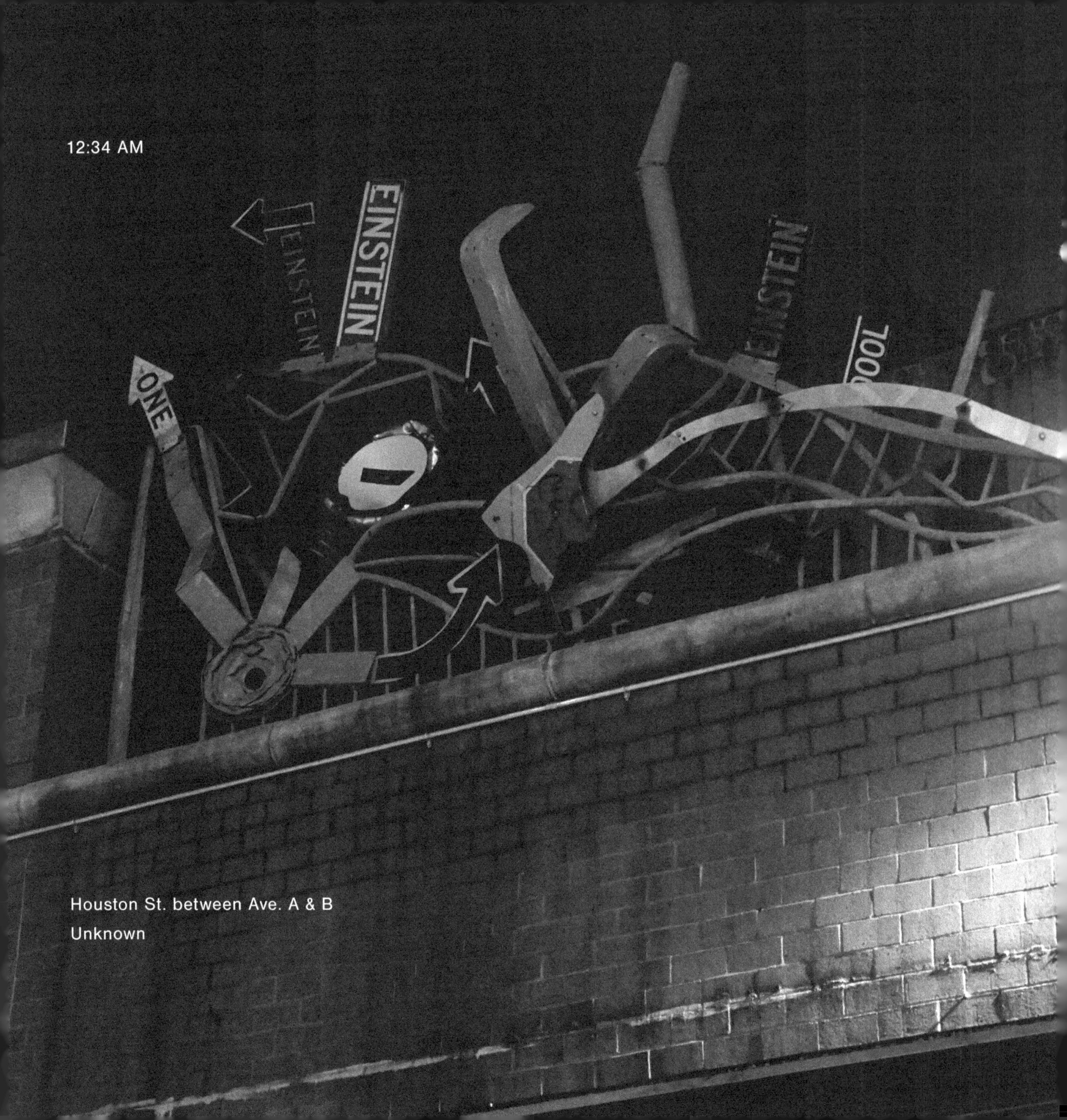

12:34 AM

Houston St. between Ave. A & B

Unknown

12:46 AM

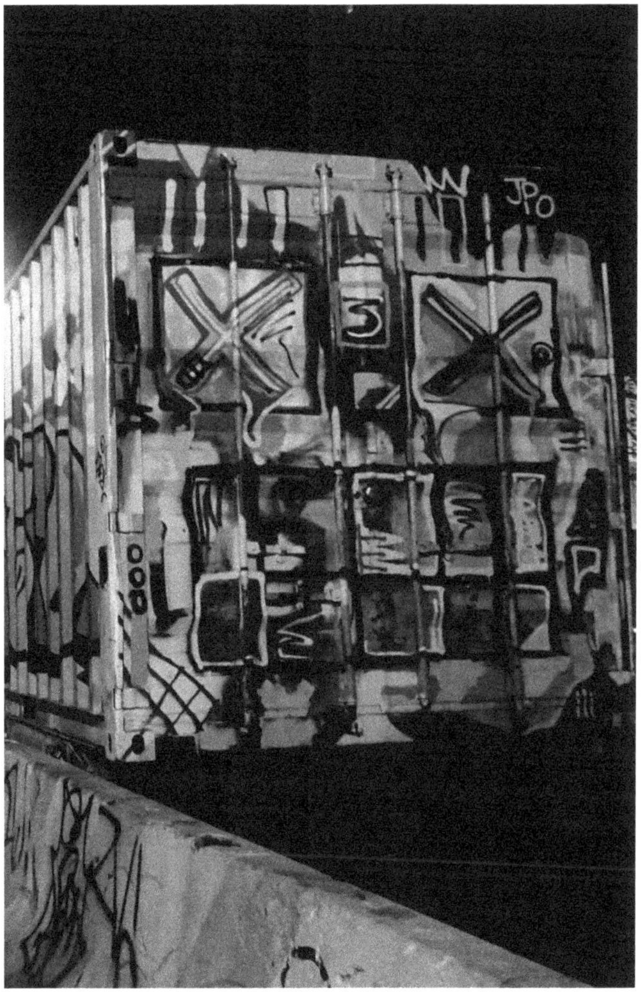

1st St. between 1st & Ave. A

JPO

12:47 AM

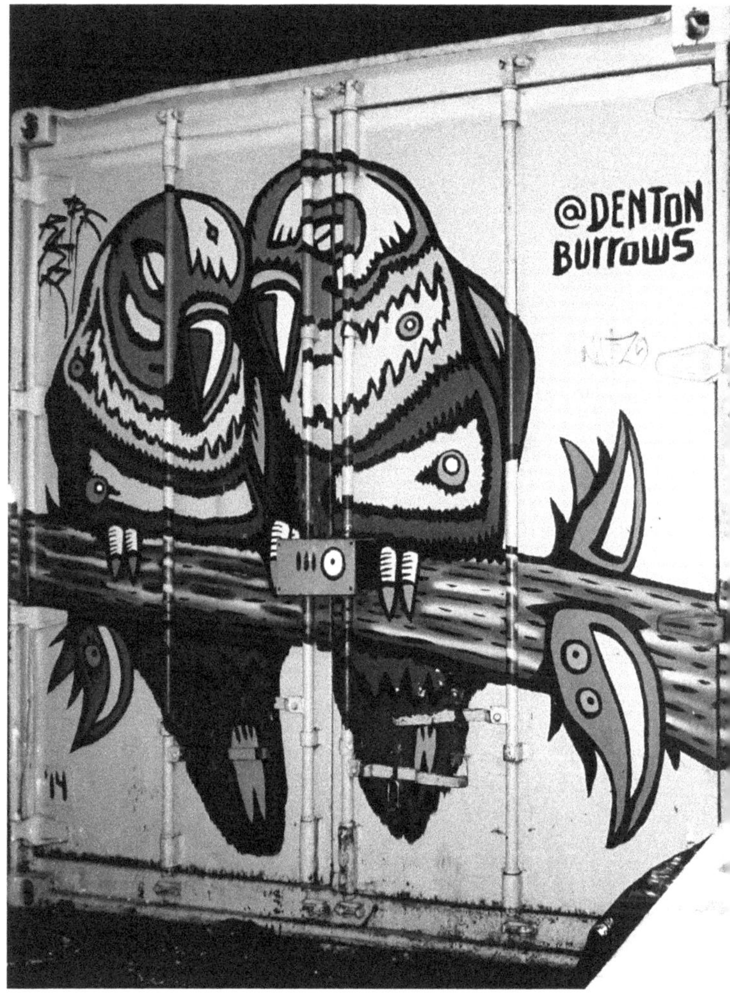

1st St. between 1st & Ave. A

Denton Burrows

12:48 AM

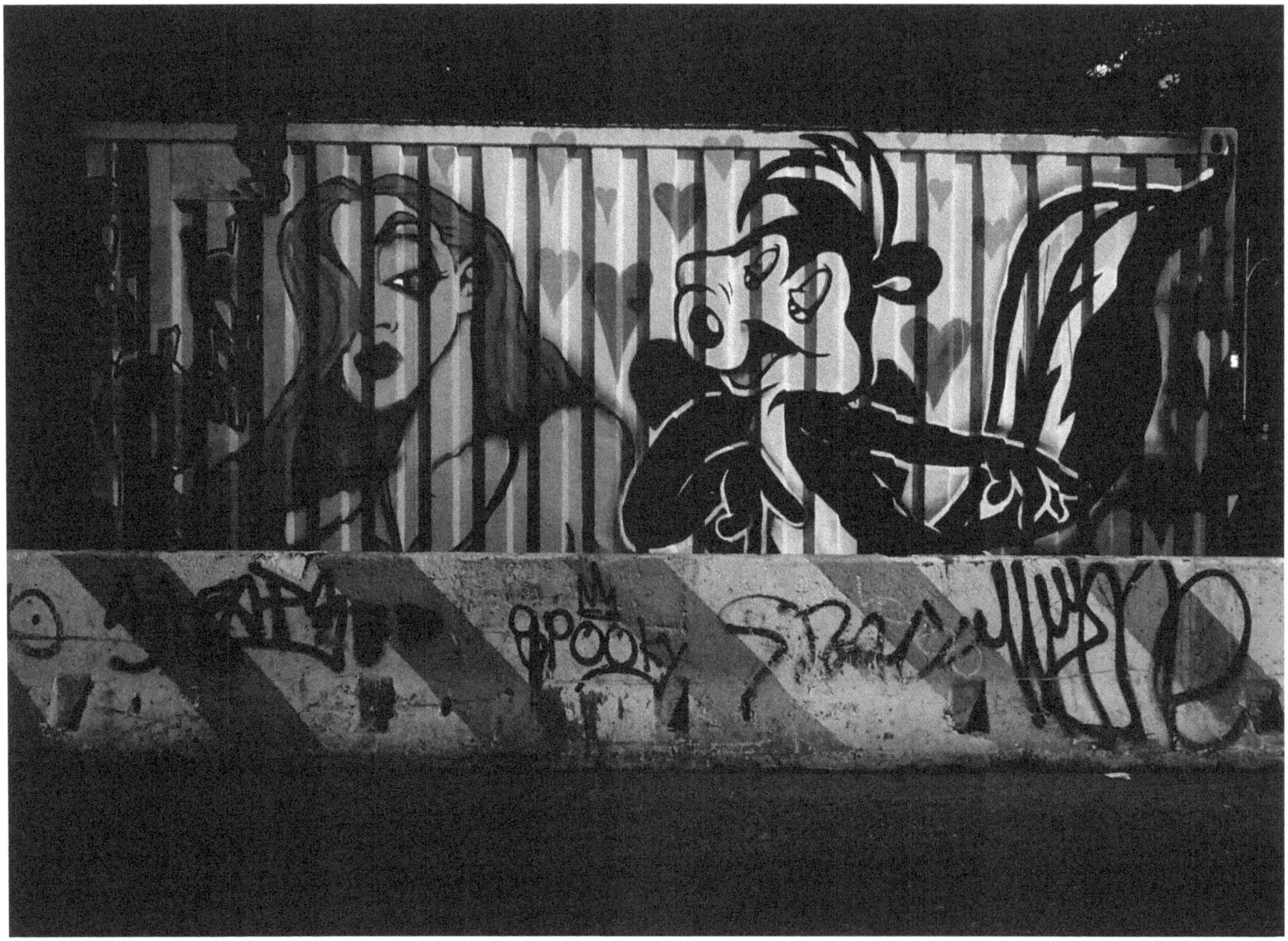

1st St. between 1st & Ave. A

Cram

12:51 AM

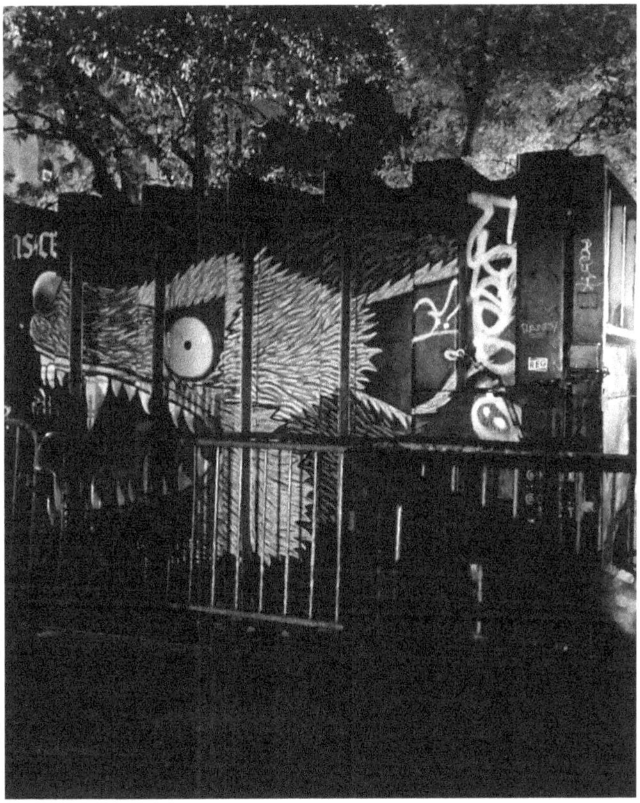

1st St. between 1st & Ave. A

Nicole Salgar & Chuck Berrett

12:55 AM

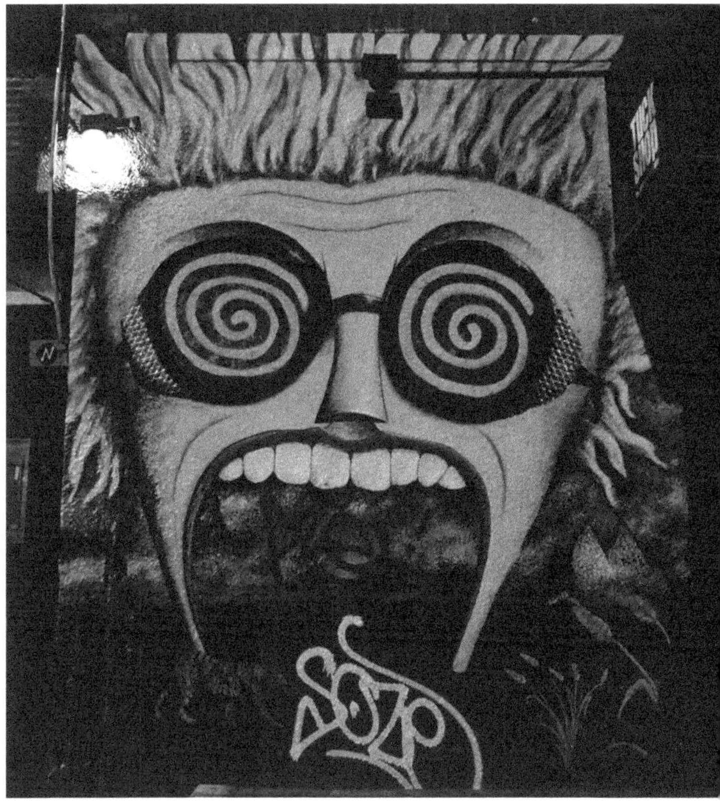

1st St. between 1st & 2nd Ave.

Unknown

12:56 AM

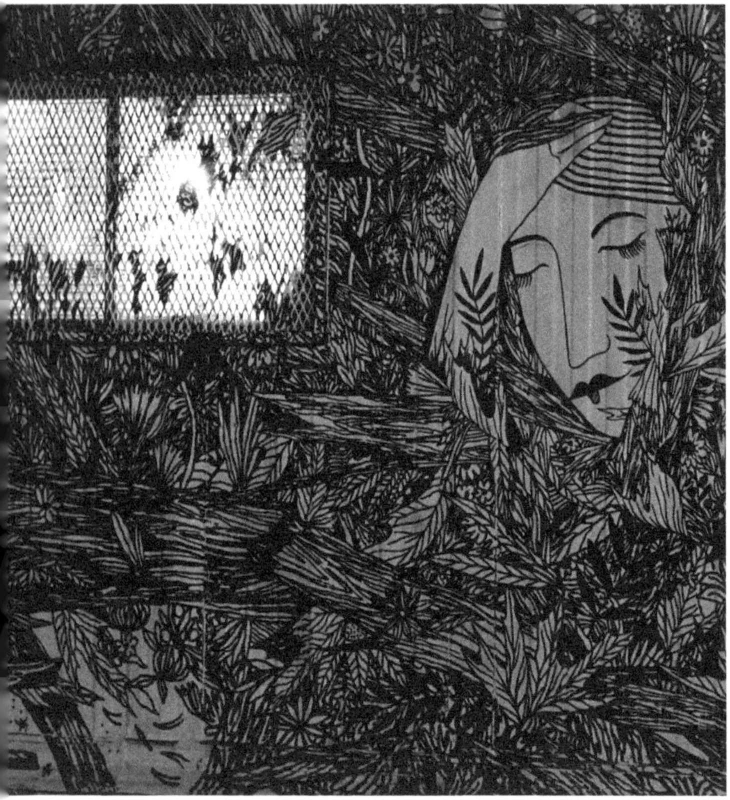

1st St. between 1st & 2nd Ave.

Hydeon

12:57 AM

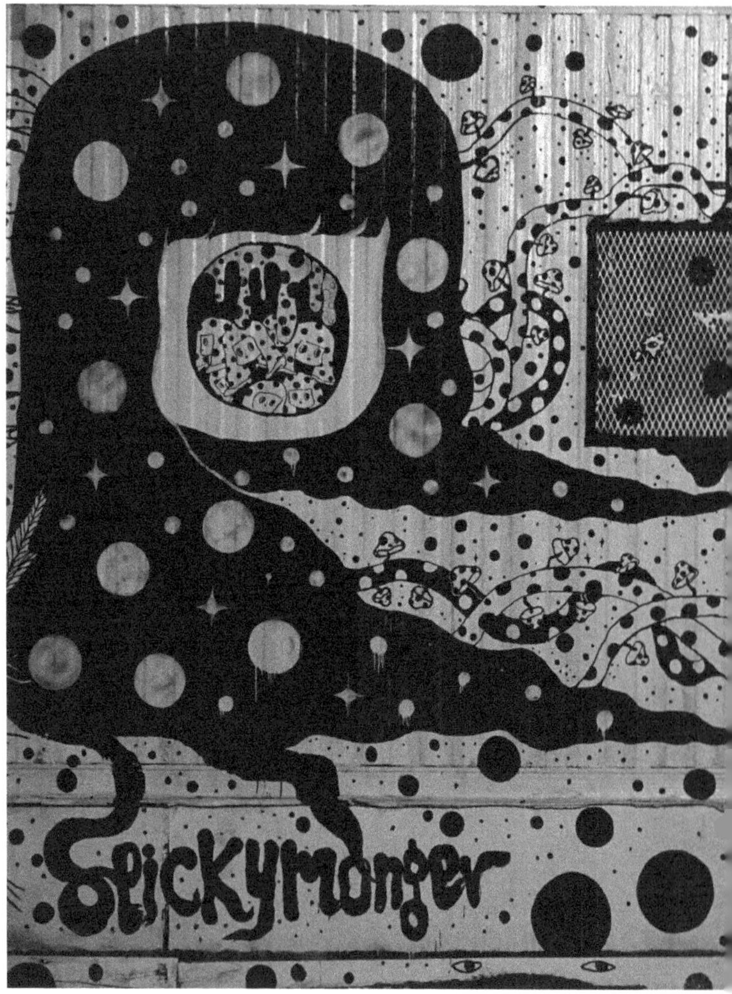

1st St. between 1st & 2nd Ave.

Stickymonger

12:57 AM

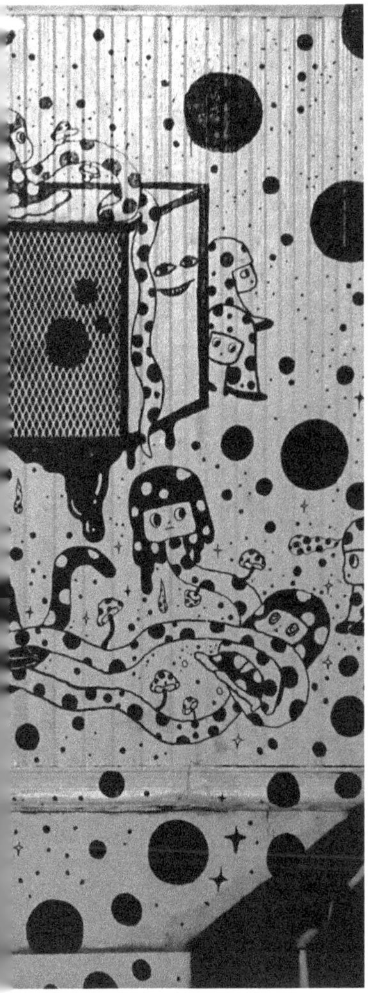

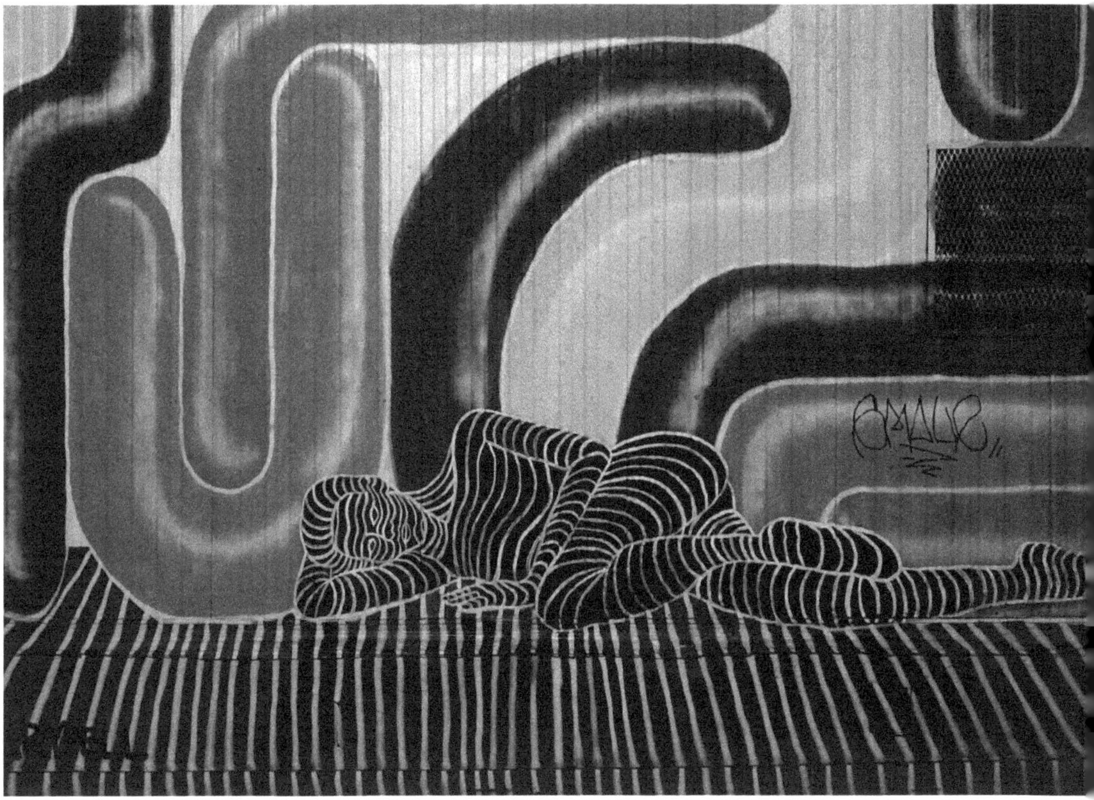

1st St. between 1st & 2nd Ave.

Jenna Krypell

1:00 AM

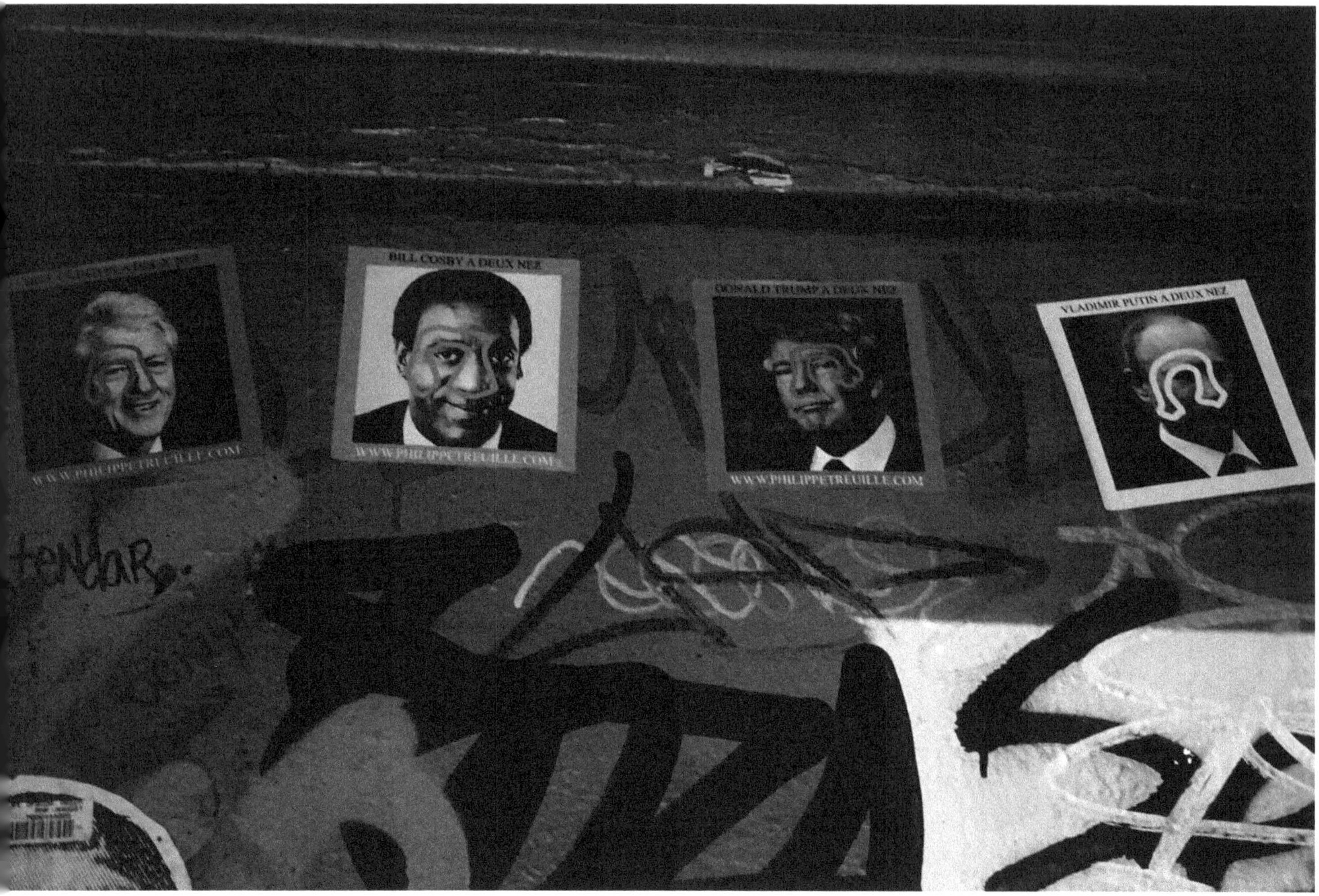

1st St. between 1st & 2nd Ave.

Philippe Treuille

1:05 AM

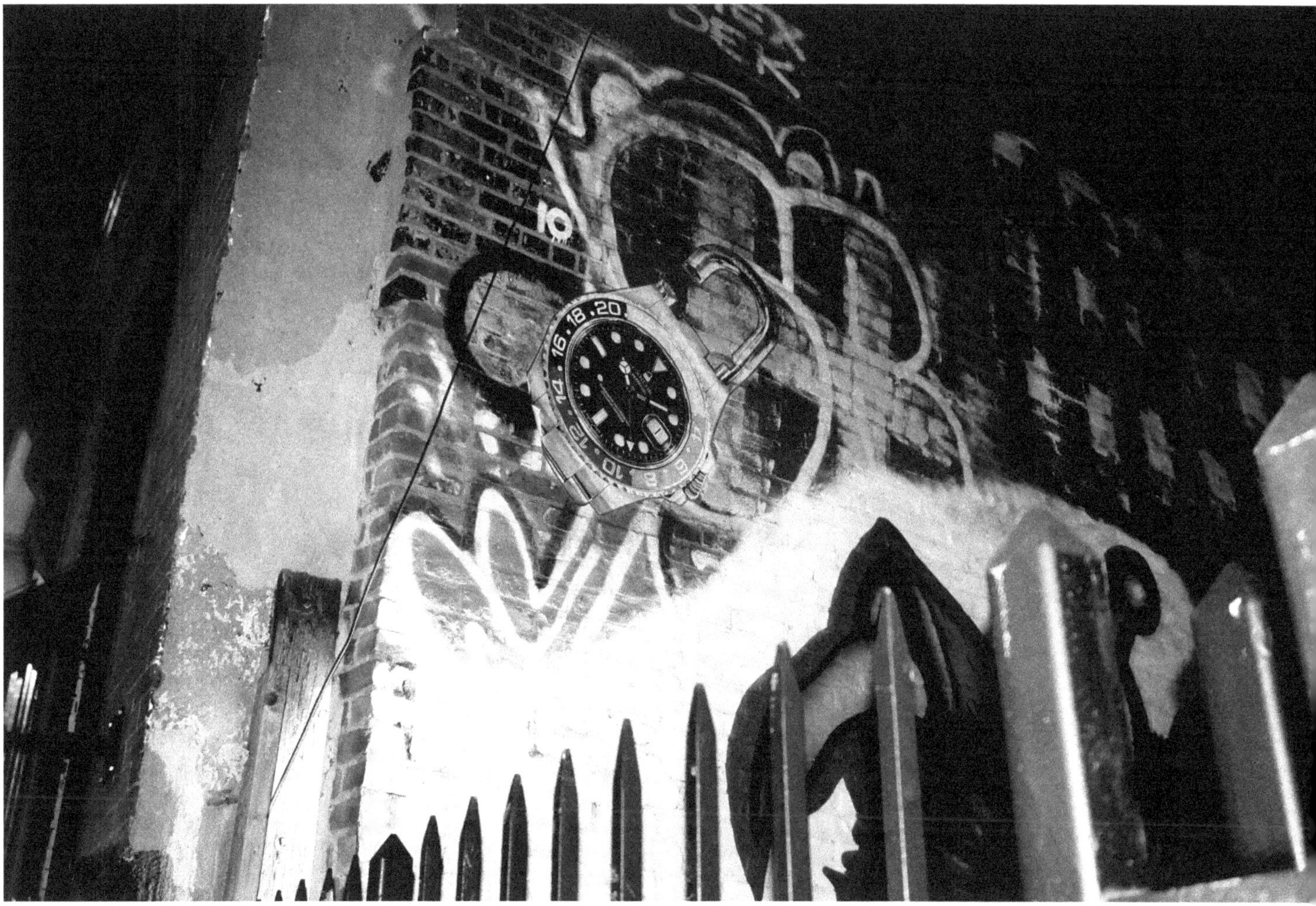

1st St. between 1st & 2nd Ave.

Unlok

1:06 AM

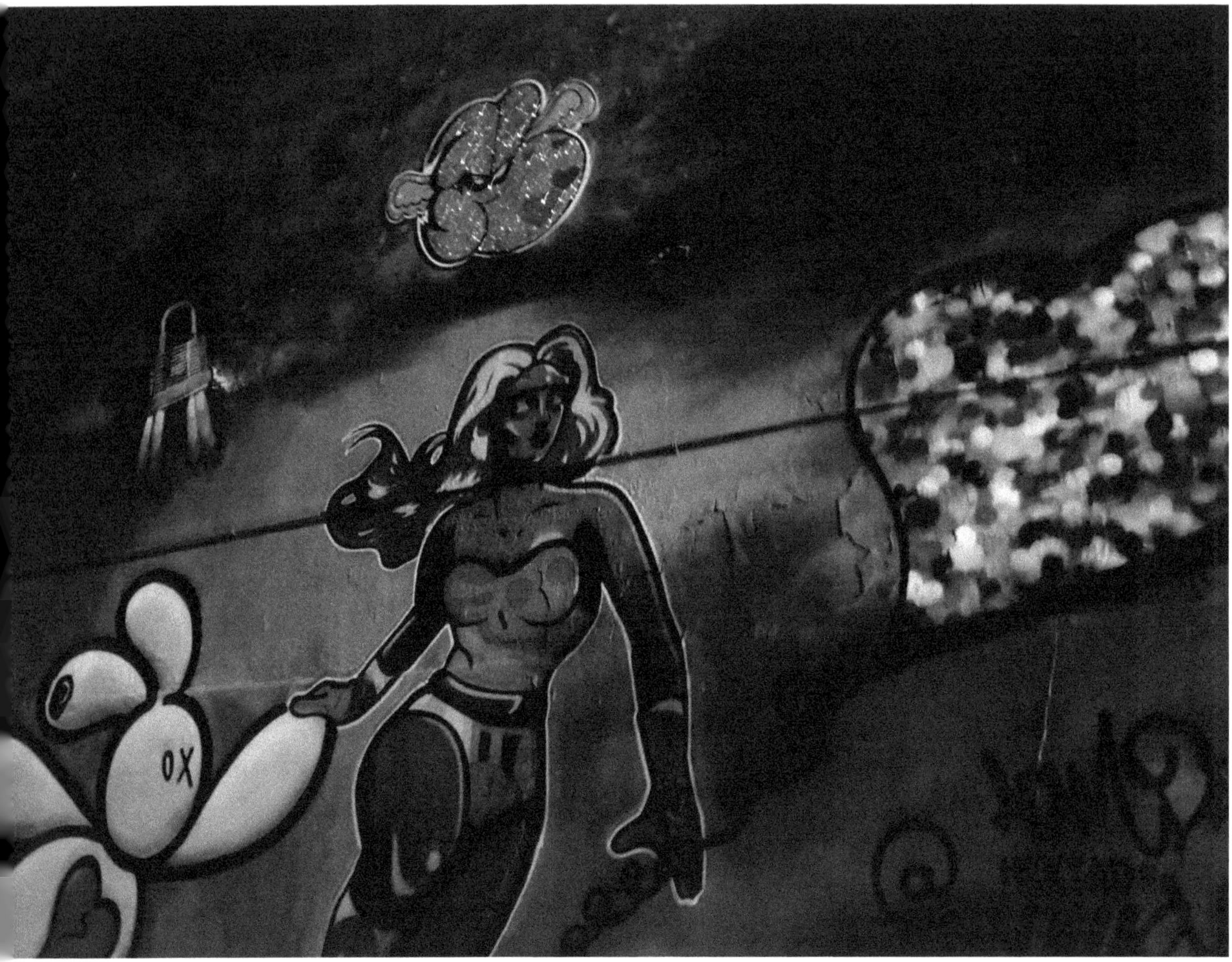

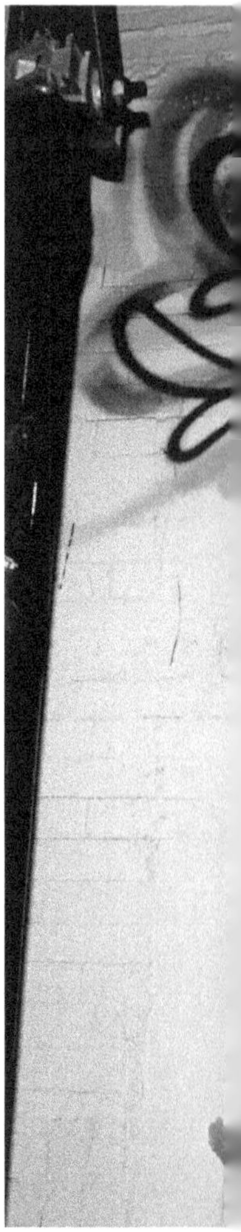

1st St. between 1st & 2nd Ave.

Unlok, Adam Dare, Madman, Kwue Molly, Hektad

1:09 AM

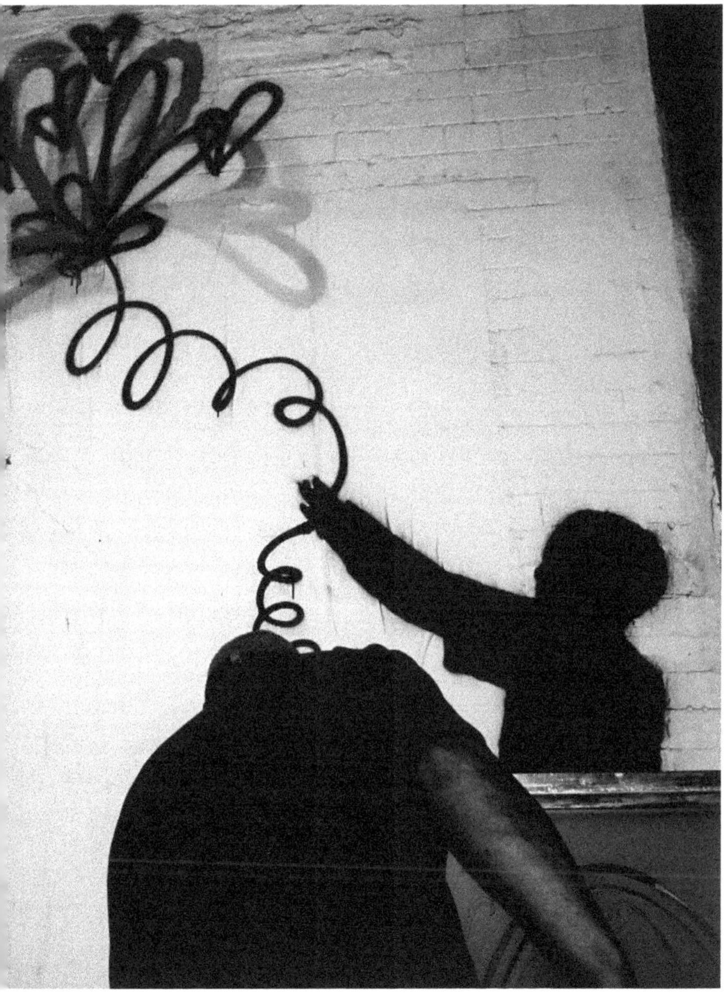

1st St. between 2nd Ave. & Bowery

Hektad

1:13 AM

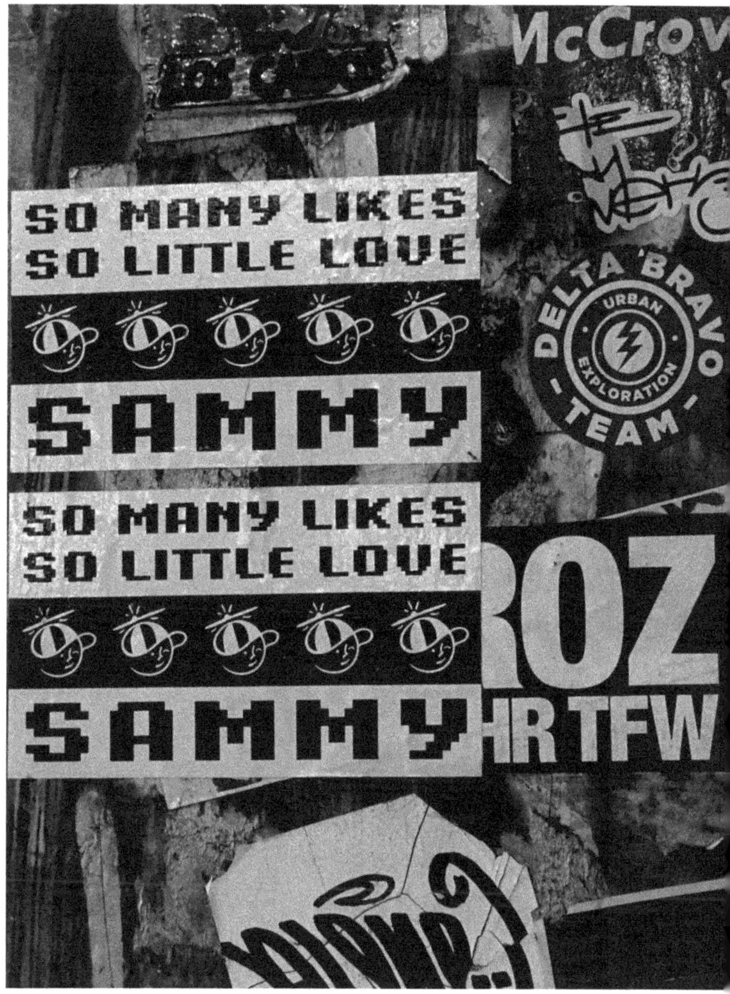

Extra Place

Sammy

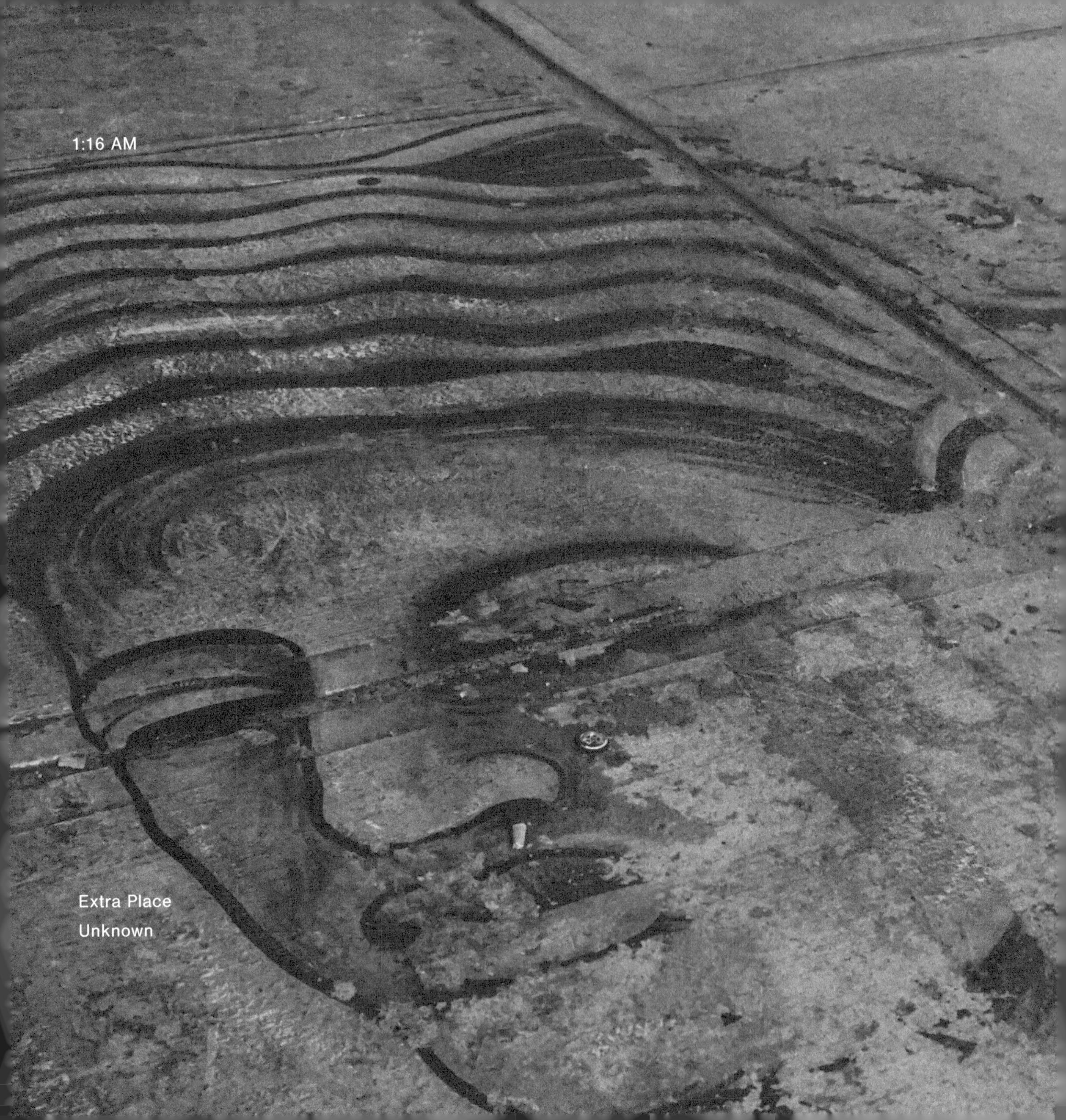

1:16 AM

Extra Place

Unknown

1:17 AM

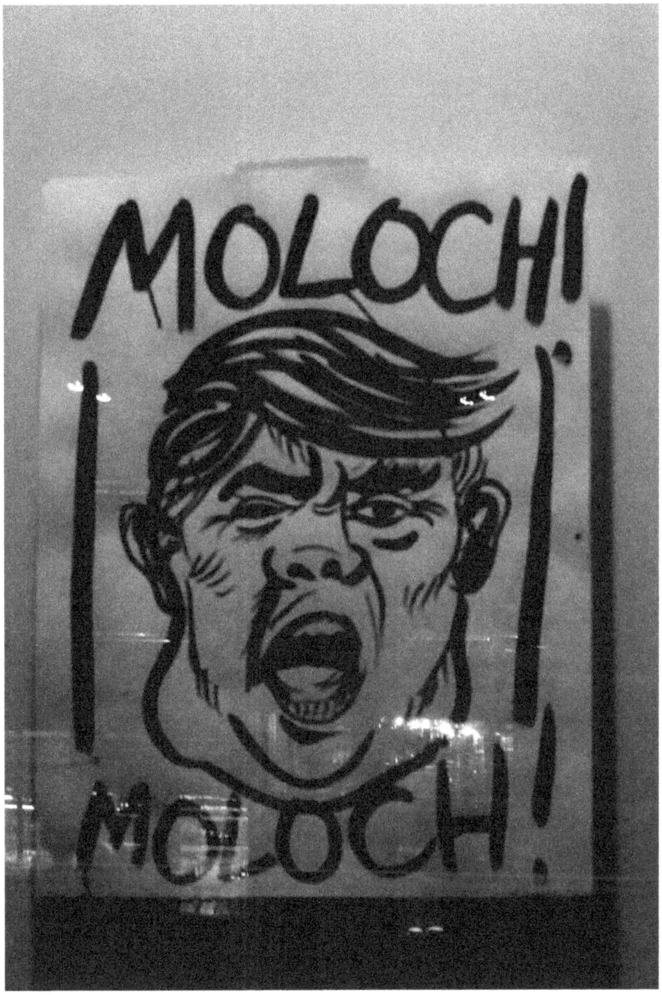

1st St. between 2nd Ave. & Bowery

Unknown

1:23 AM

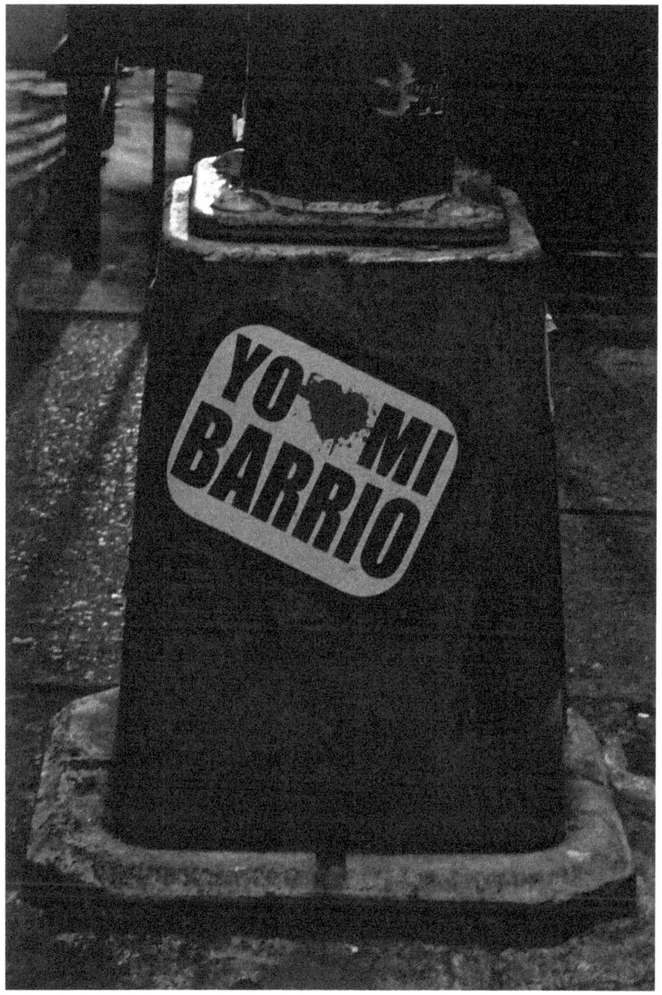

2nd St. between 2nd Ave. & Bowery

Unknown

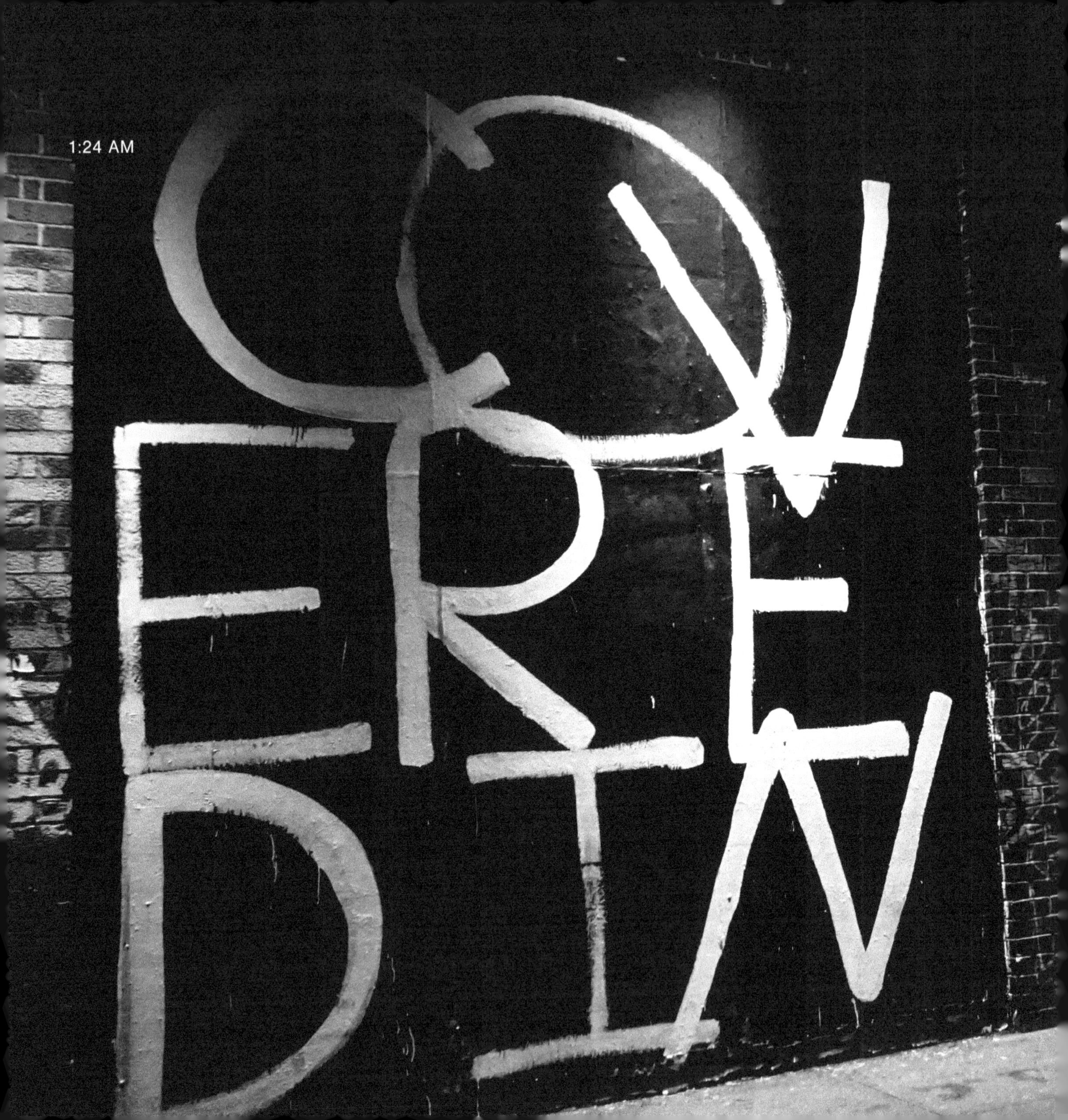

1:24 AM

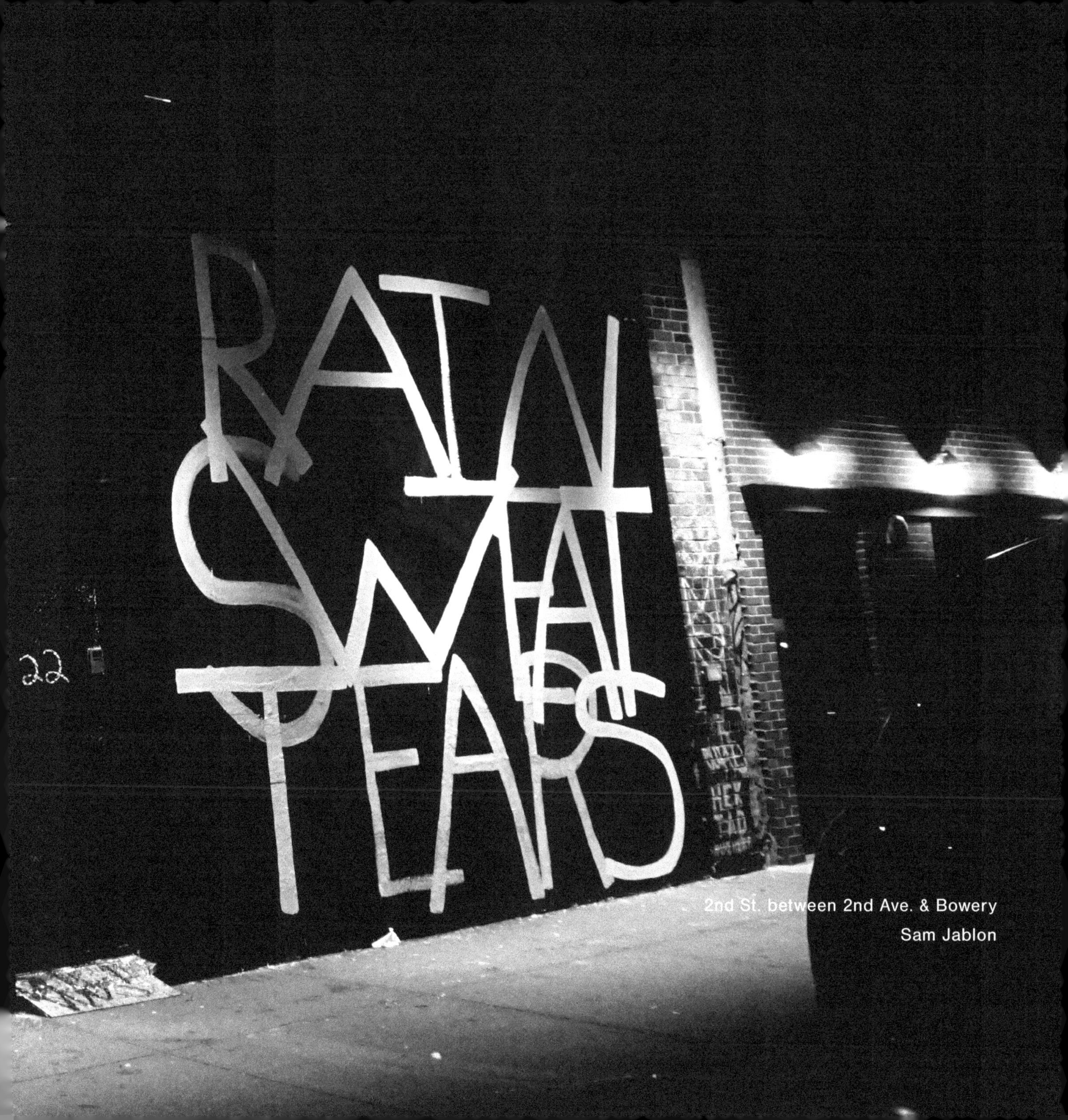

2nd St. between 2nd Ave. & Bowery

Sam Jablon

1:29 AM

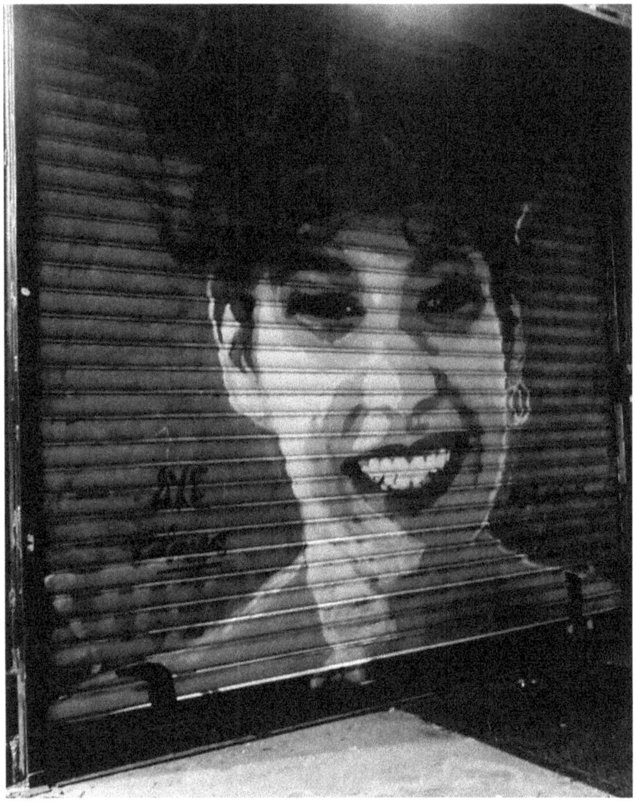

2nd St. between 1st & 2nd Ave.

Axe Colours

1:35 AM

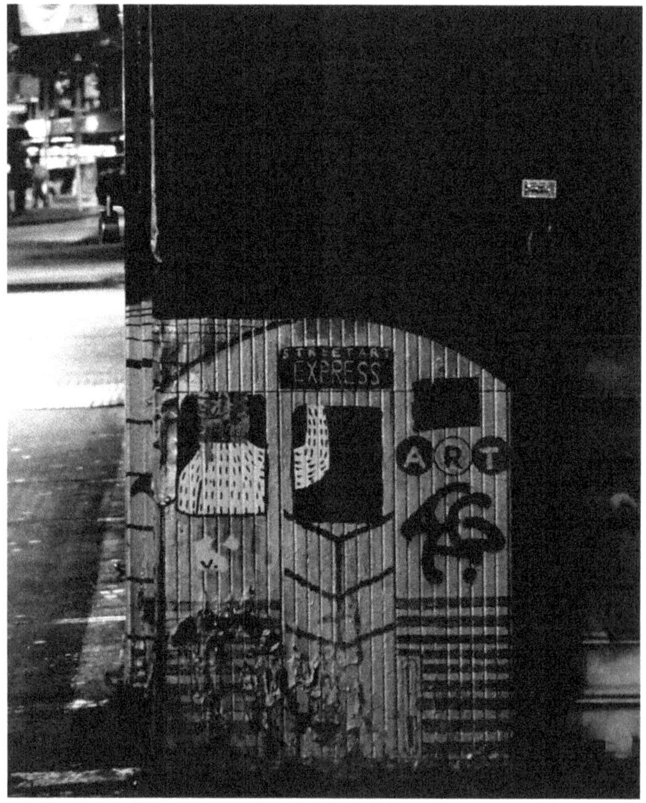

2nd St. between 1st & 2nd Ave.

Adrian Wilson, Brandon Sines

1:38 AM

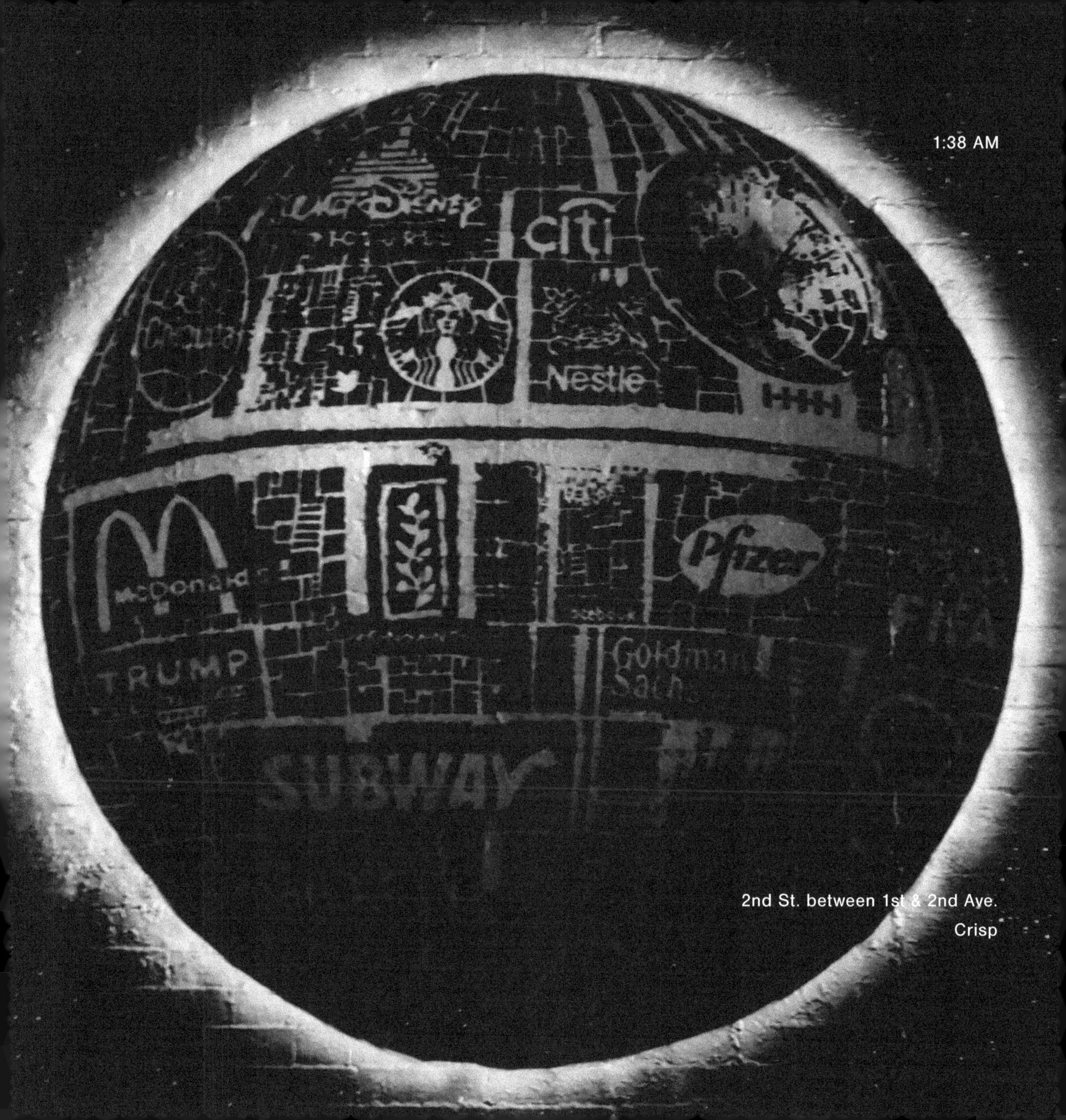

2nd St. between 1st & 2nd Ave.

Crisp

1:42 AM

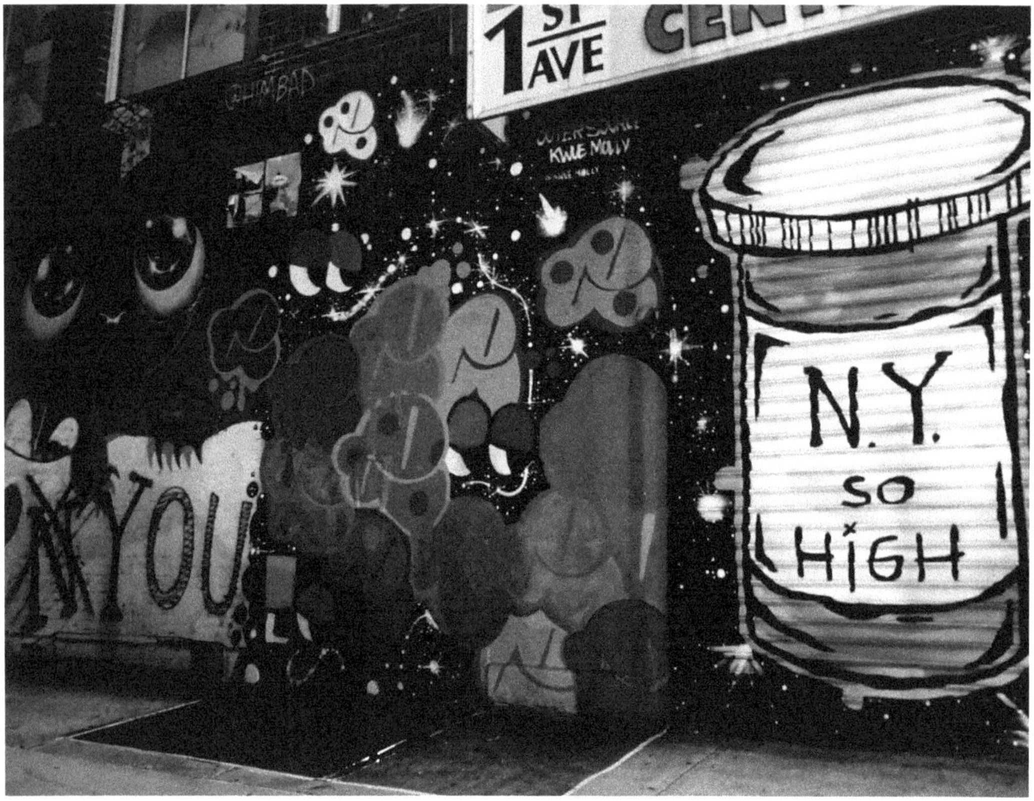

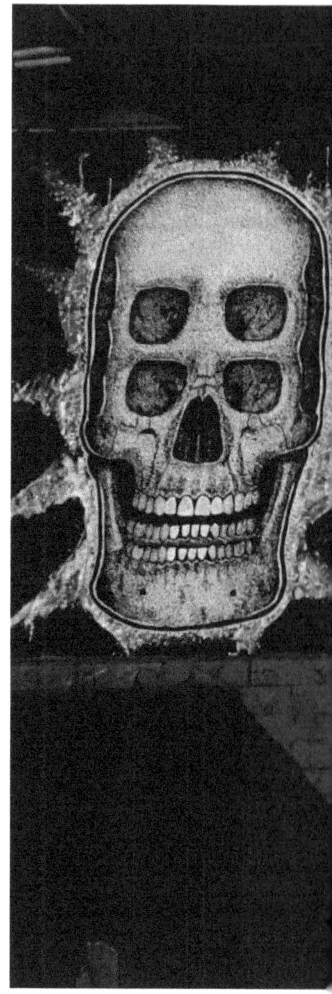

2nd St. between 1st & 2nd Ave.
Himbad, Kwue Molly, Dirt Cobain

1:43 AM

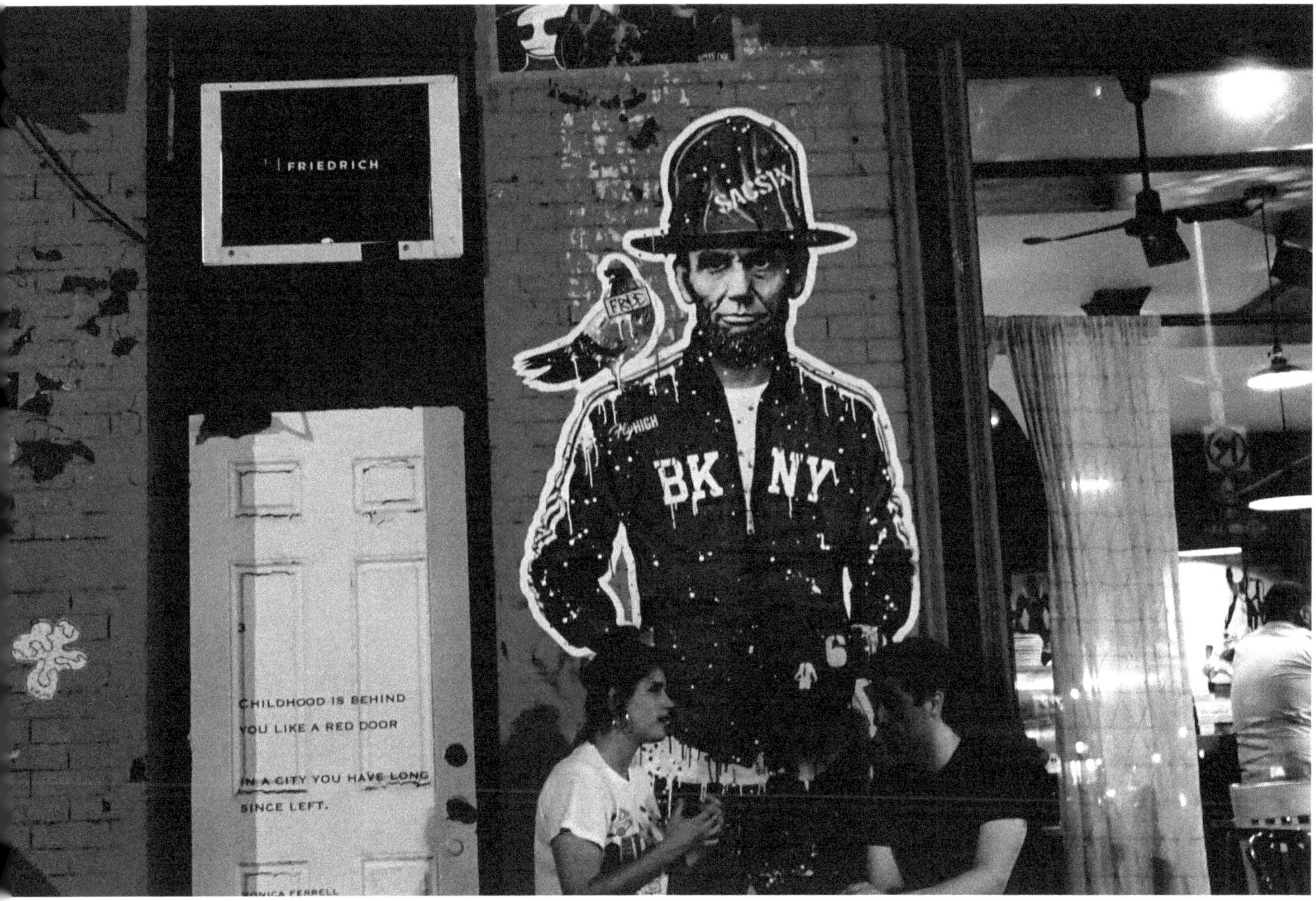

2nd St. between 1st & Ave. A

Dr. Scott, “Monnica Farrel”, Sacsix

1:45 AM

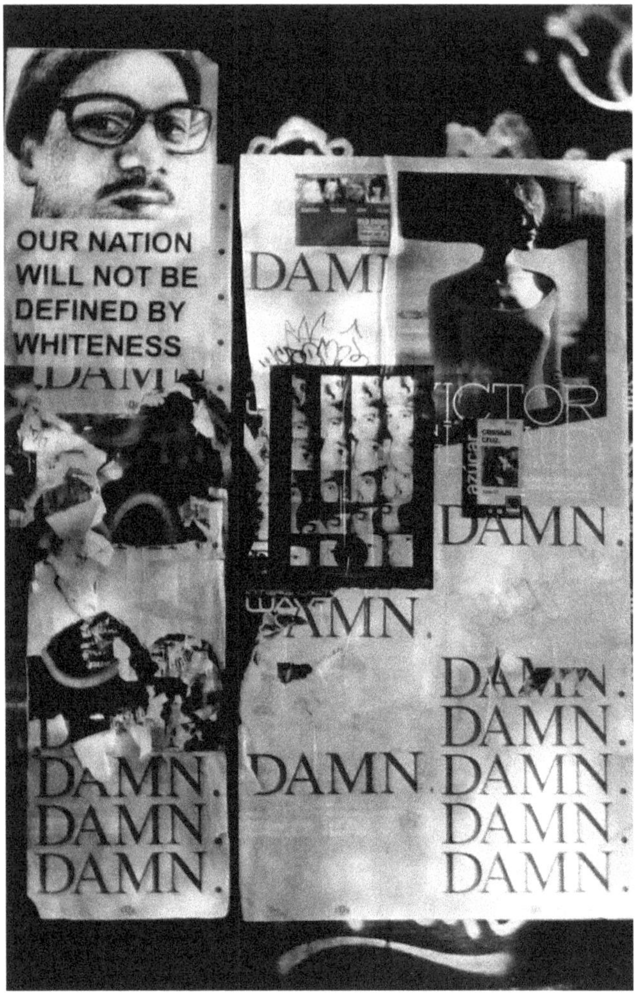

2nd St. between 1st & Ave. A

Unknown

1:46 AM

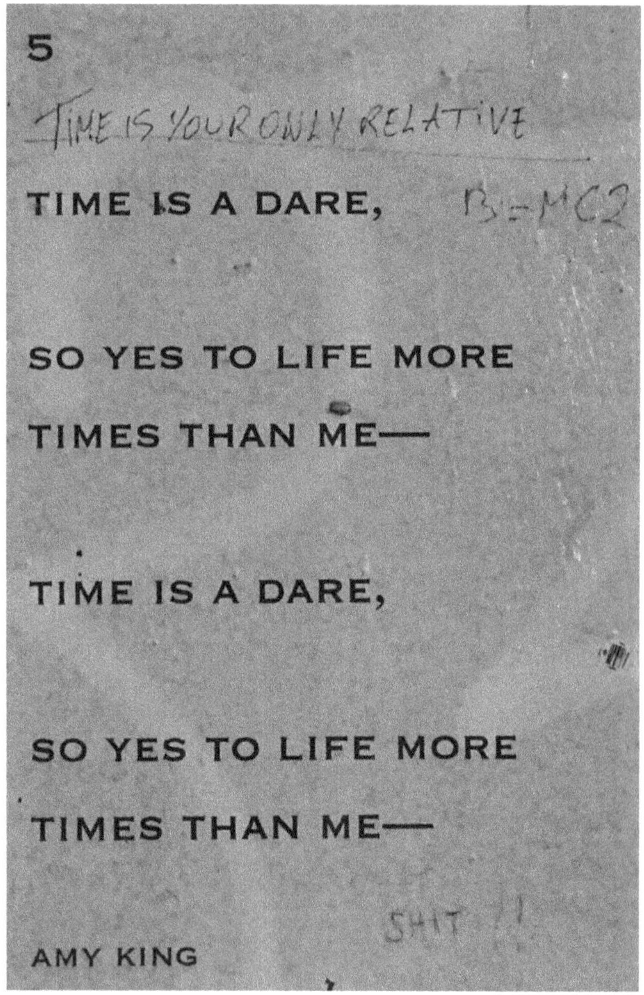

2nd St. between 1st & Ave. A

"Amy King"

1:48 AM

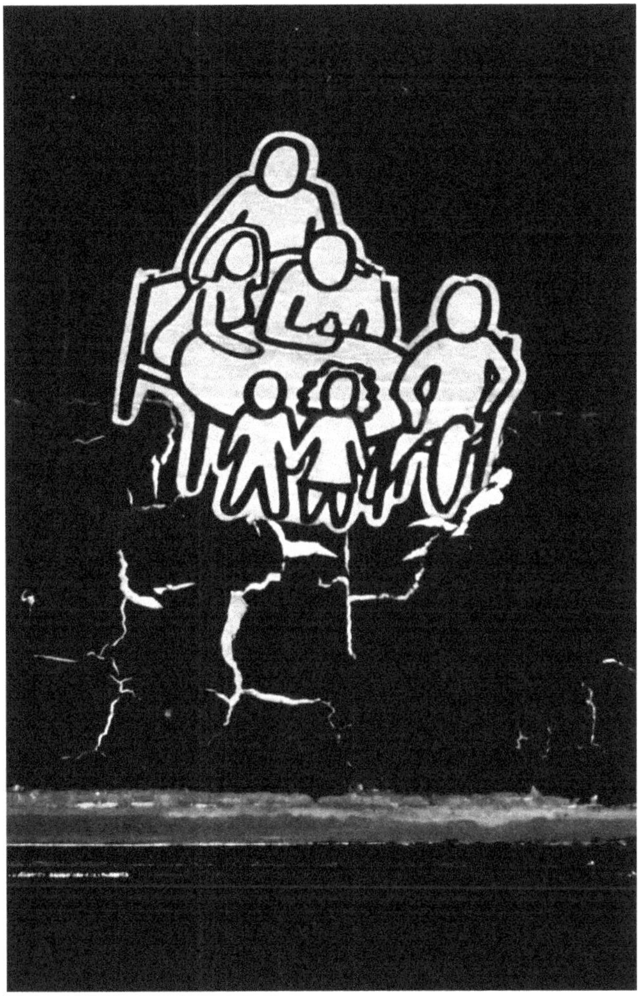

2nd St. between 1st & Ave. A

Fumero

1:49 AM

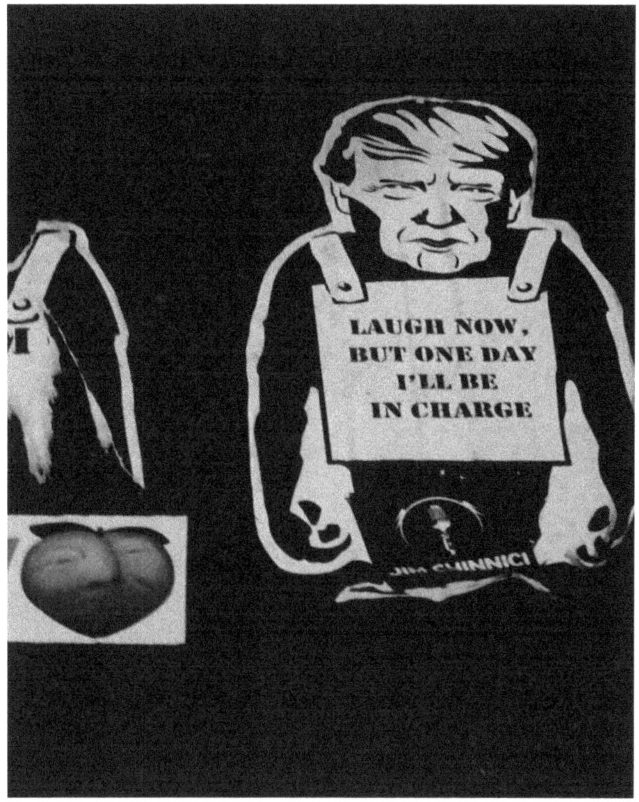

2nd St. between 1st & Ave. A

Con$umr

1:50 AM

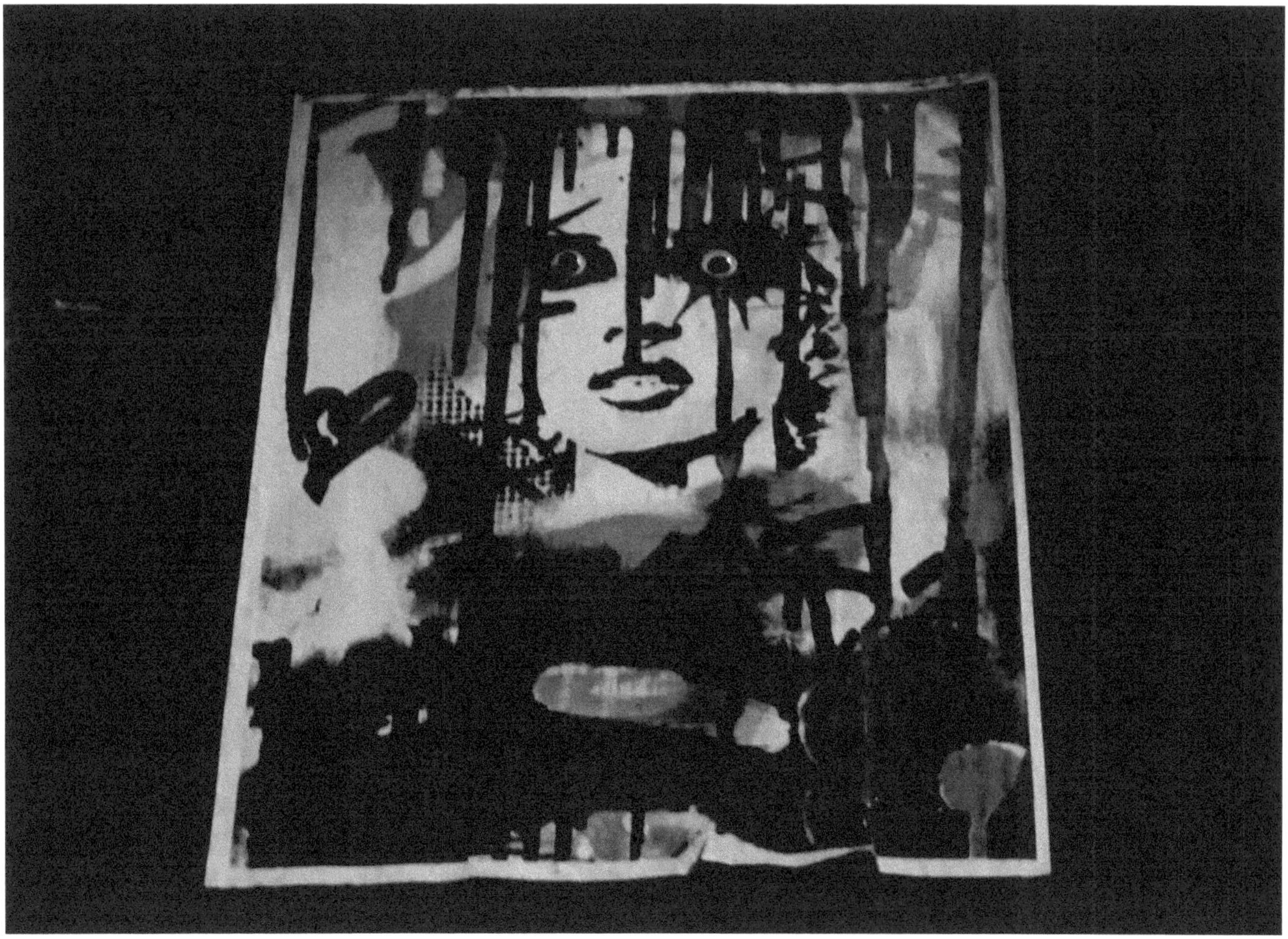

2nd St. between 1st & Ave. A

Unknown

1:52 AM

2nd St. between Ave. A & B

Bunny M

1:59 AM

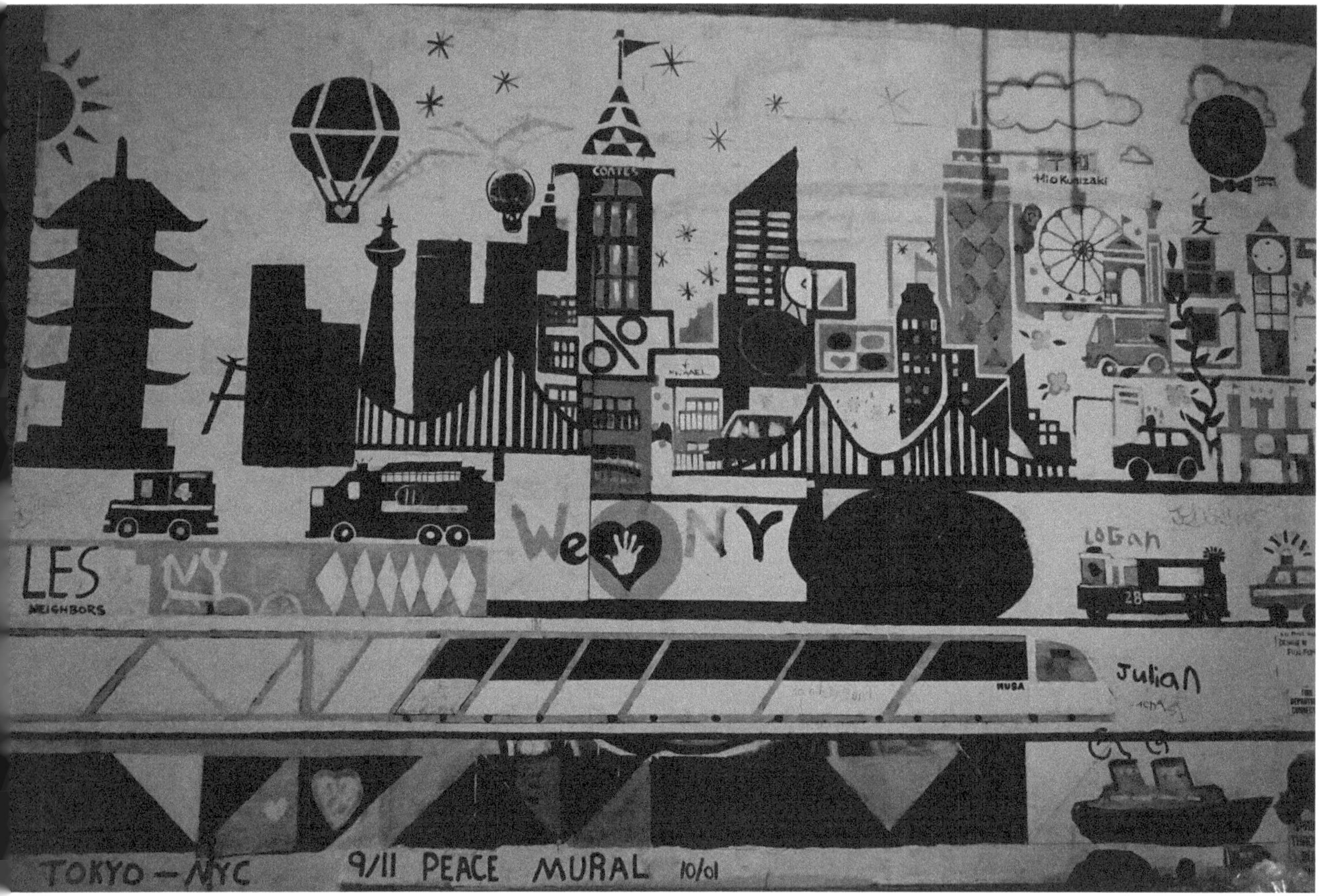

2nd St. between Ave. A & B
Coats, Michael, Mio Kunizaki, Logan, Julian, Damien Lopez,
Fujii Fumiya

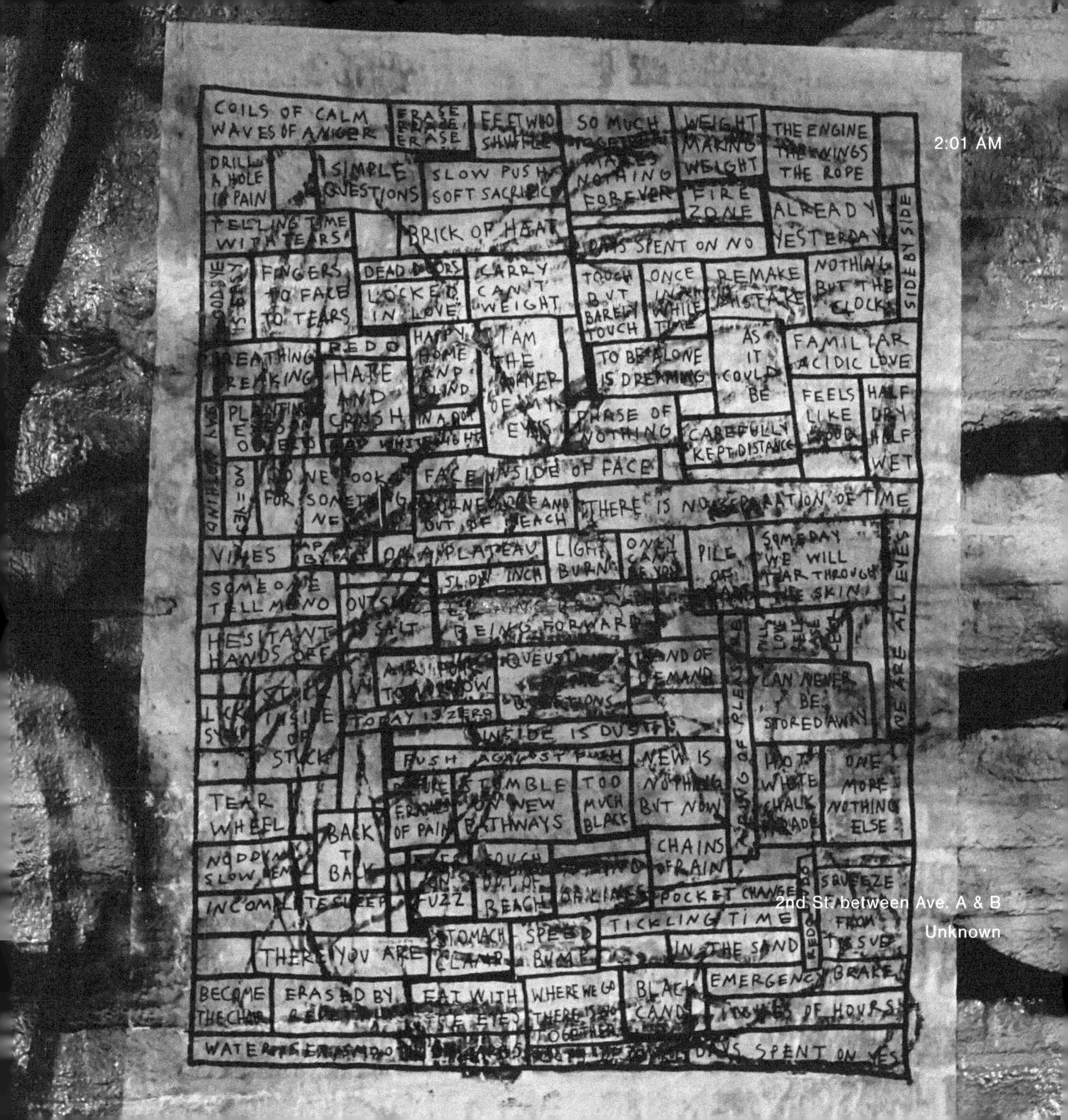

2:01 AM

2nd St. between Ave. A & B

Unknown

2:10 AM

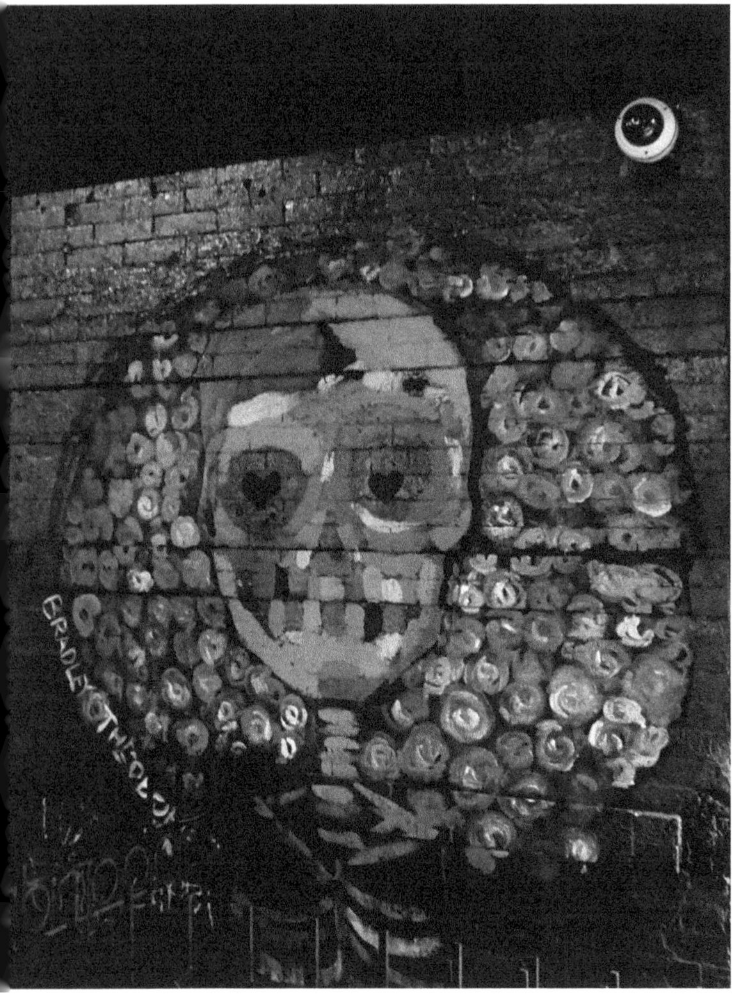

2nd St. between Ave. B & C

Bradley Theodore

2:14 AM

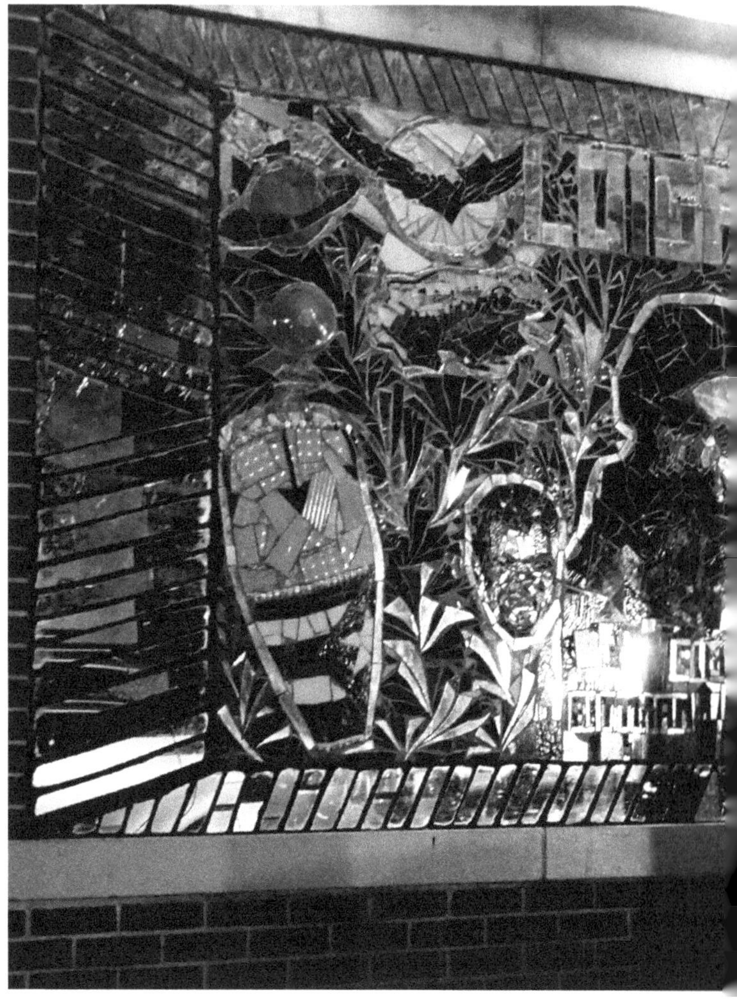

3rd St. between Ave. C & D

Carlos Pinto

2:18 AM

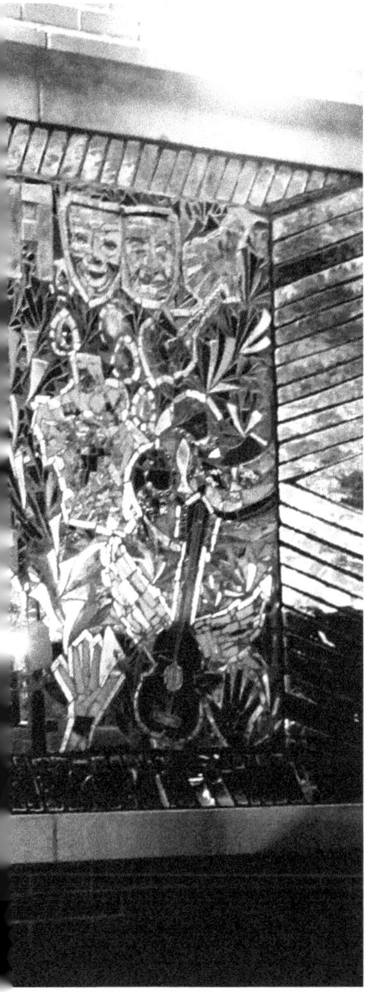

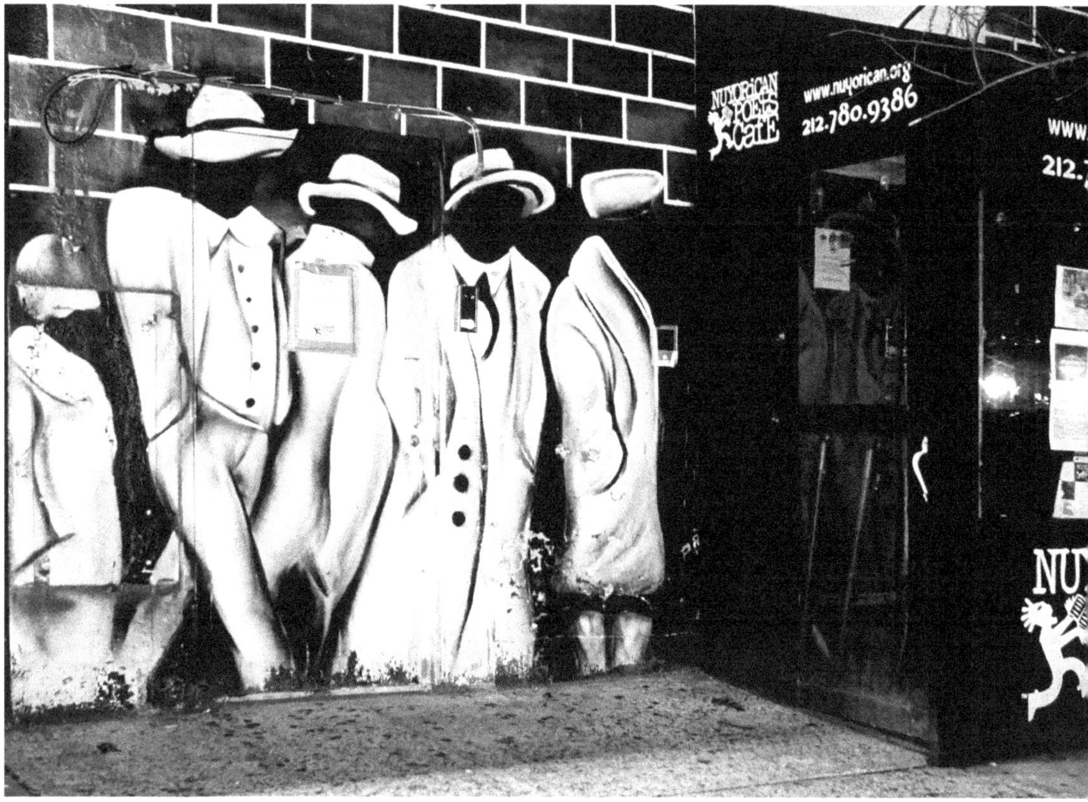

3rd St. between Ave. B & C

Joe Whippler

2:21 AM

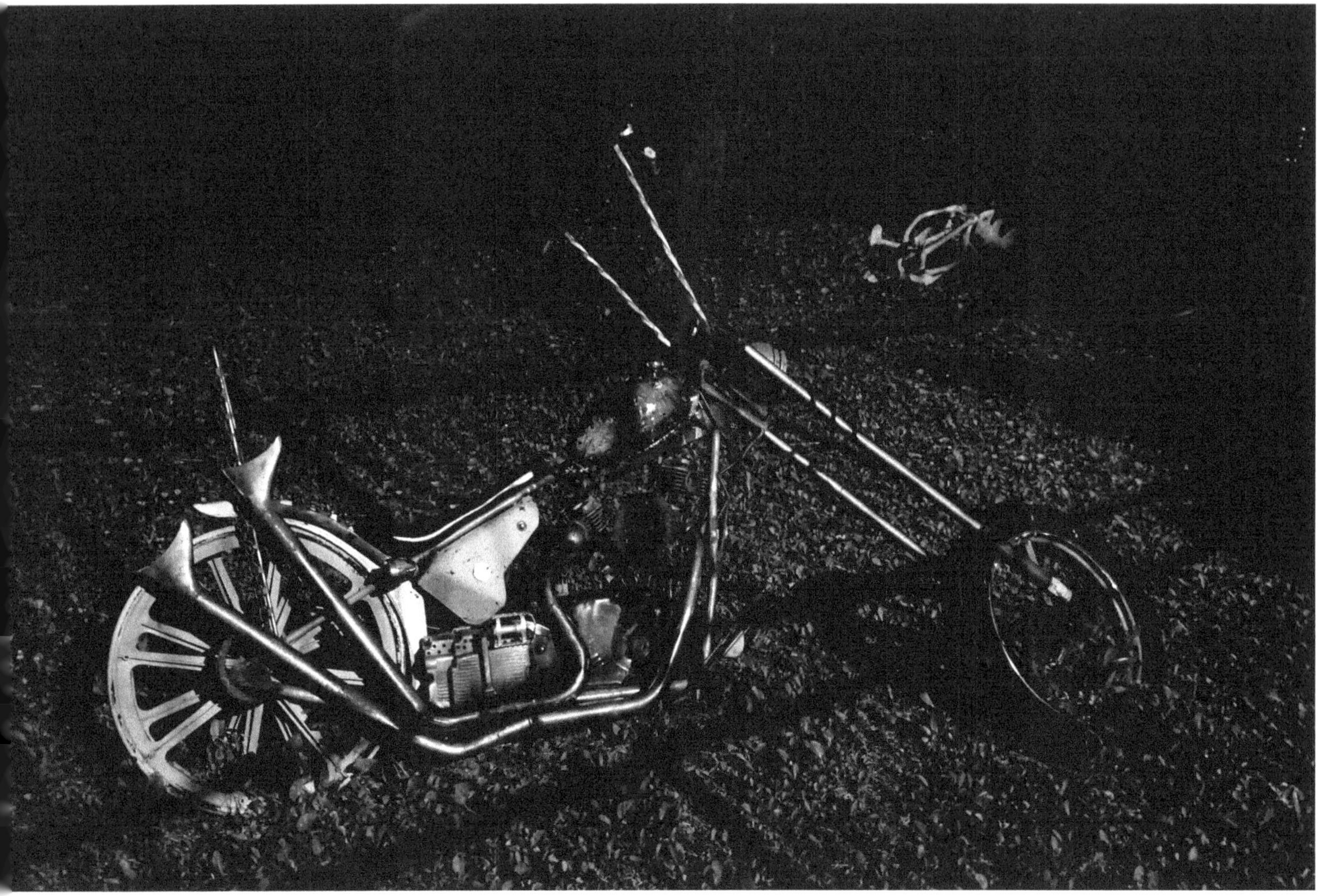

3rd St. between Ave. B & C

Linus Coraggio

2:23 AM

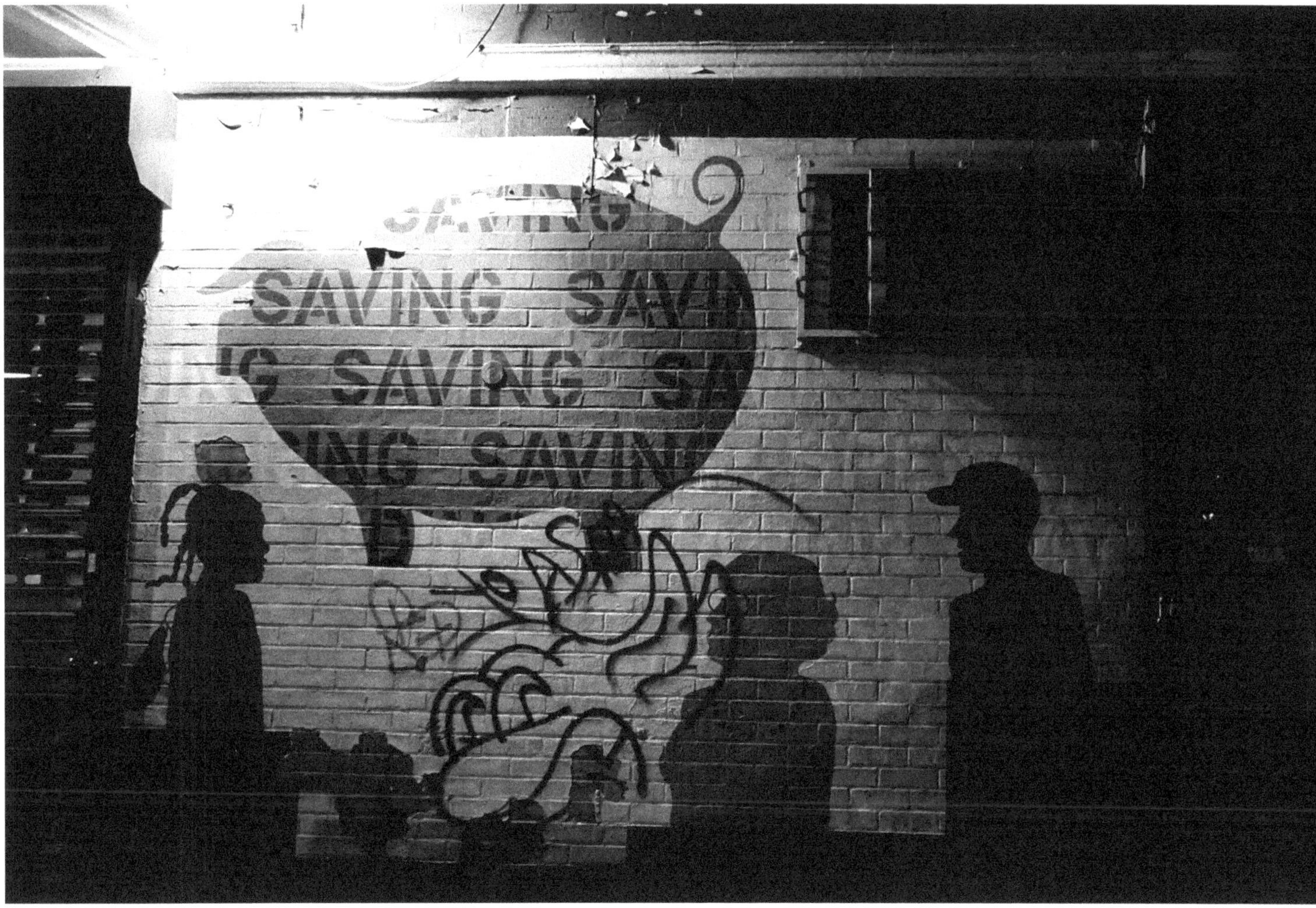

3rd St. between Ave. B & C

Janet Braun-Reinitz & Rochcelle Shicoff

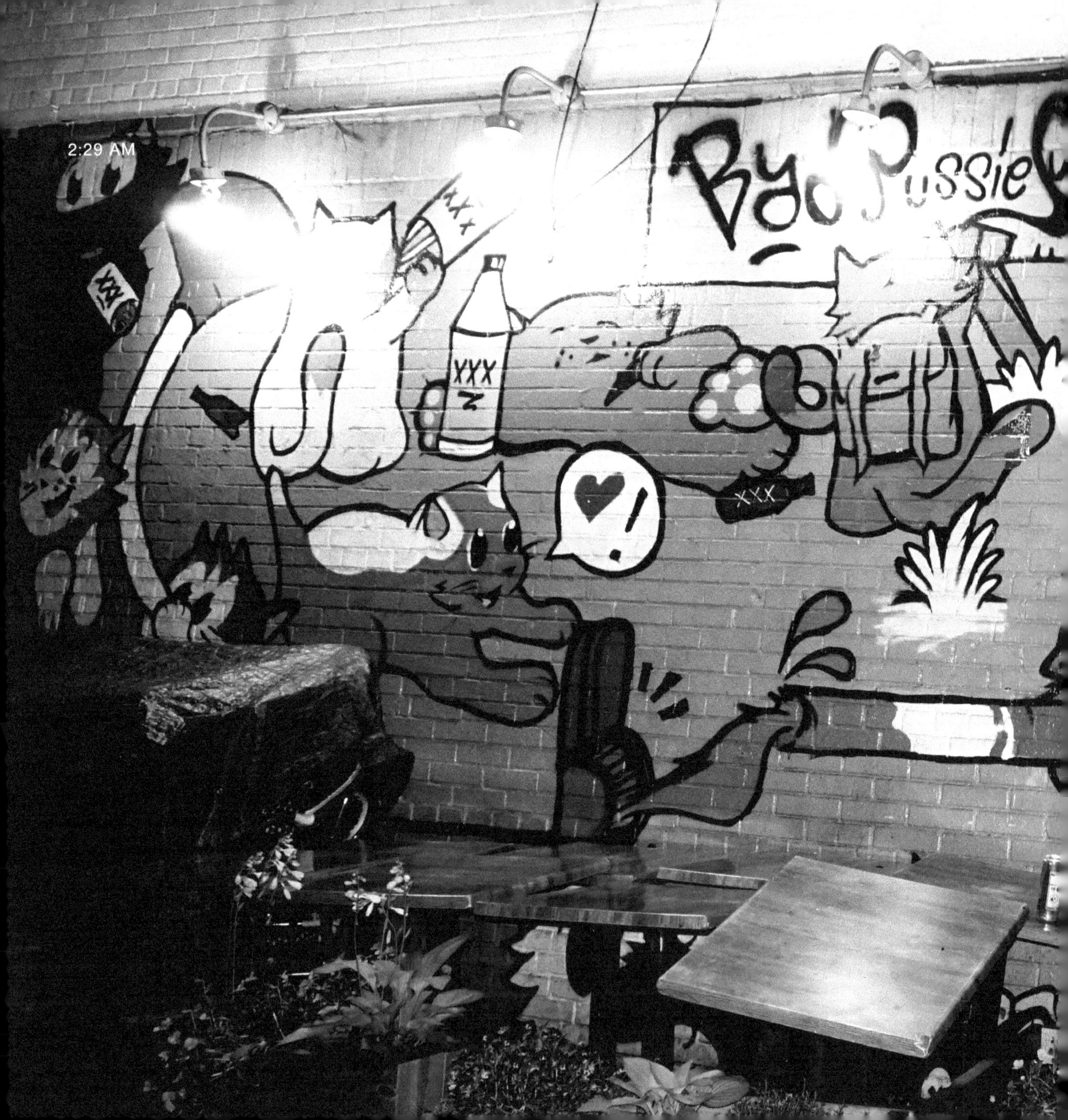
2:29 AM

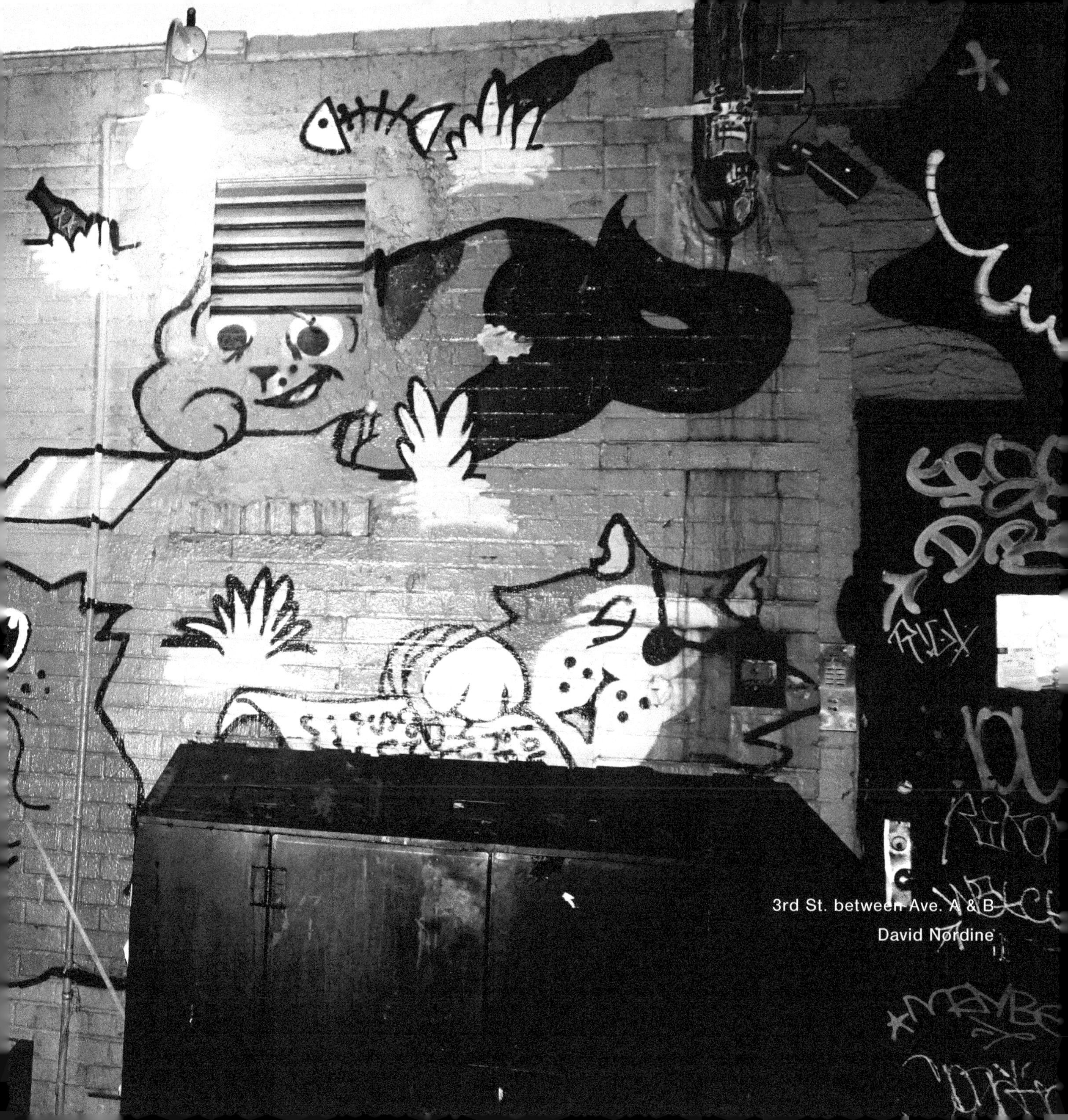

3rd St. between Ave. A & B

David Nordine

2:32 AM

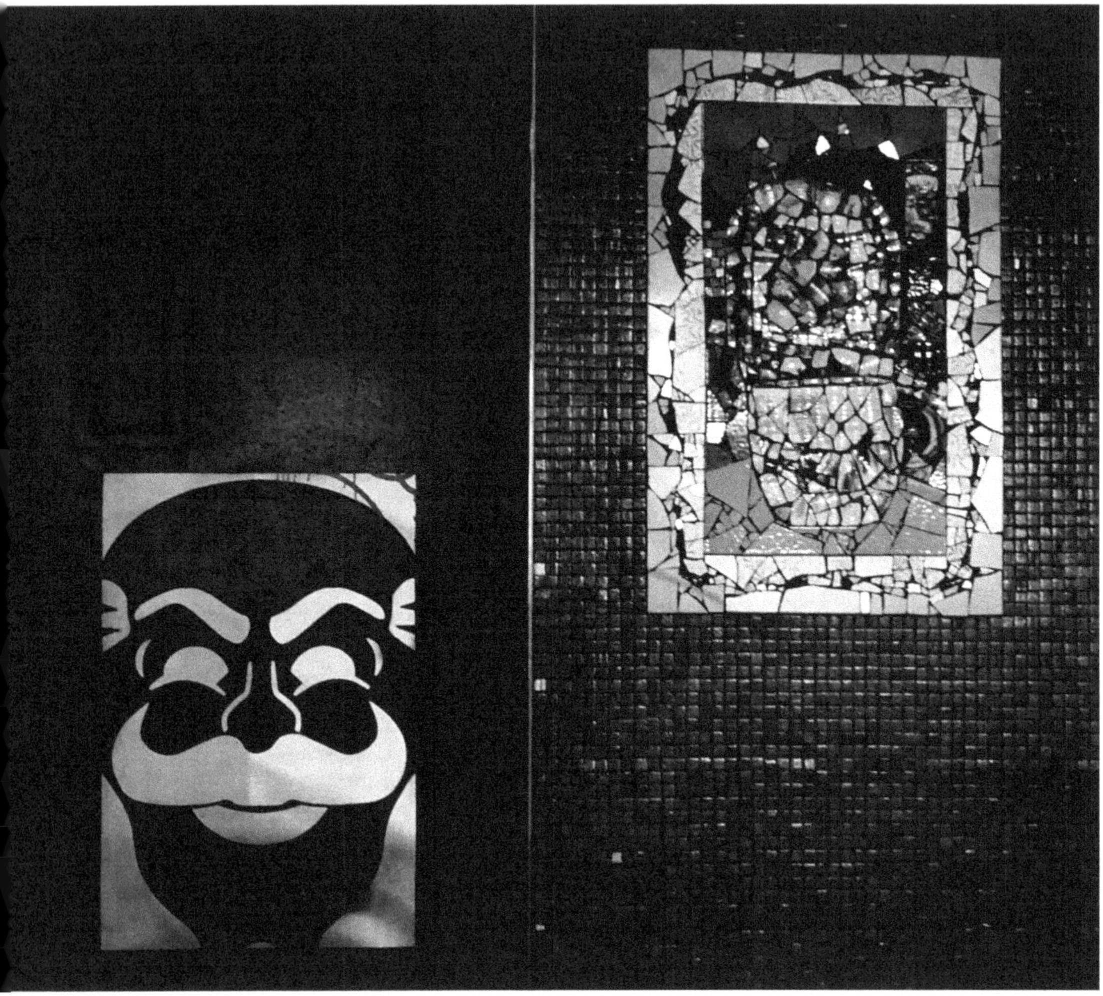

3rd St. between Ave. A & B

Unknown

2:35 AM

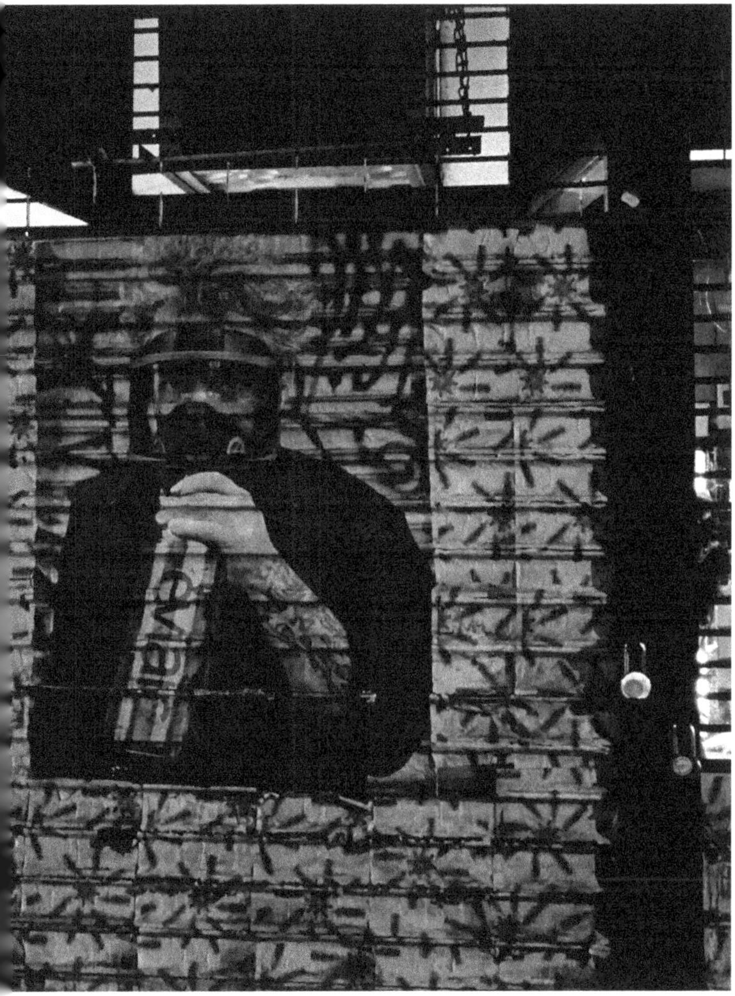

3rd St. between 1st & Ave. A

Raemann

2:39 AM

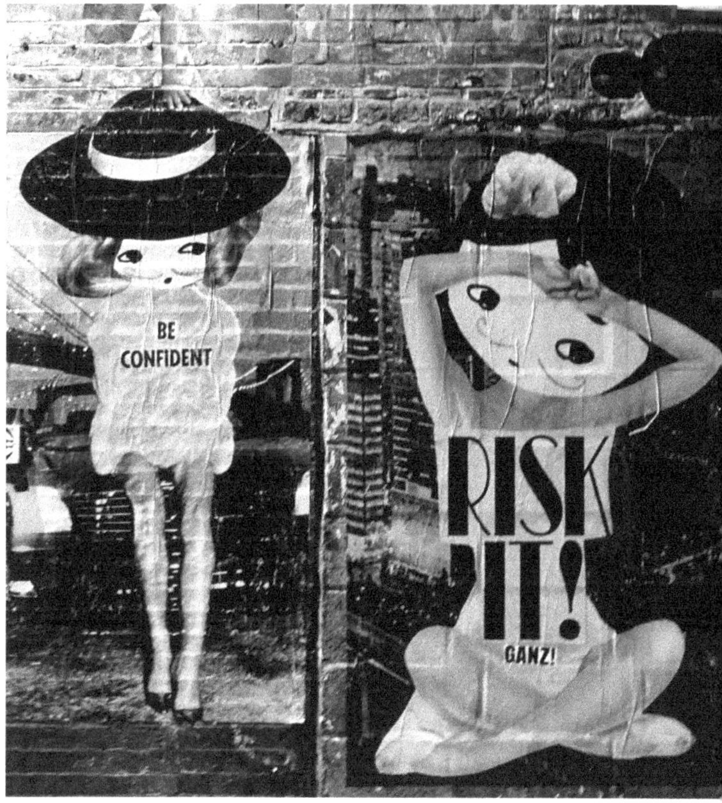

3rd St. between 1st & 2nd Ave.

Libby Schoettle

2:40 AM

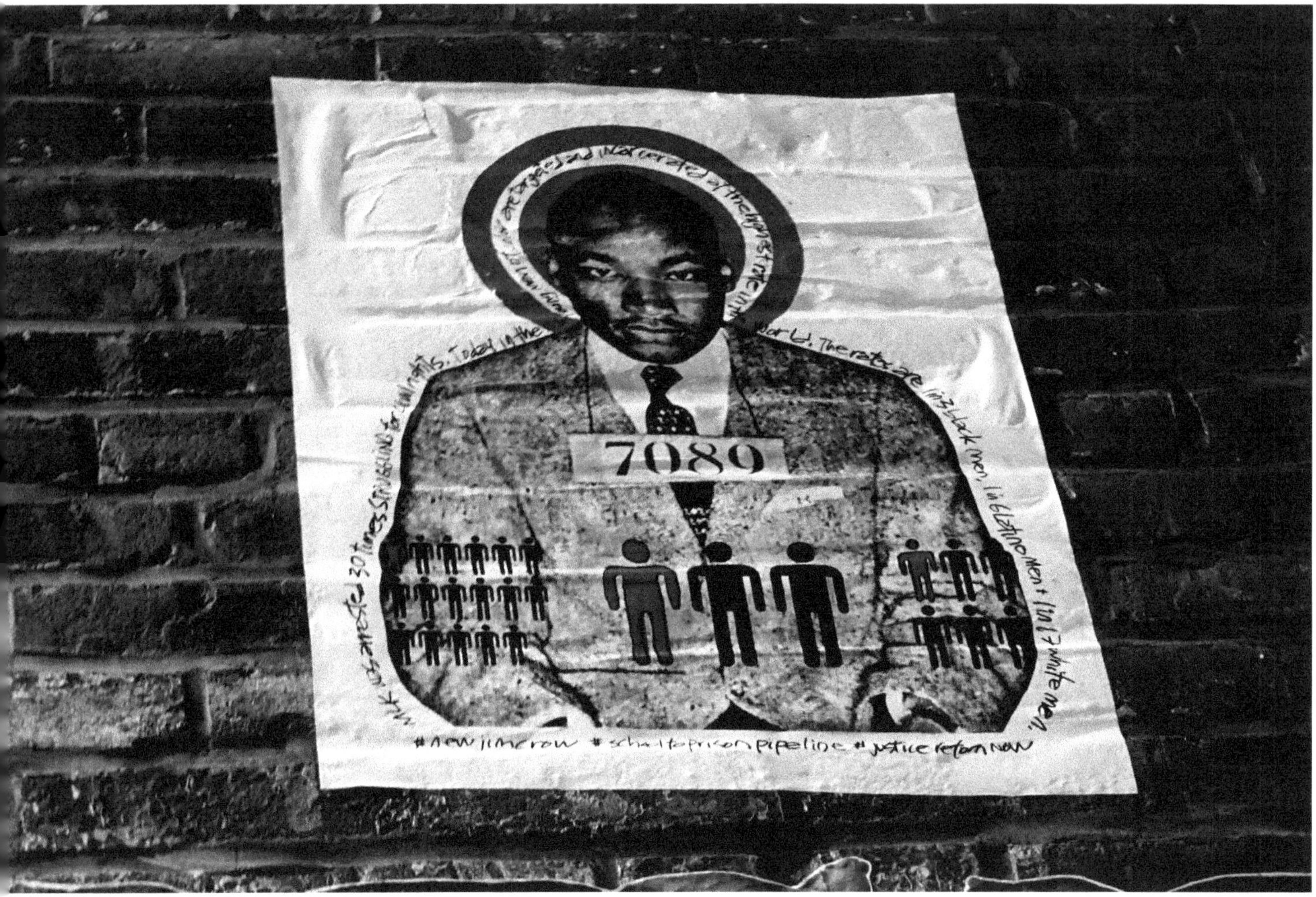

3rd St. between 1st & 2nd Ave.

Unknown

2:42 AM

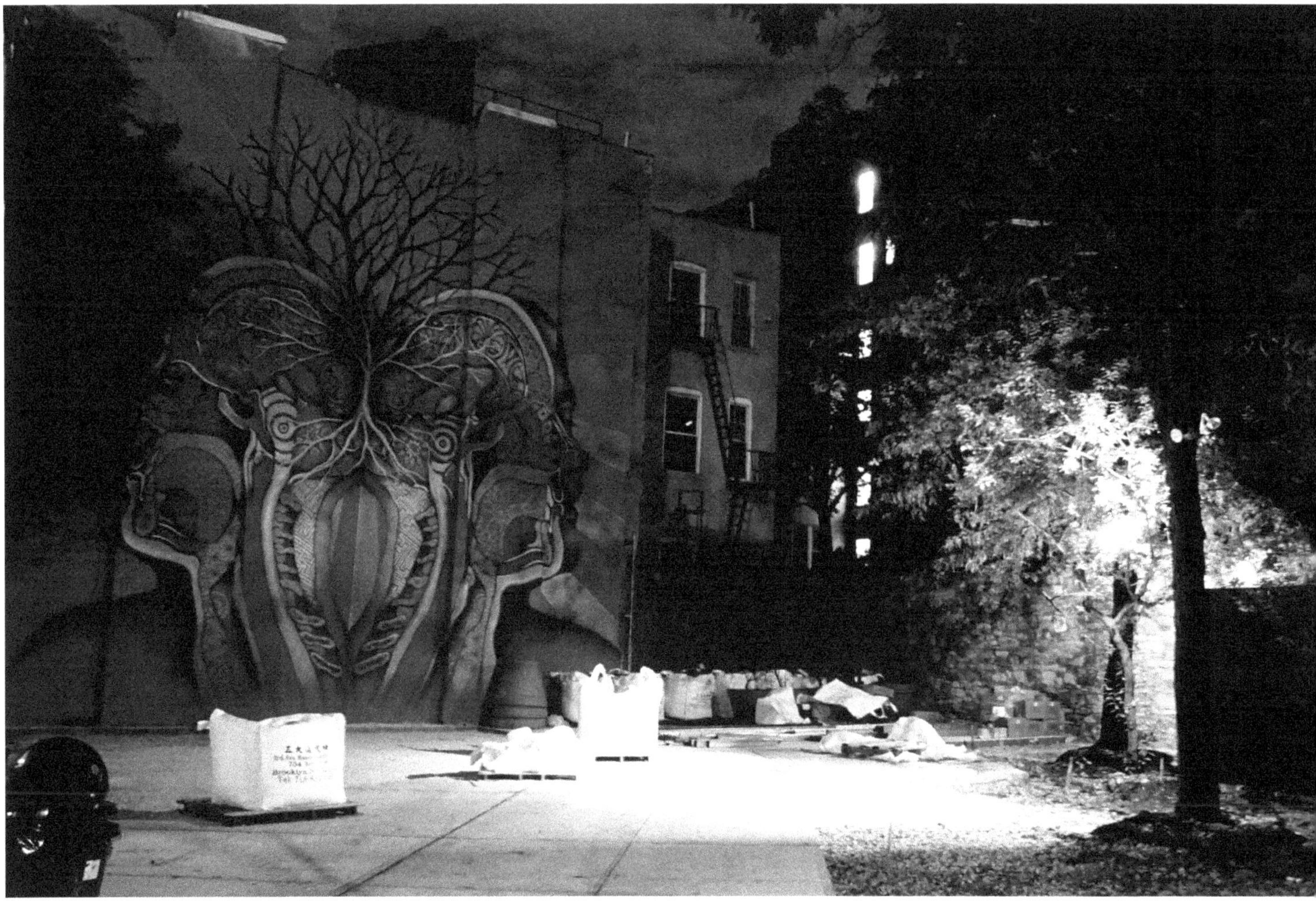

3rd St. between 2nd Ave. & Bowery

Beau Stanton

2:44 AM

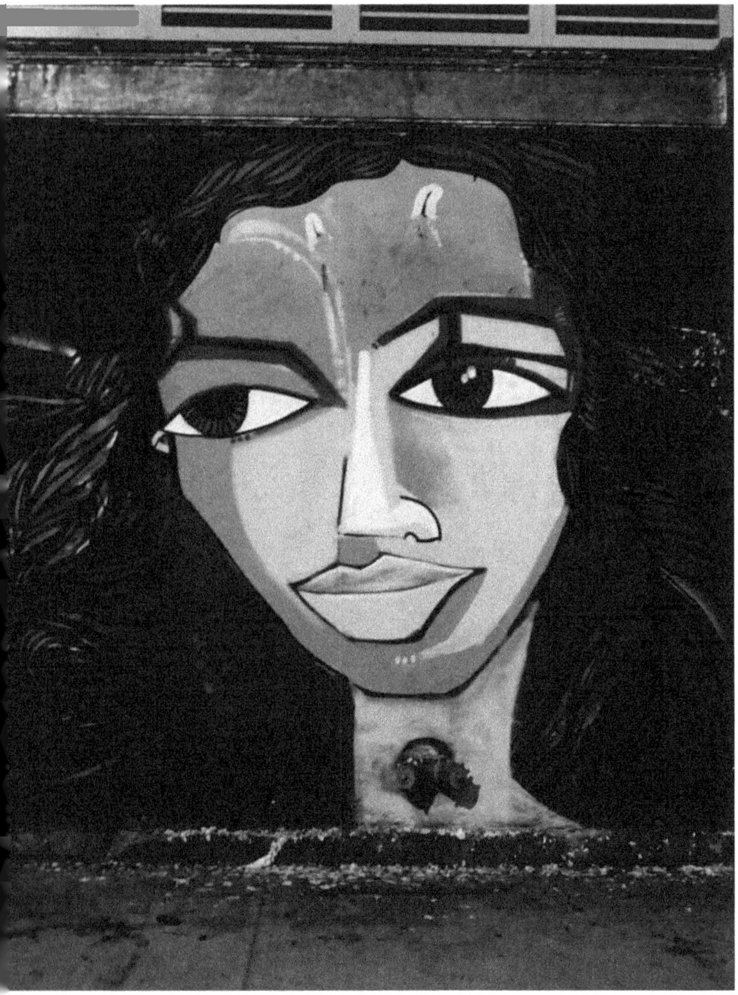

3rd St. between 2nd Ave. & Bowery

Alice Mizrachi

2:53 AM

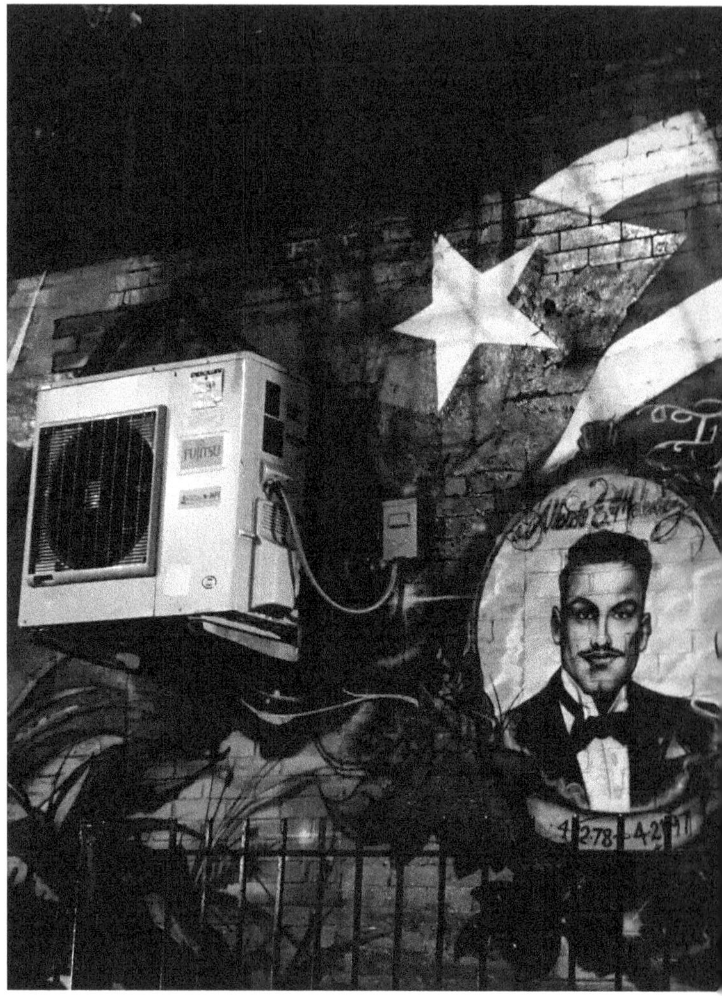

4th St. between Ave. C & D

Charlie Doves

2:56 AM

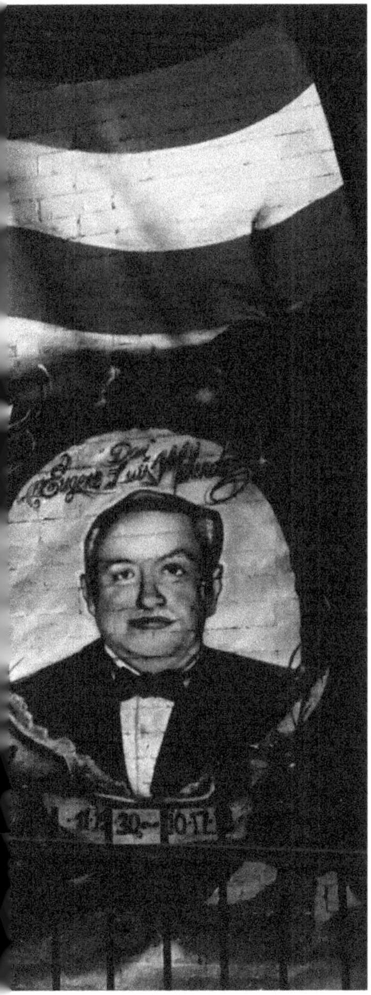

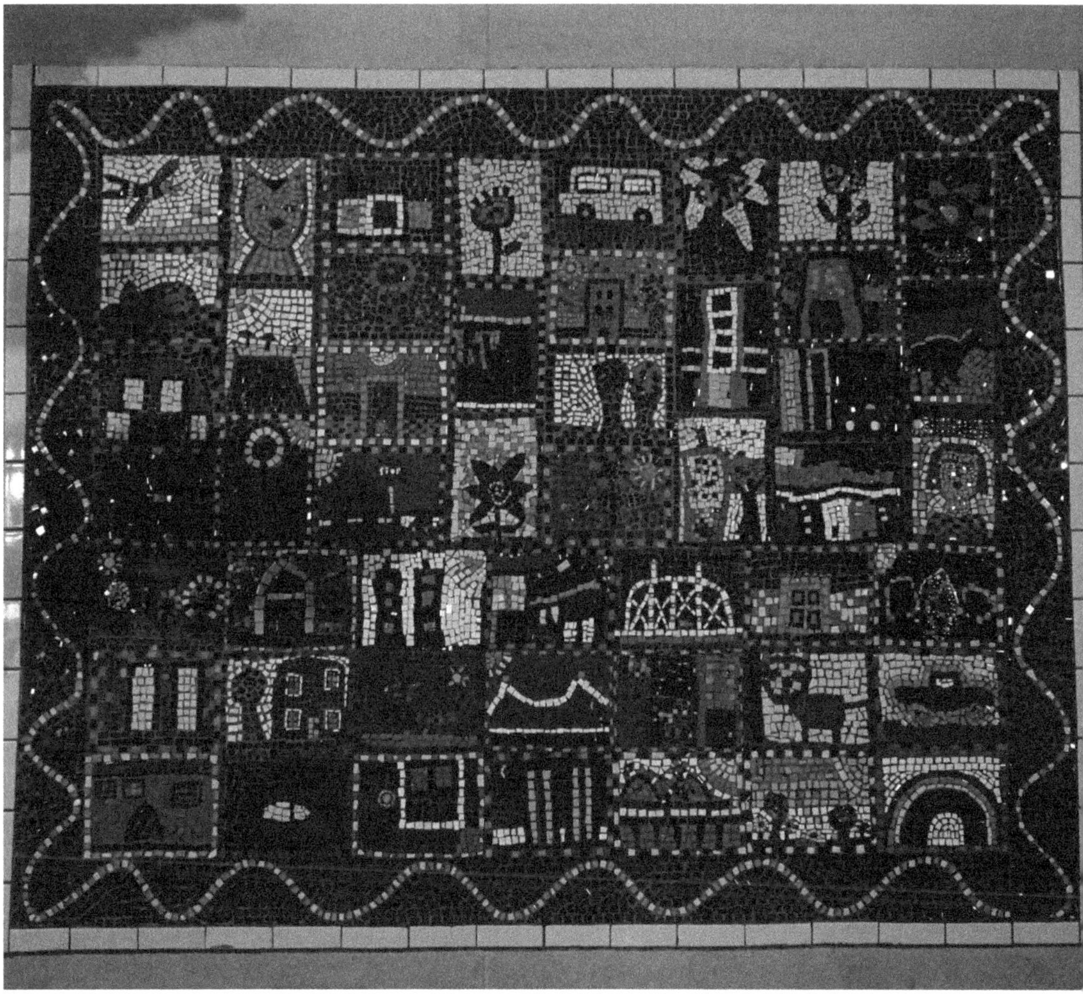

4th St. between Ave. C & D

Susan Greenstein, Marissa Perez, and

3rd Grade Classes of 1999-2000 at PS 15

3:03 AM

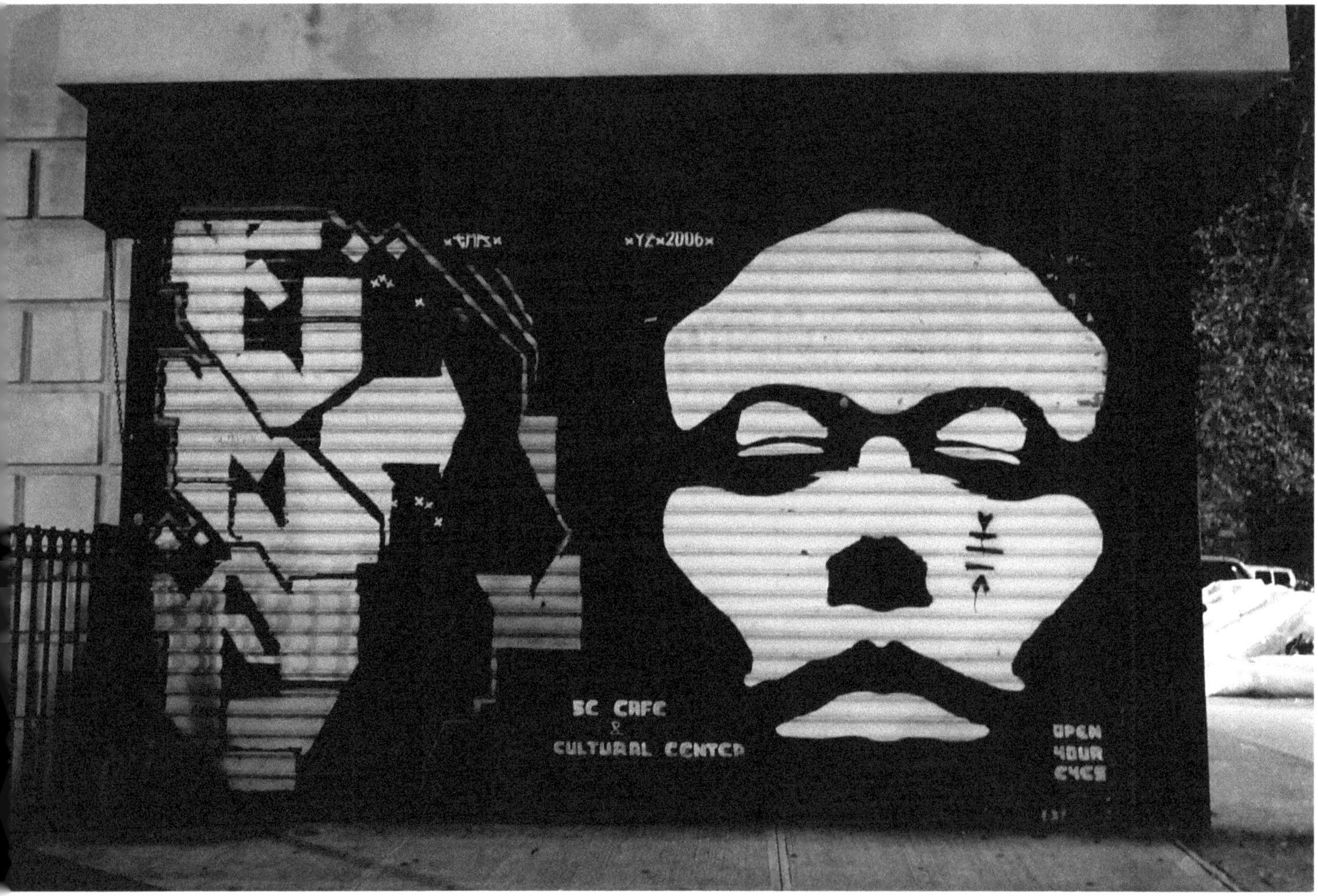

5th St. between Ave. C & D

Ema, Yeseult

3:15 AM

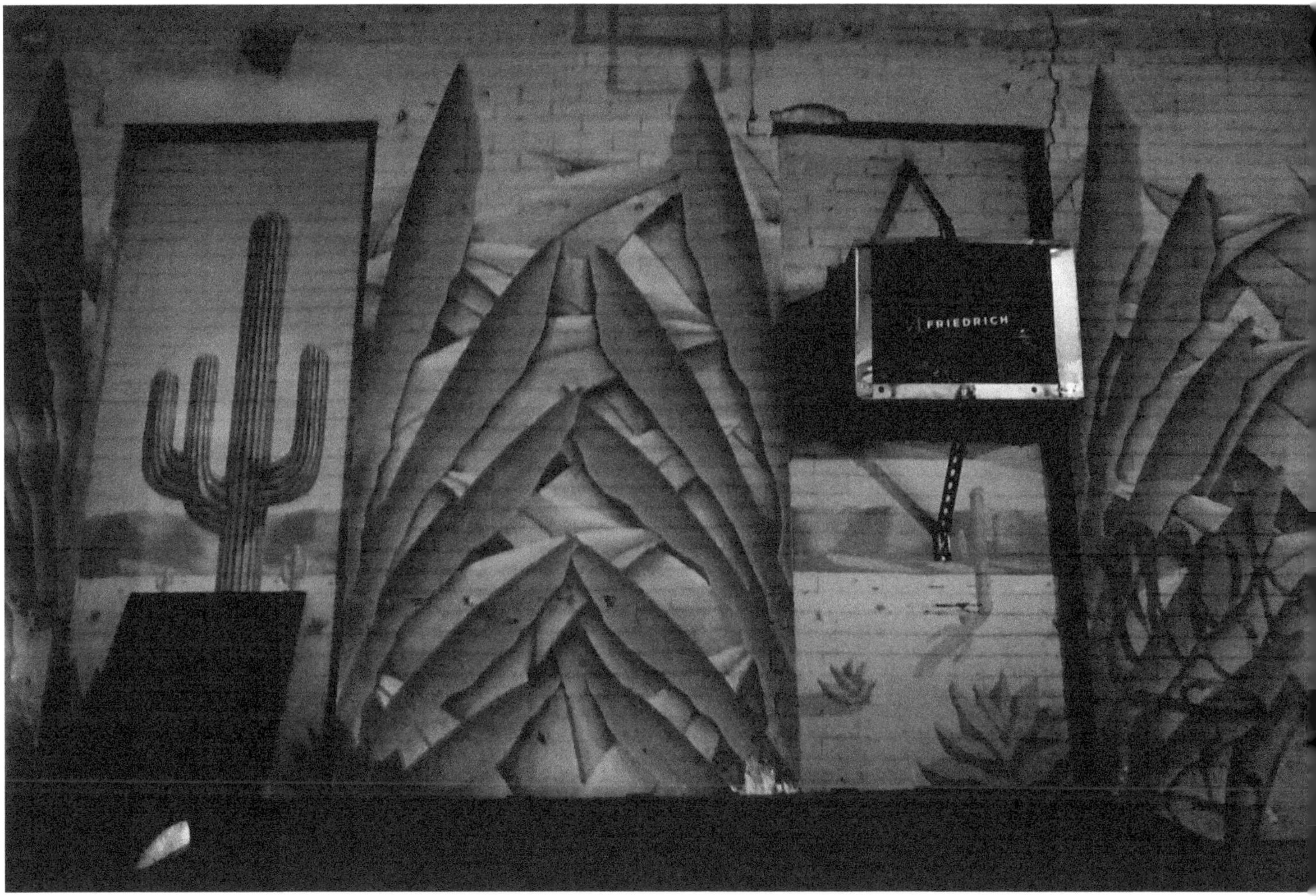

5th St. between 1st & 2nd Ave.

Unknown

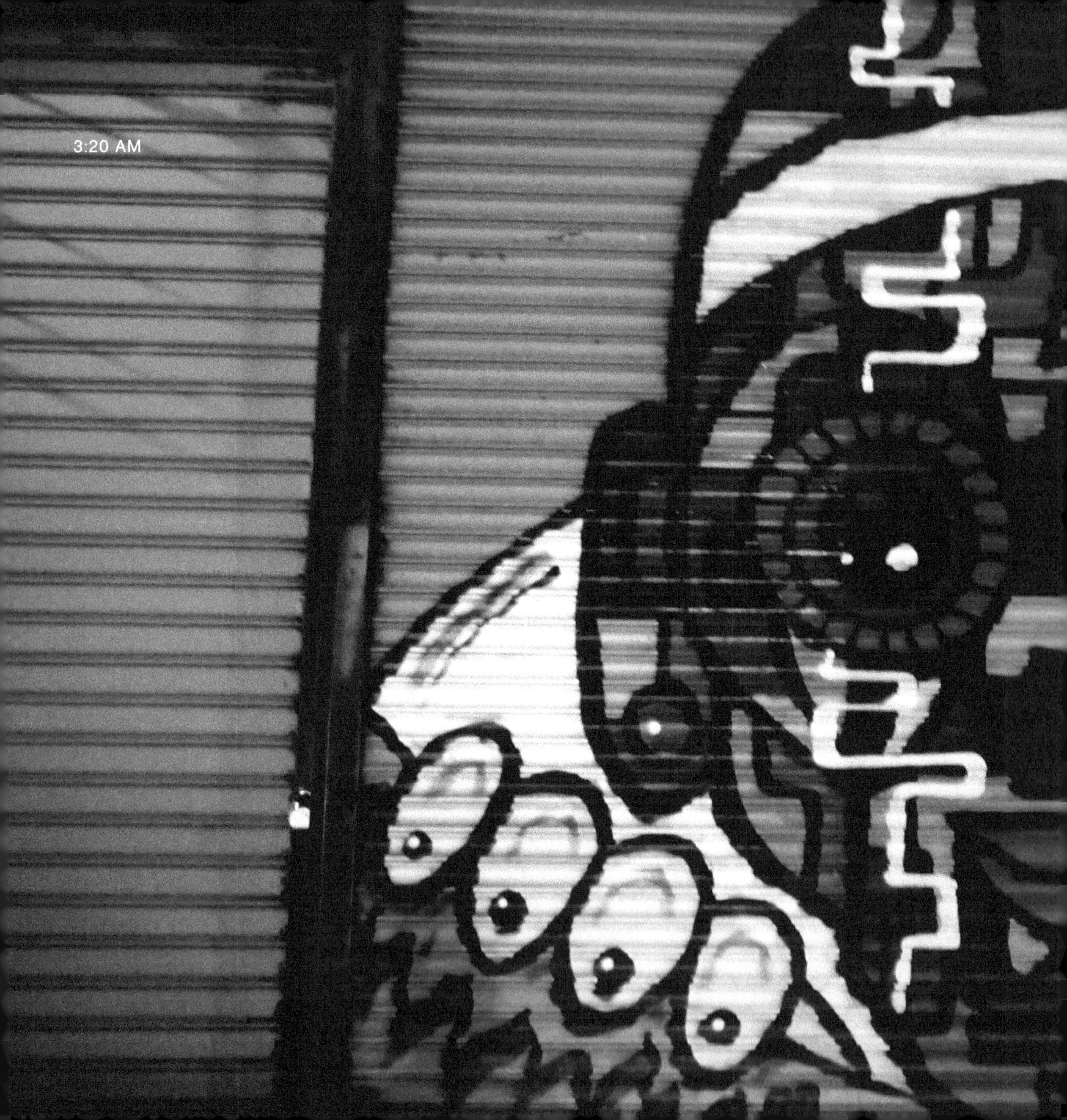
3:20 AM

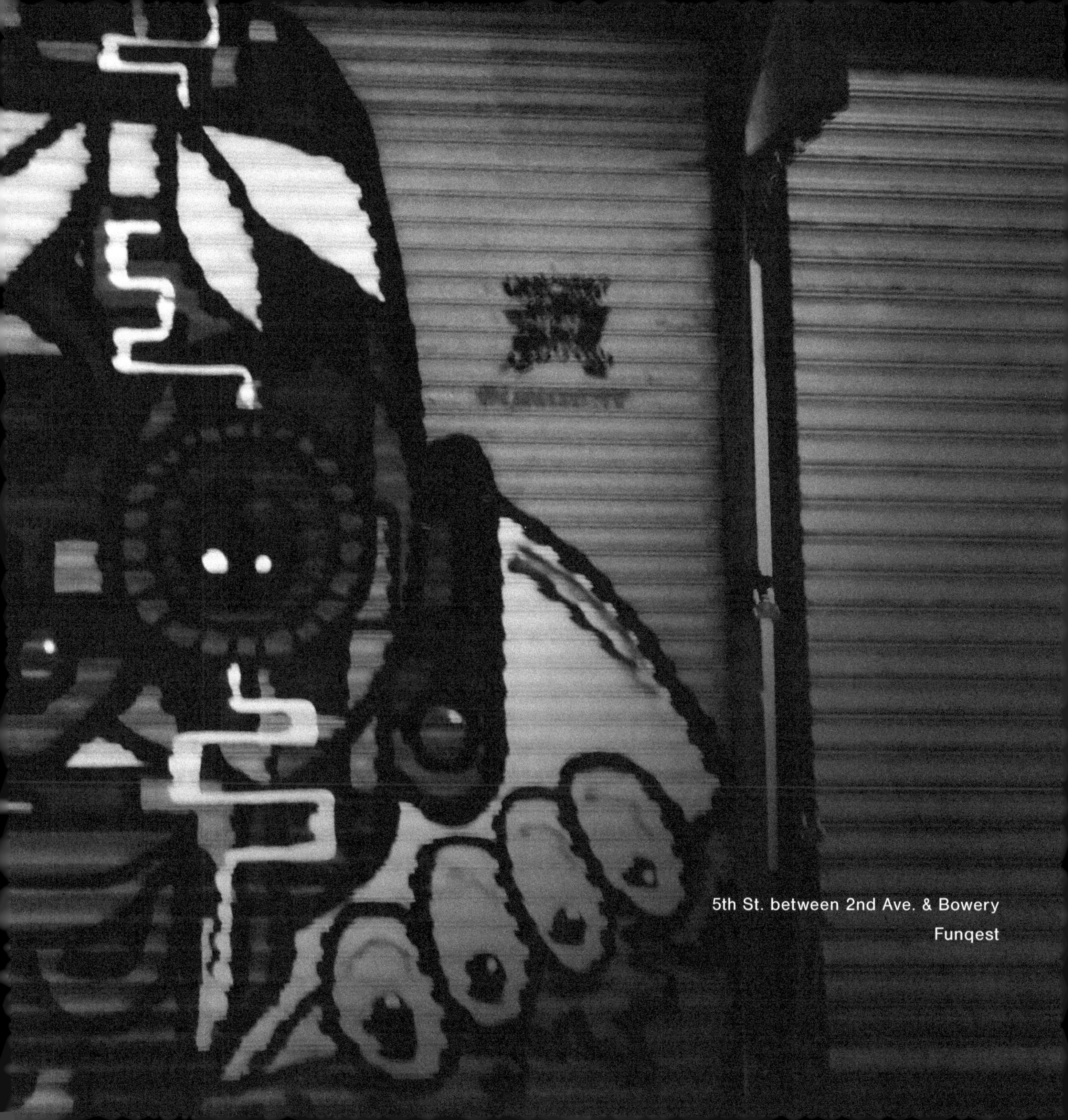

5th St. between 2nd Ave. & Bowery

Funqest

3:22 AM

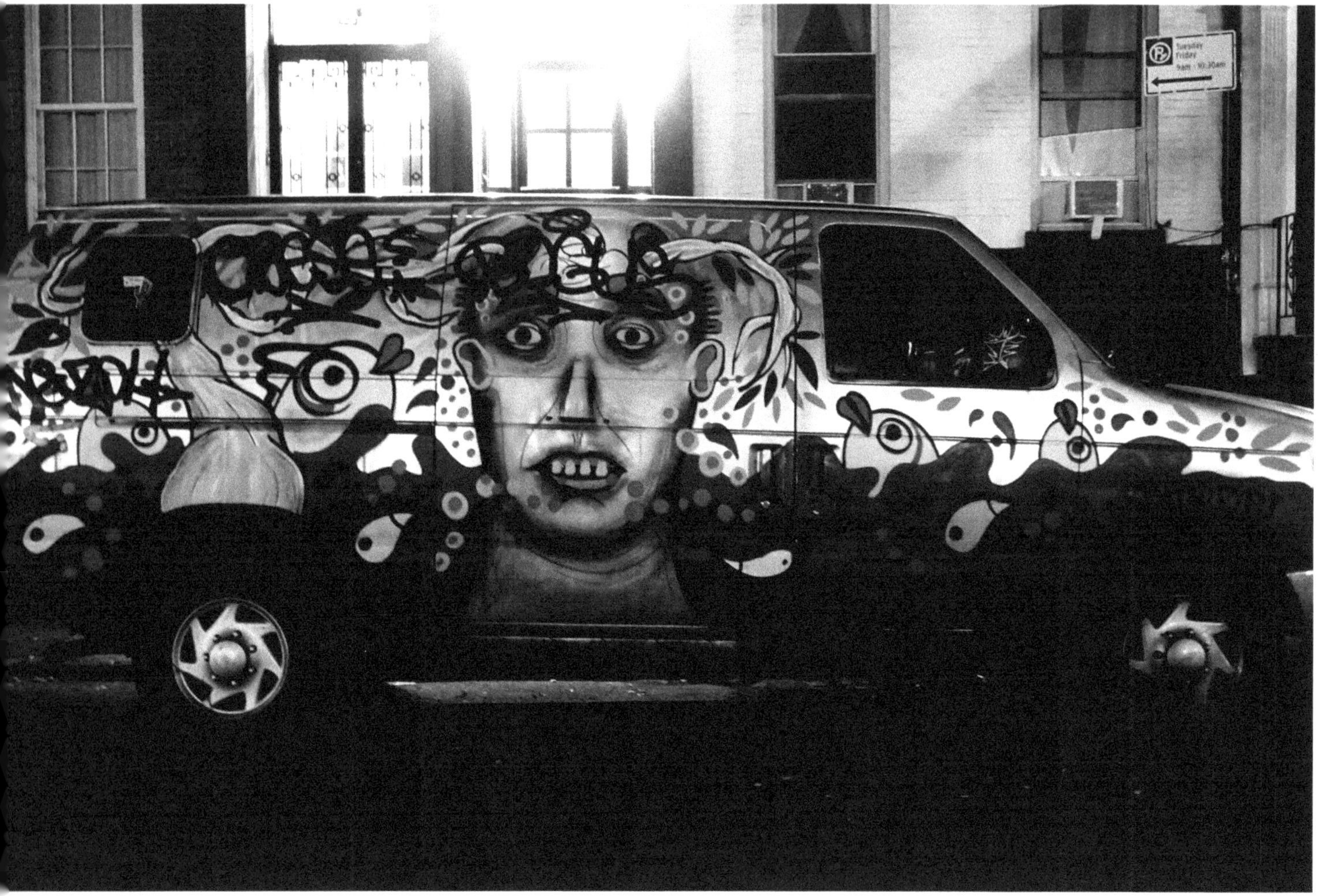

5th St. between 2nd Ave. & Bowery

Urbanimal

3:29 AM

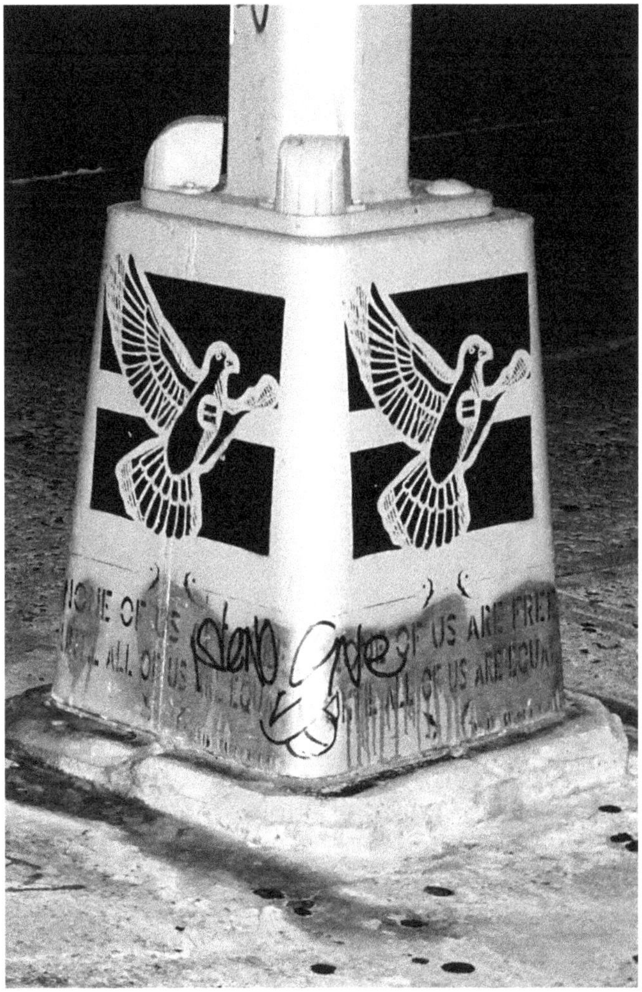

Taras Shevchenko Place

B.D. White

3:31 AM

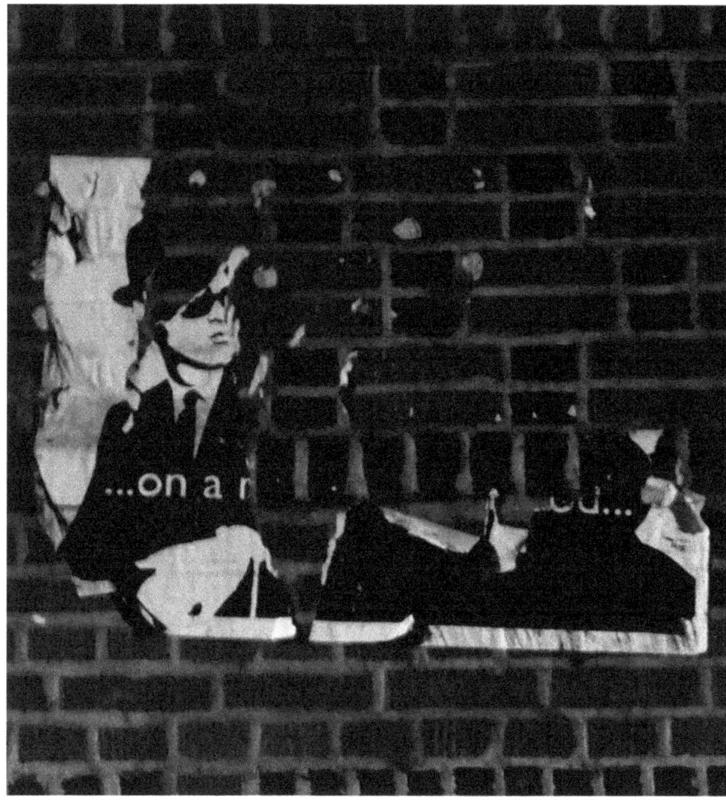

6th St. between 2nd Ave. & Bowery

Cost

3:35 AM

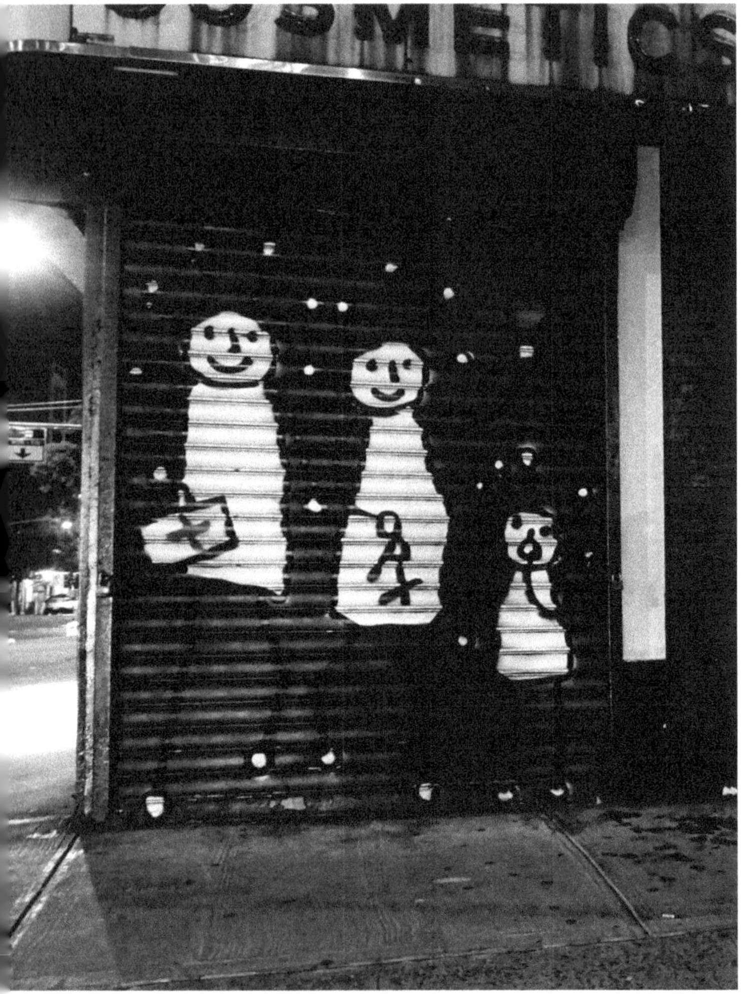

6th St. between 2nd Ave. & Bowery

Paul Kostabi

3:36 AM

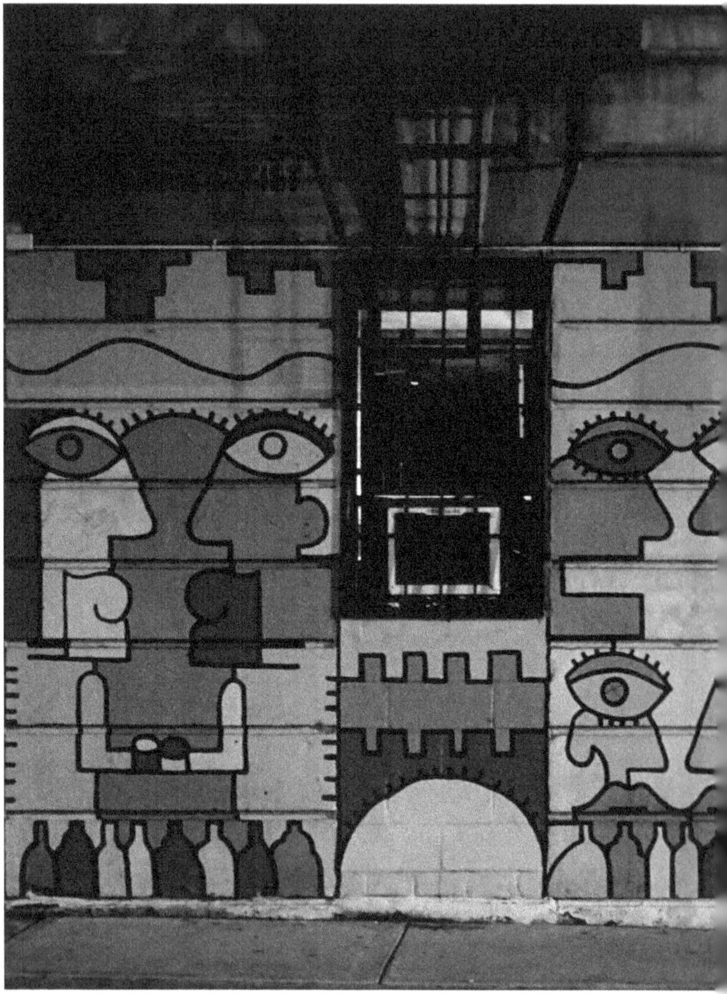

6th St. between 1st & 2nd Ave.

Billy the Artist

3:38 AM

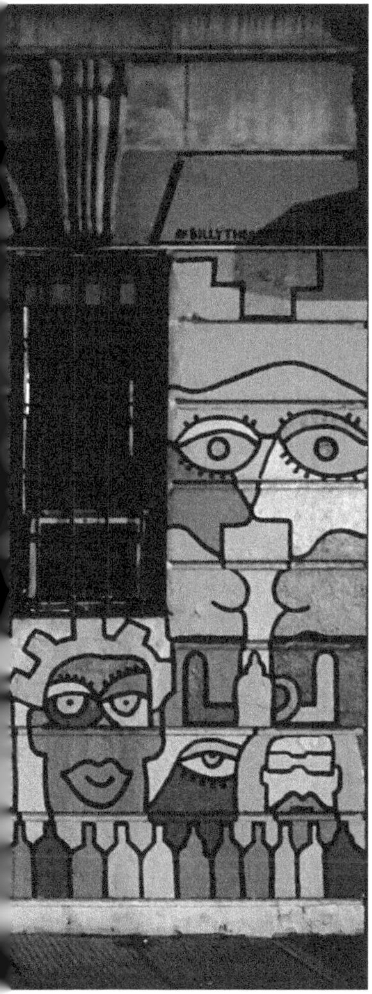

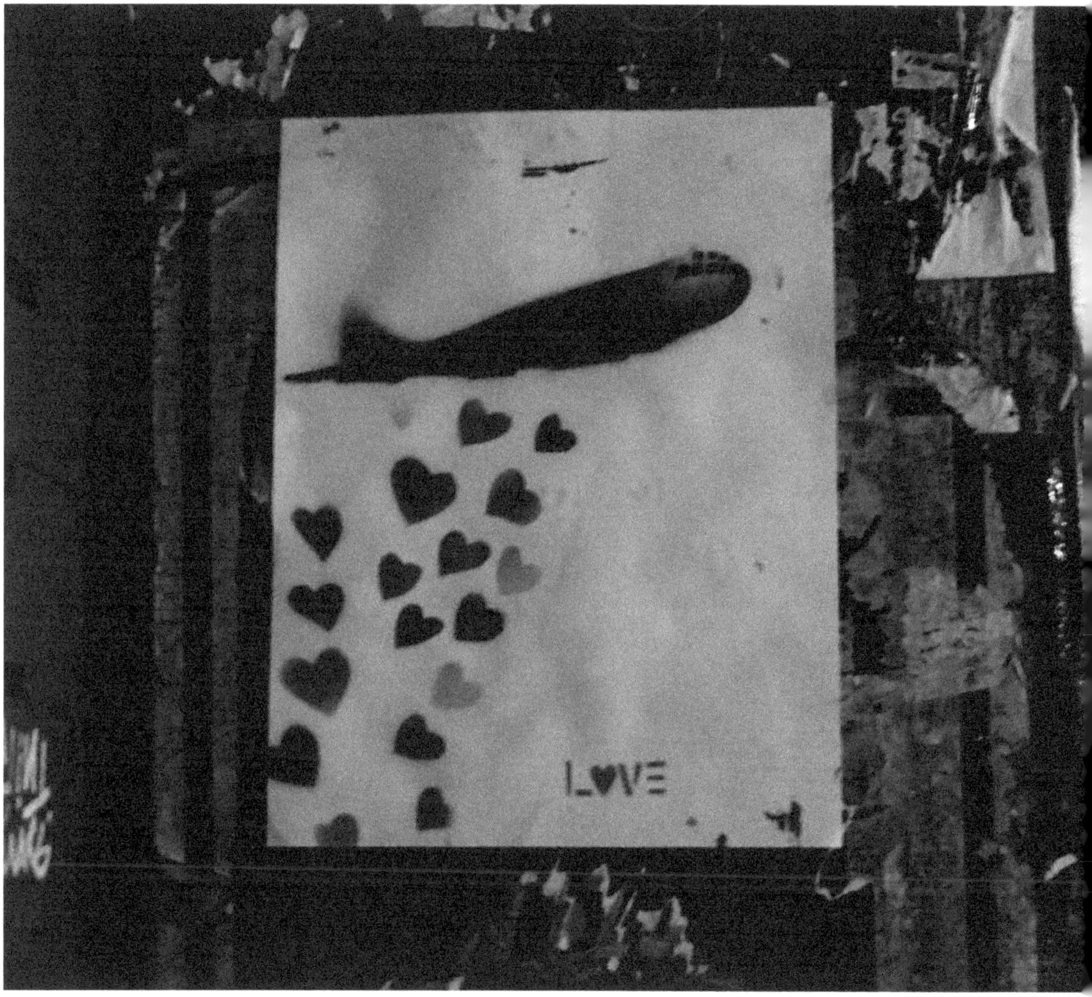

6th St. between 1st & 2nd Ave.

DLove

3:39 AM

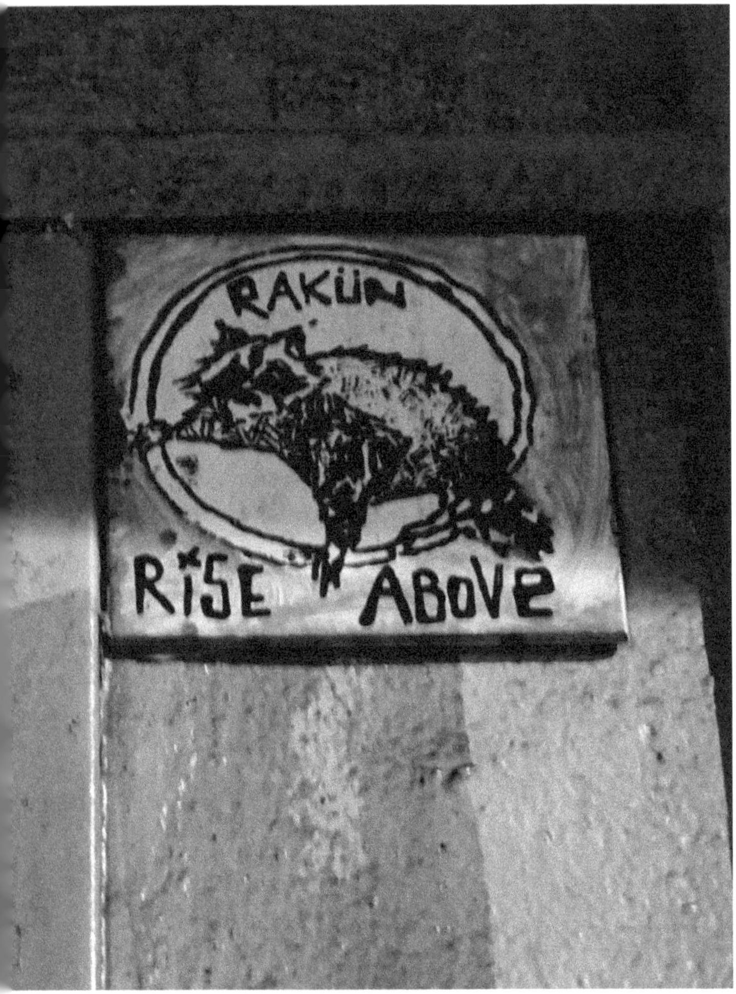

6th St. between 1st & 2nd Ave.

Unknown

3:40 AM

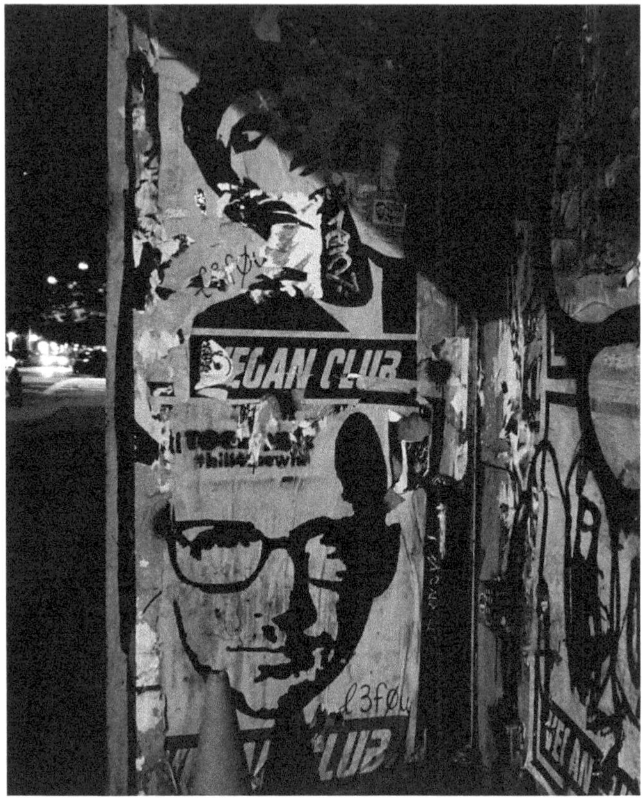

6th St. between 1st & 2nd Ave.

Le Fou

4:00 AM

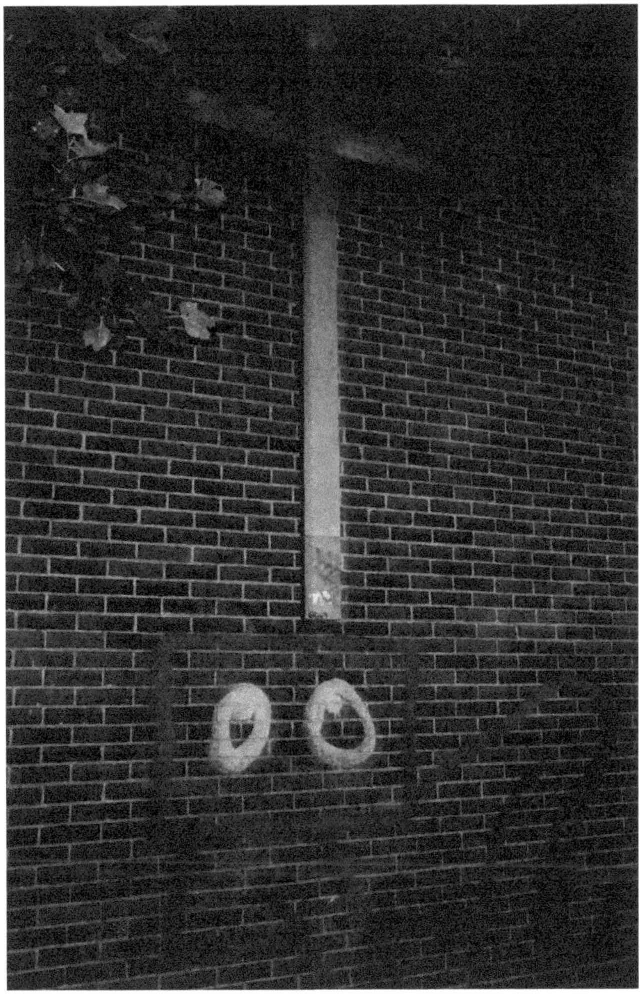

6th St. between Ave. C & D

Unknown

4:07 AM

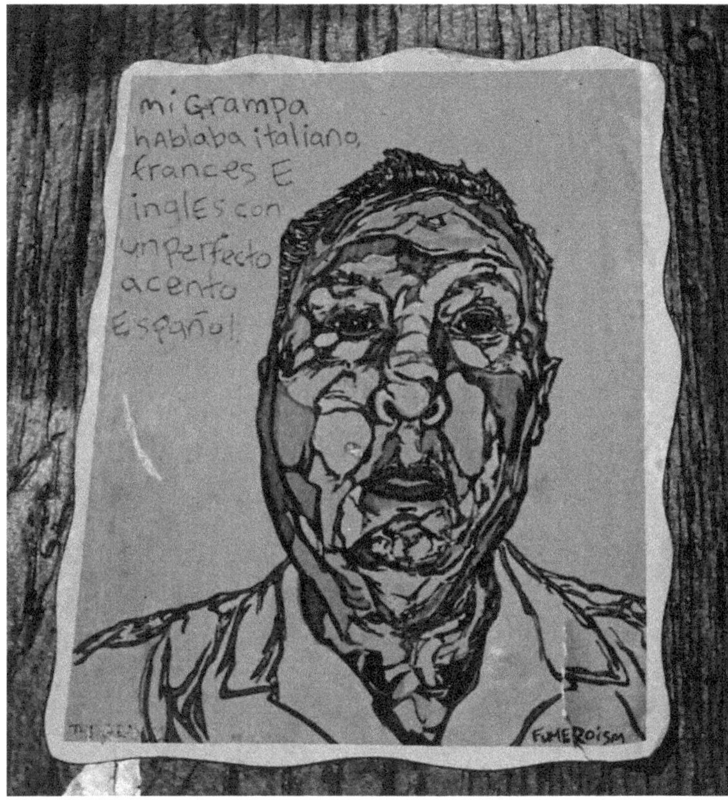

7th St. between Ave. B & C

Fumero

4:22 AM

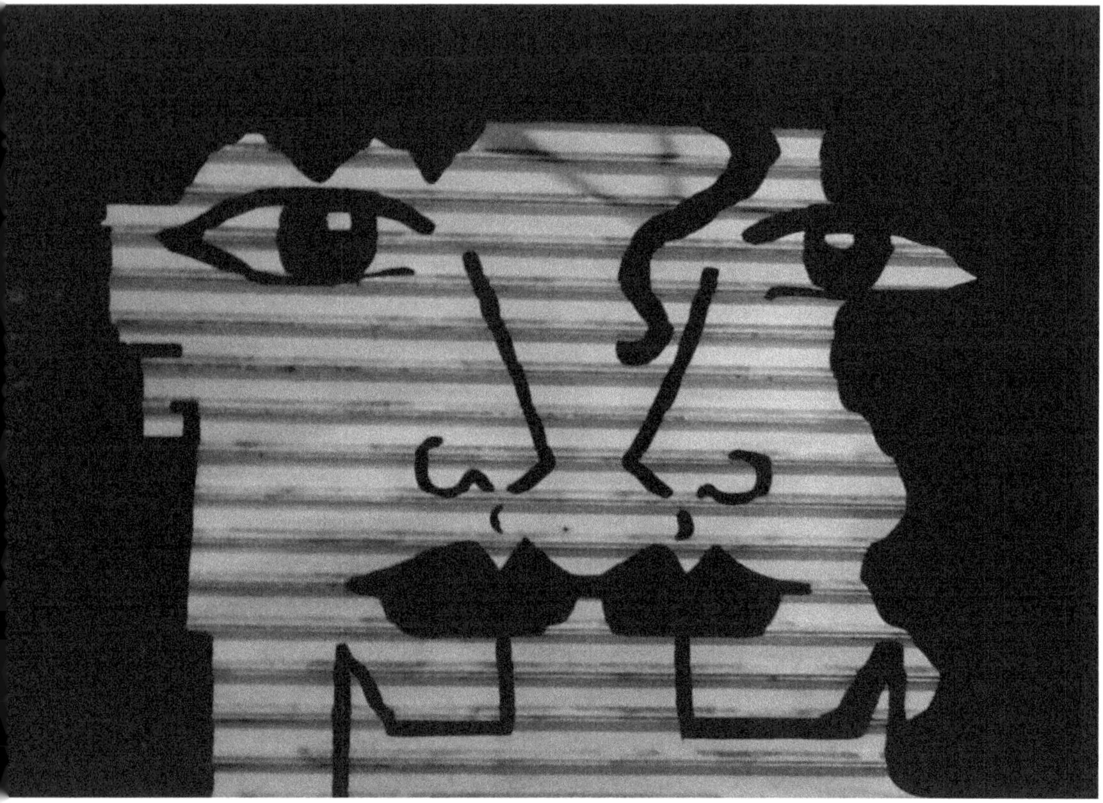

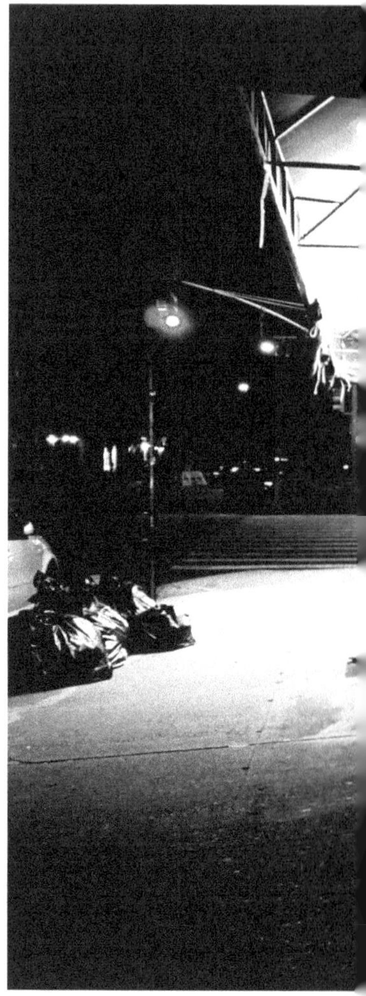

7th St. between 1st & Ave. A

Anna Laurini

4:25 AM

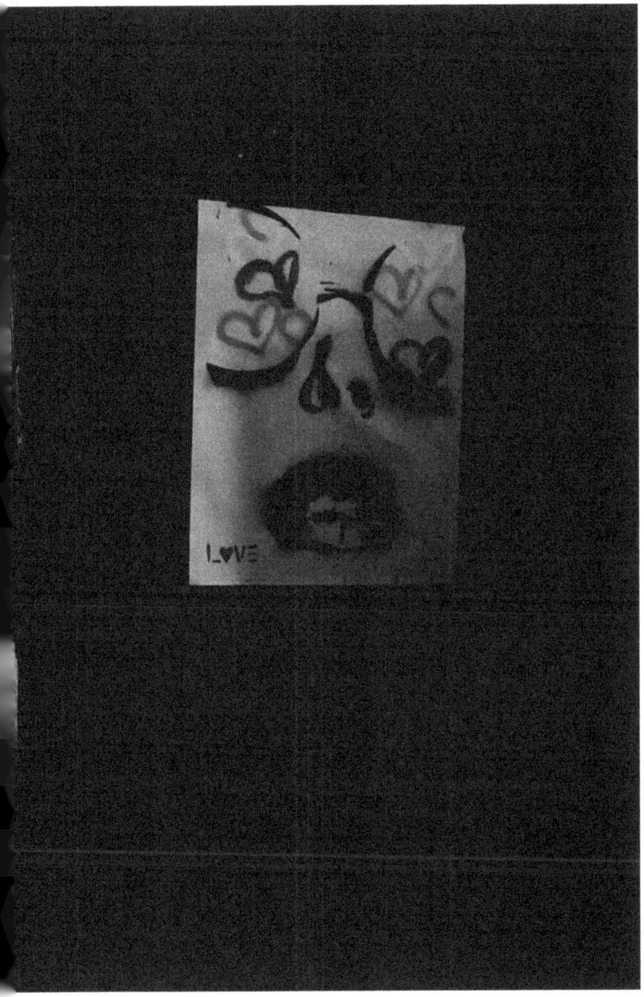

7th St. between 1st & Ave. A

DLove

4:27 AM

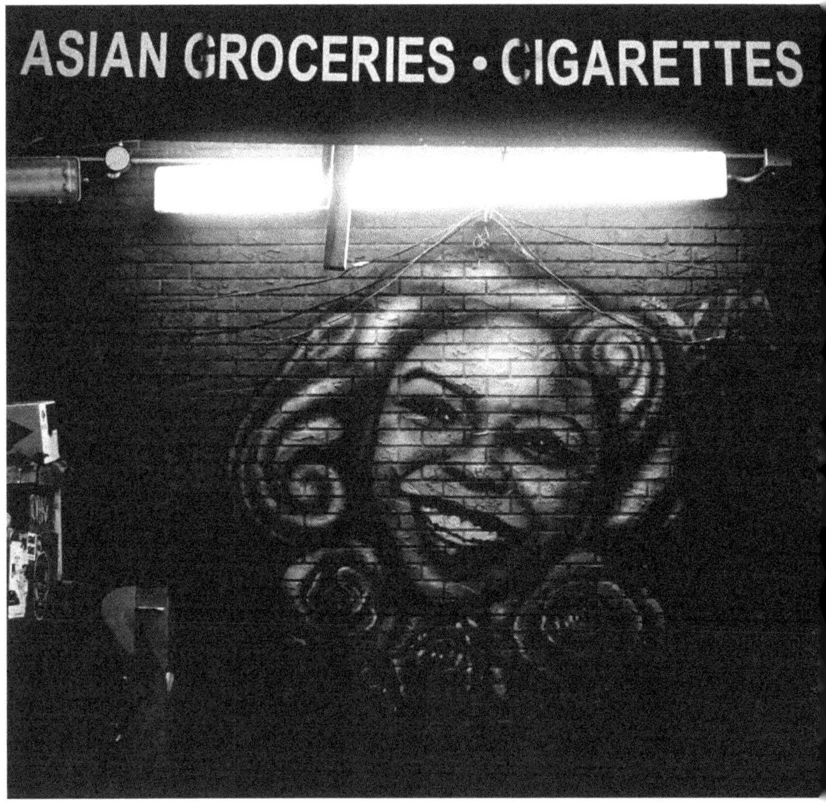

7th St. between 1st & 2nd Ave.

Muckrock

4:27 AM

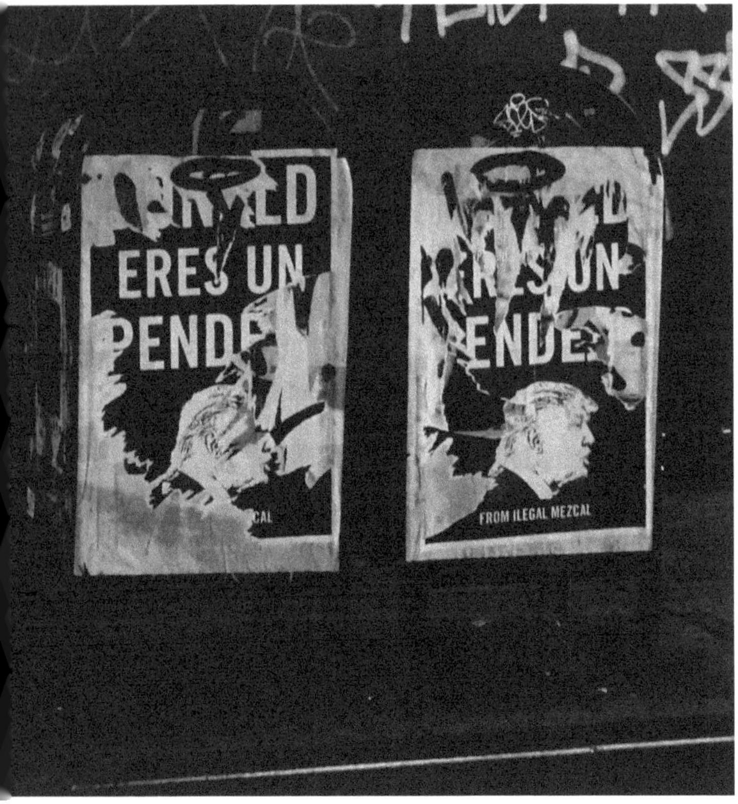

7th St. between 1st & 2nd Ave.

“Ilegal Mezcal”

4:29 AM

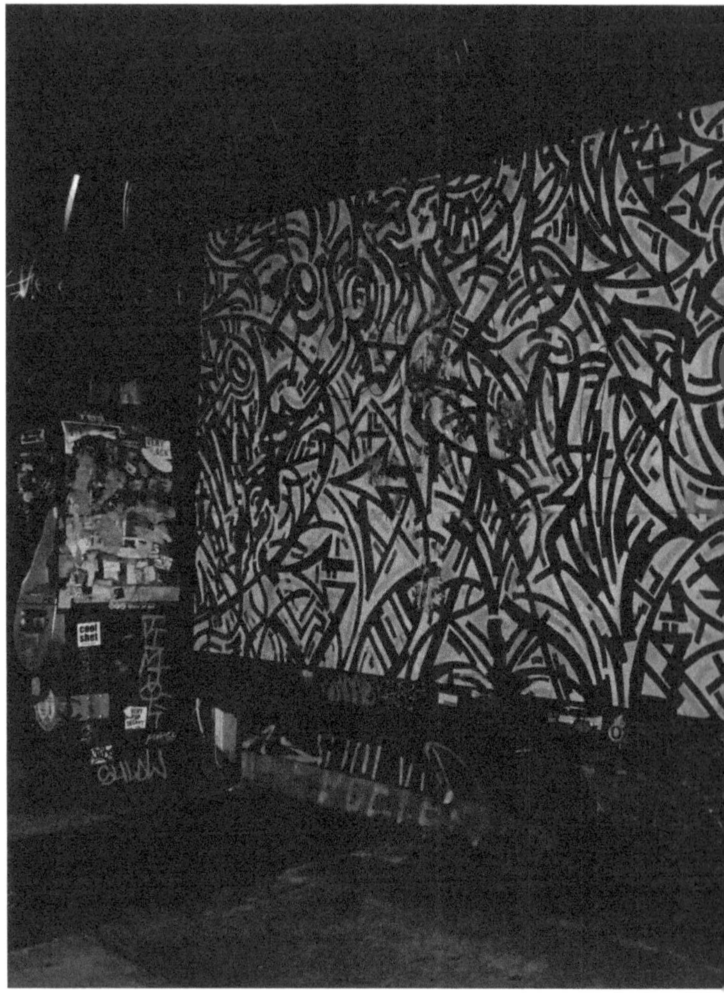

7th St. between 1st & 2nd Ave.

Cram

4:38 AM

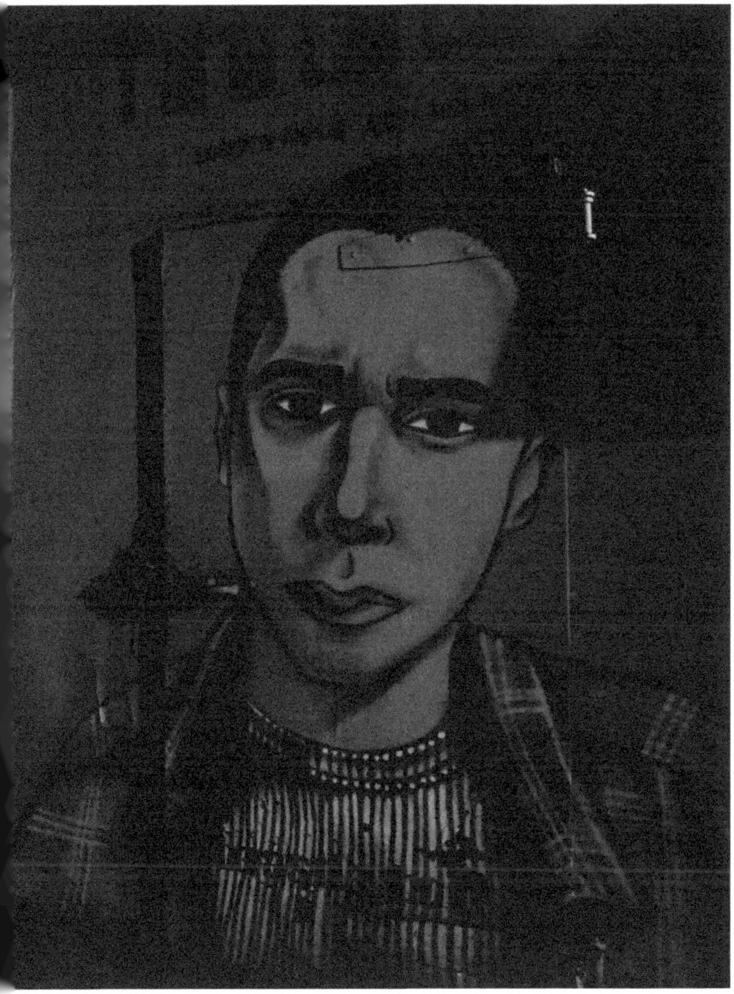

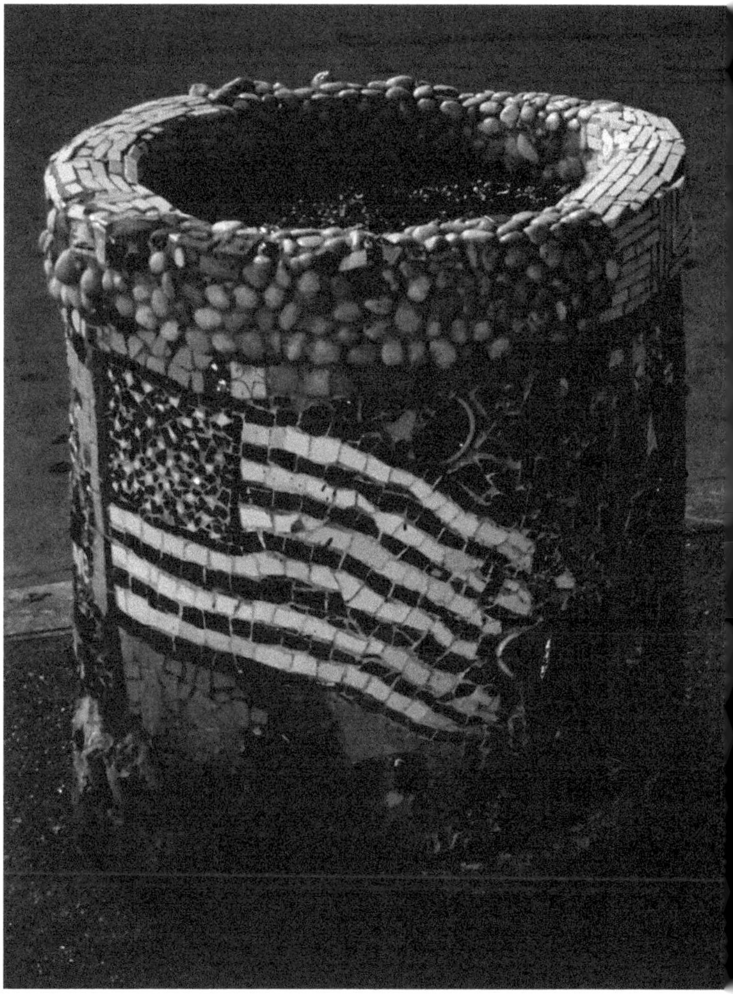

St. Mark's Place between 3rd & 4th Ave.

The Mosaic Man

4:47 AM

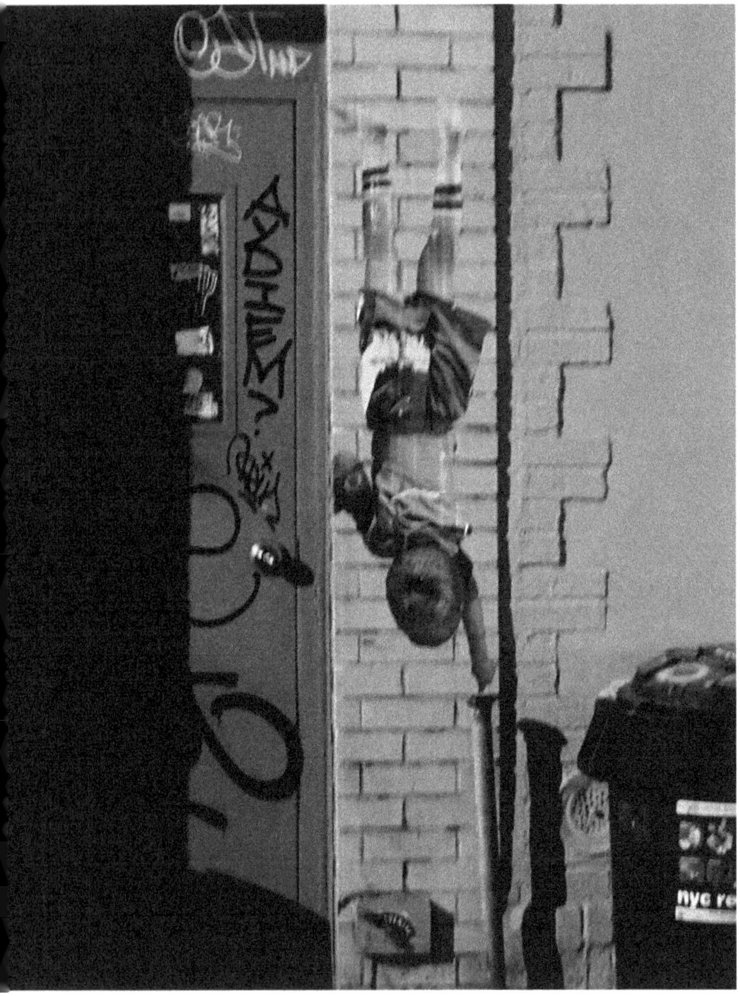

St. Mark's Place between 1st & 2nd Ave.

Thomas Allen

4:49 AM

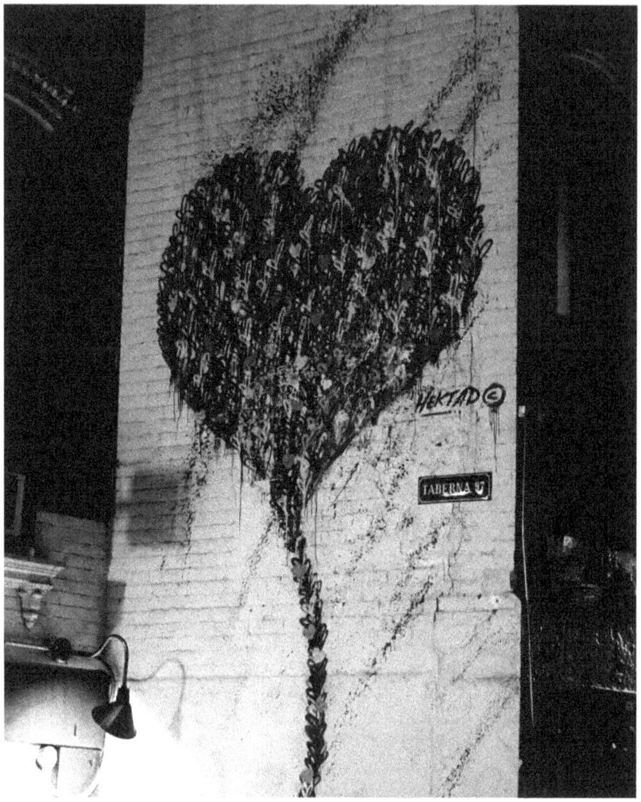

St. Mark's Place between 1st & Ave. A

Hektad

4:51 AM

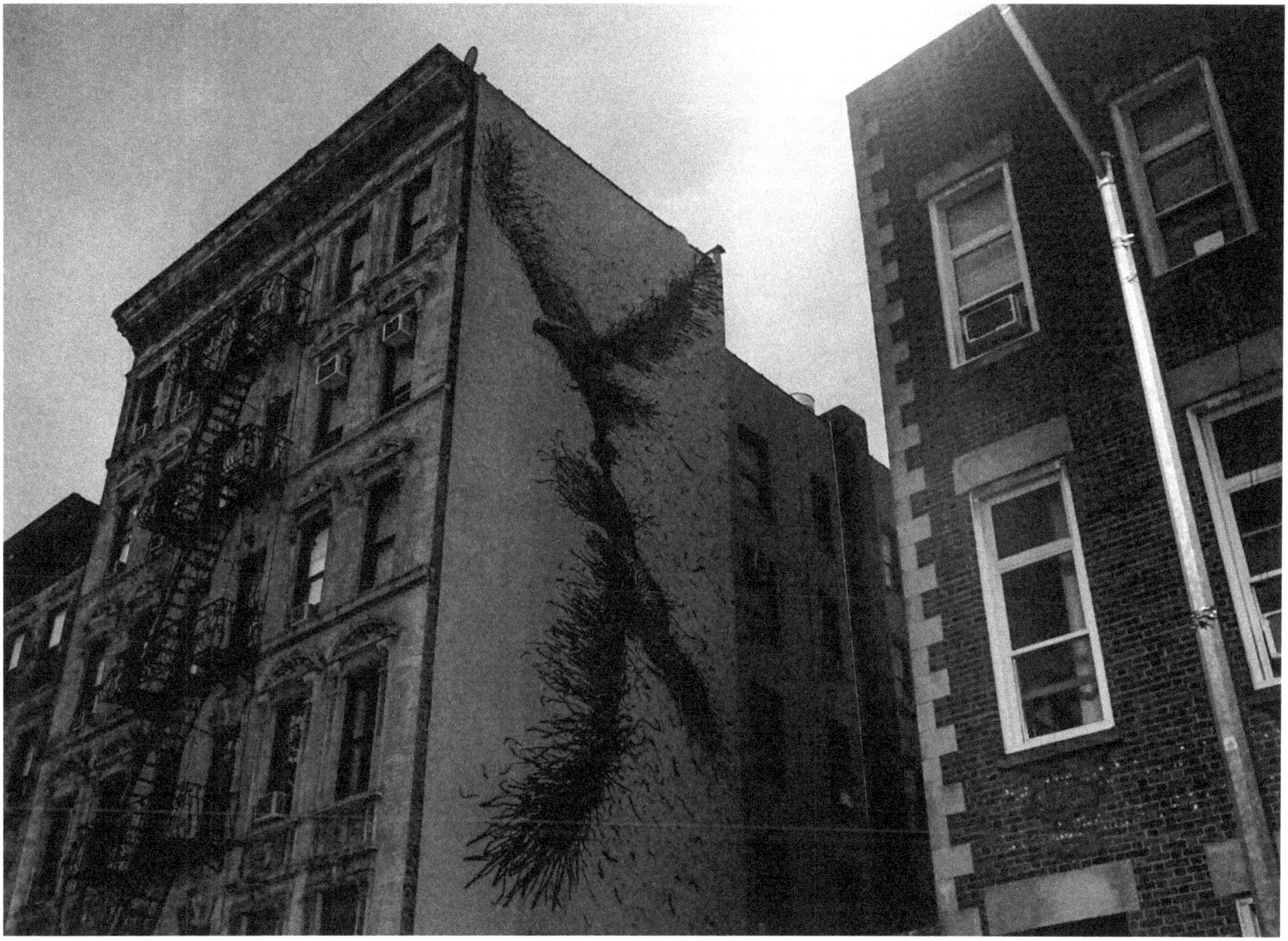

St. Mark's Place between 1st & Ave. A

Daleast

4:52 AM

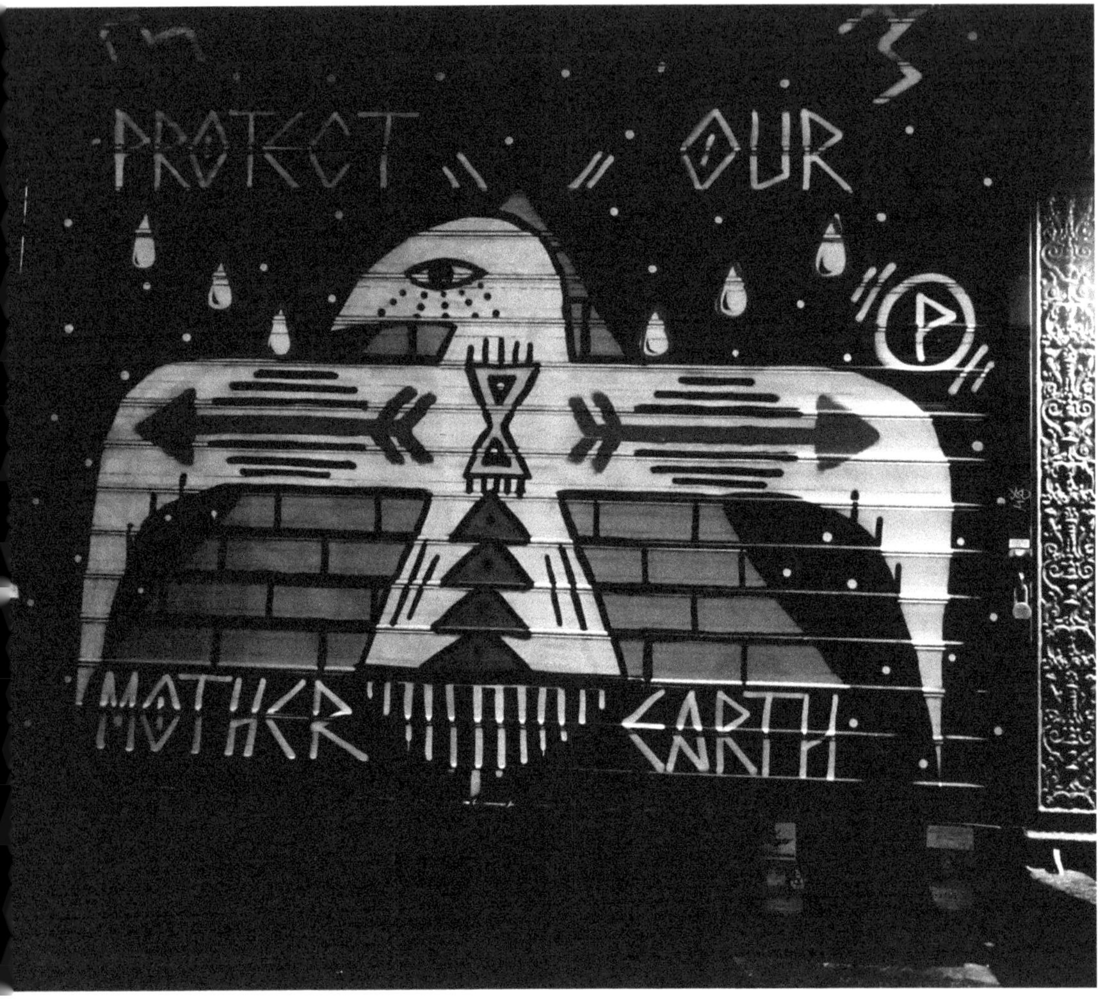

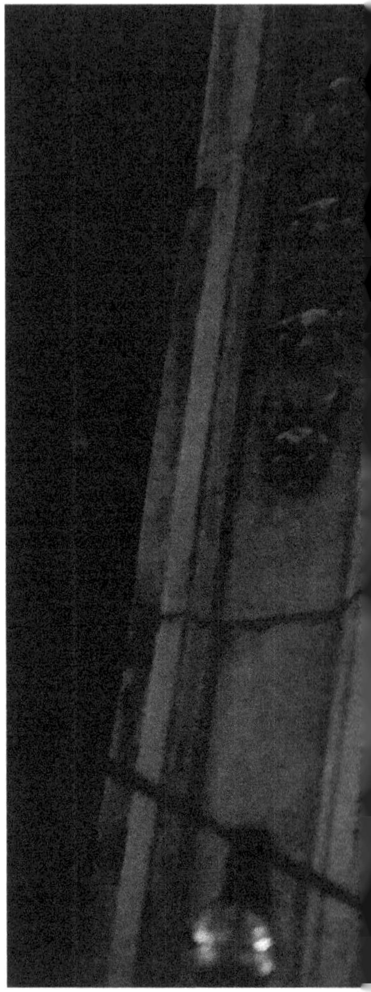

St. Mark's Place between 1st & Ave. A

Pixote

4:54 AM

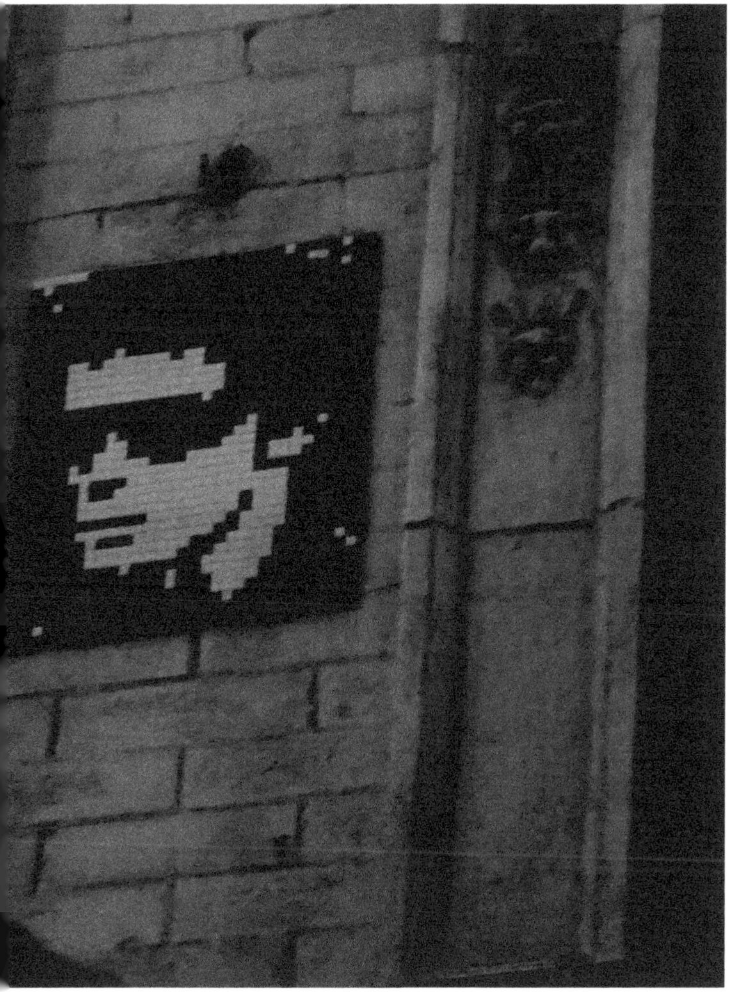

St. Mark's Place between 1st & Ave. A

Invader

4:58 AM

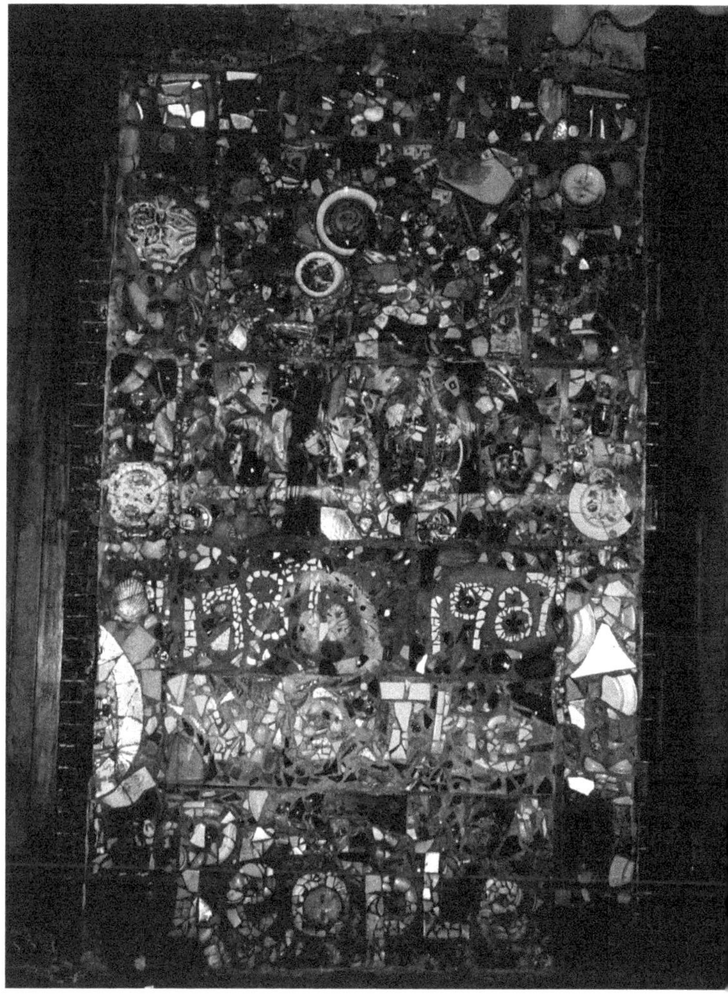

St. Mark's Place between 1st & Ave. A

The Mosaic Man

4:59 AM

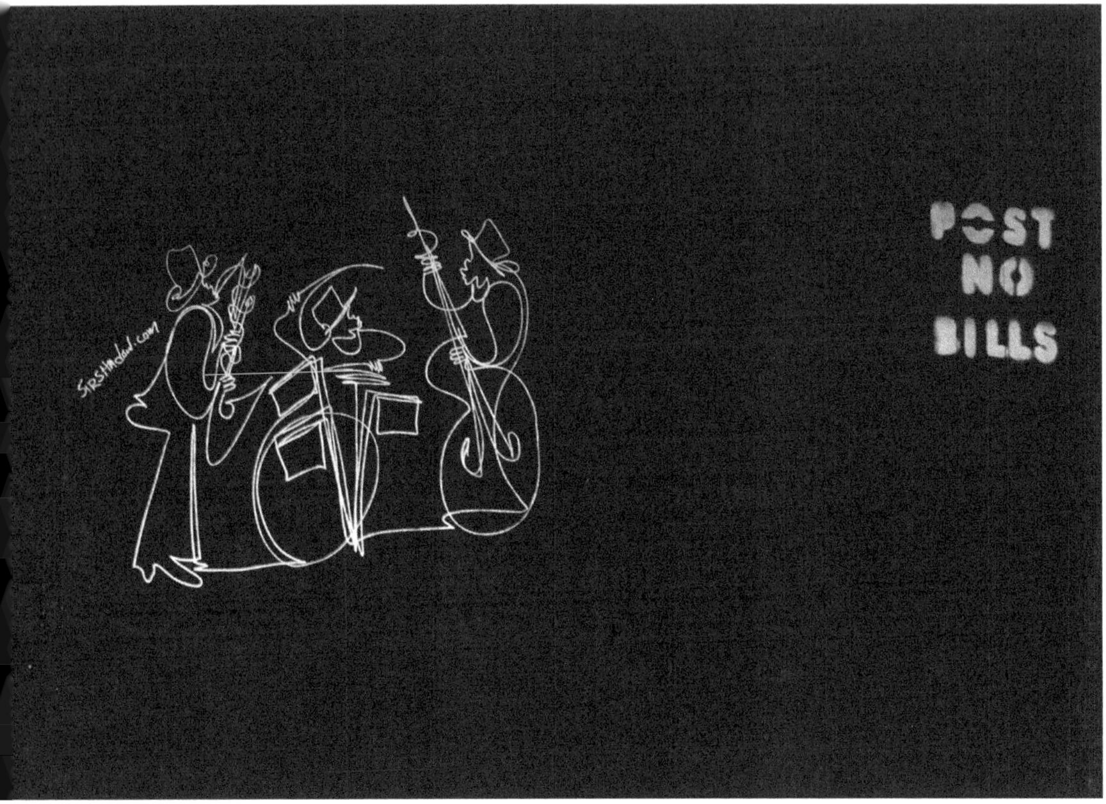

St. Mark's Place between 1st & Ave. A

Sir Shadow

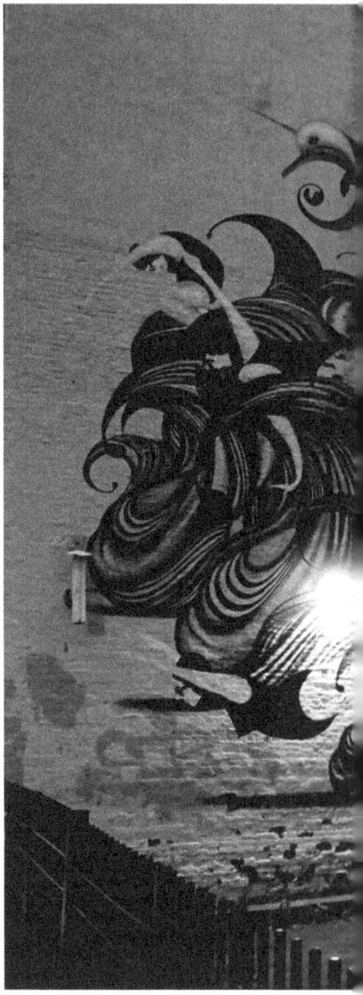

5:06 AM

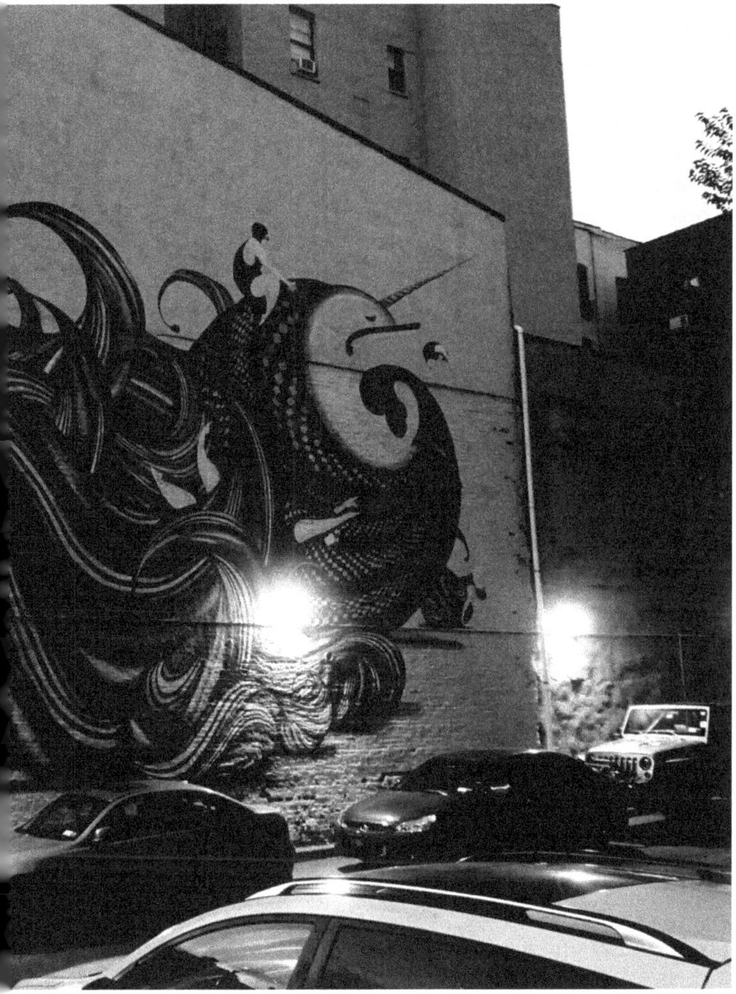

8th St. between Ave. B & C

Gary Fernandez

5:12 AM

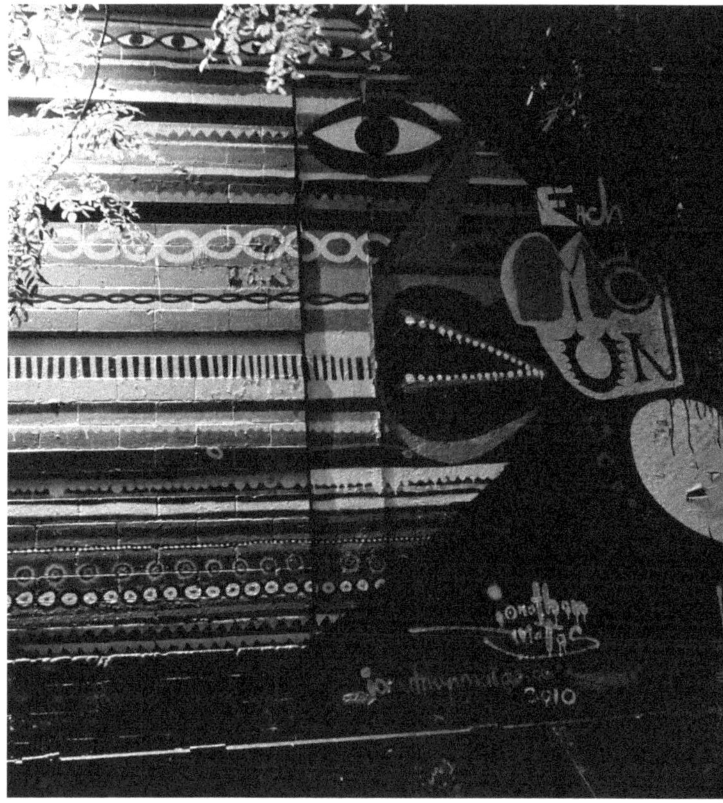

9th St. between Ave. C & D

Jonathan Matas

5:14 AM

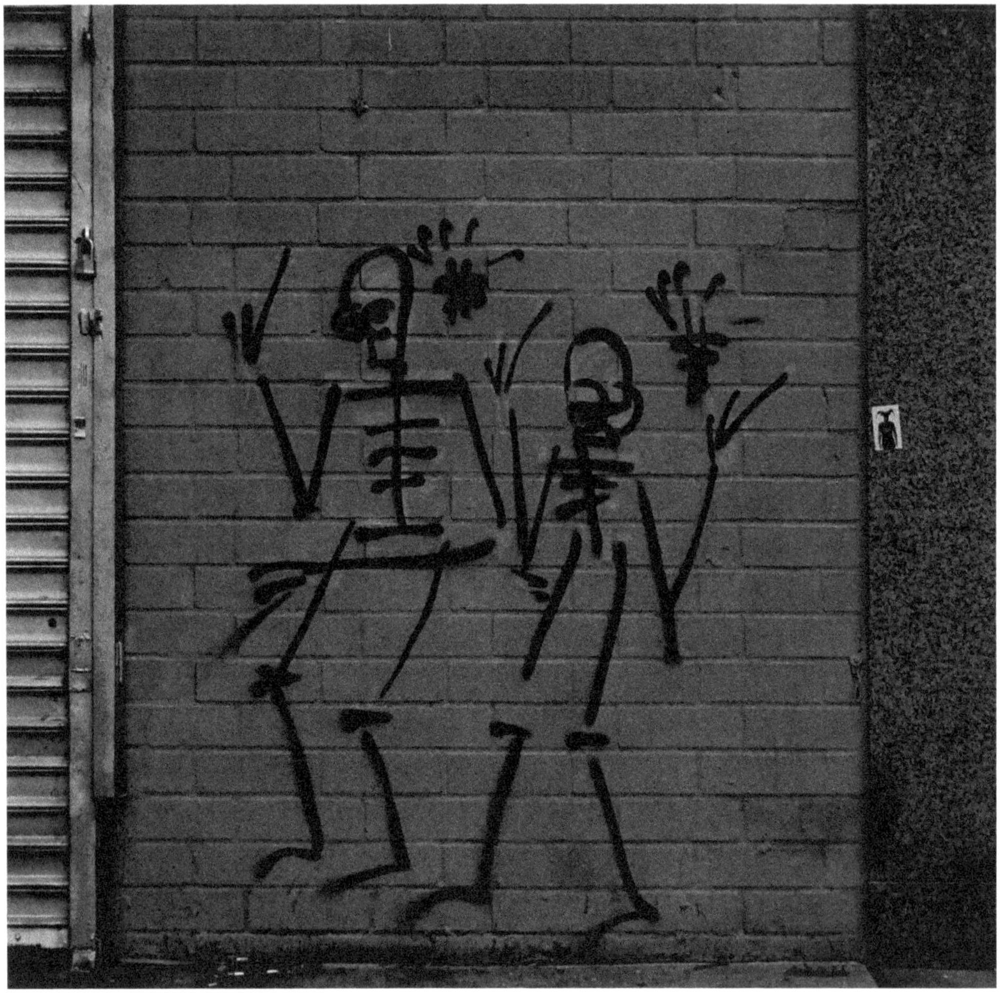

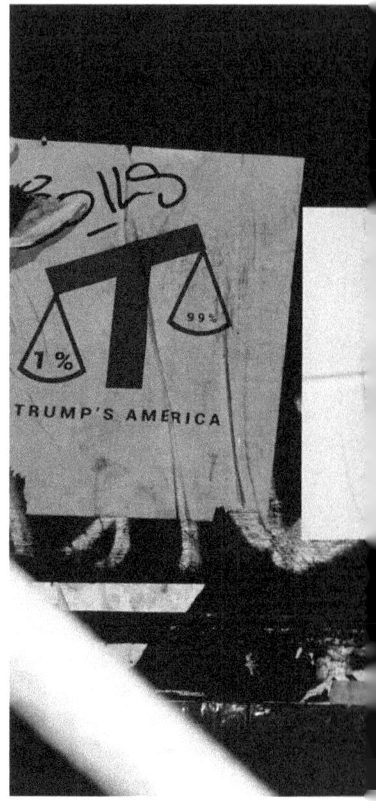

9th St. between Ave. B & C

Gianni Lee

5:18 AM

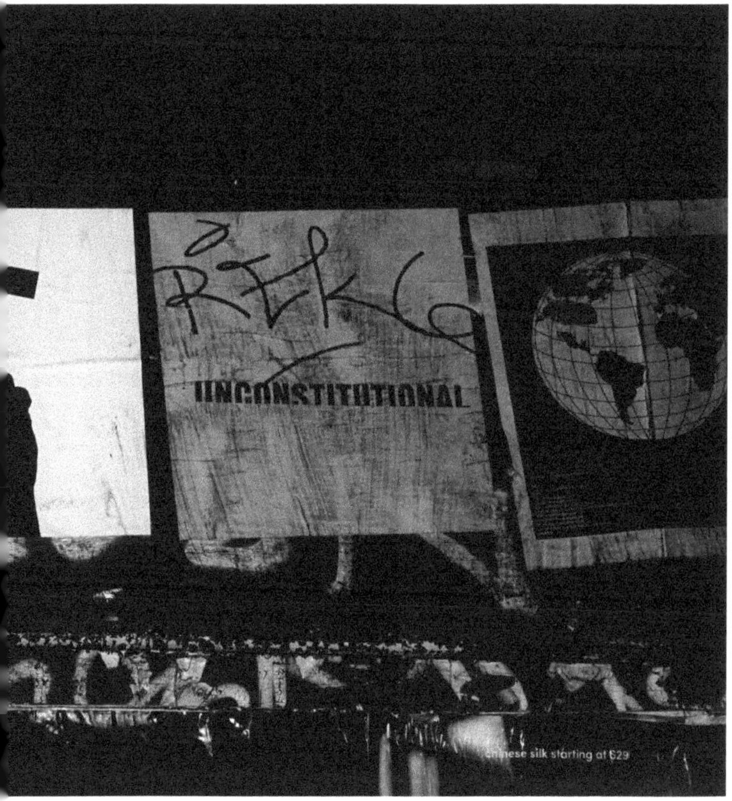

9th St. between Ave. B & C

Unknown

5:23 AM

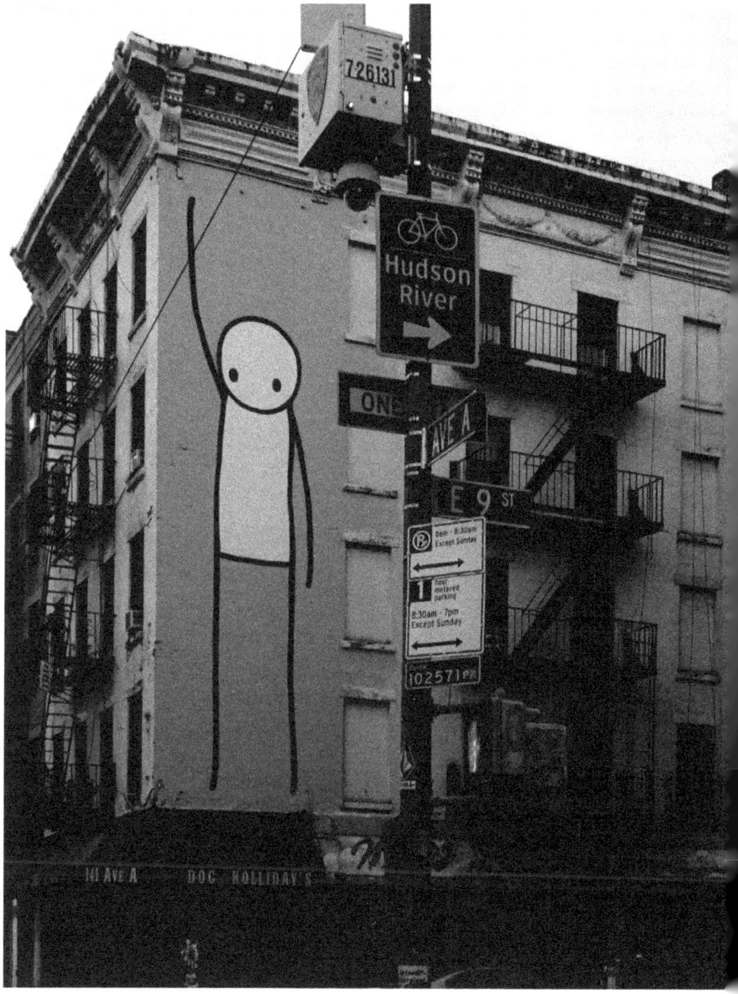

9th St. between 1st & Ave. A

Stik

5:24 AM

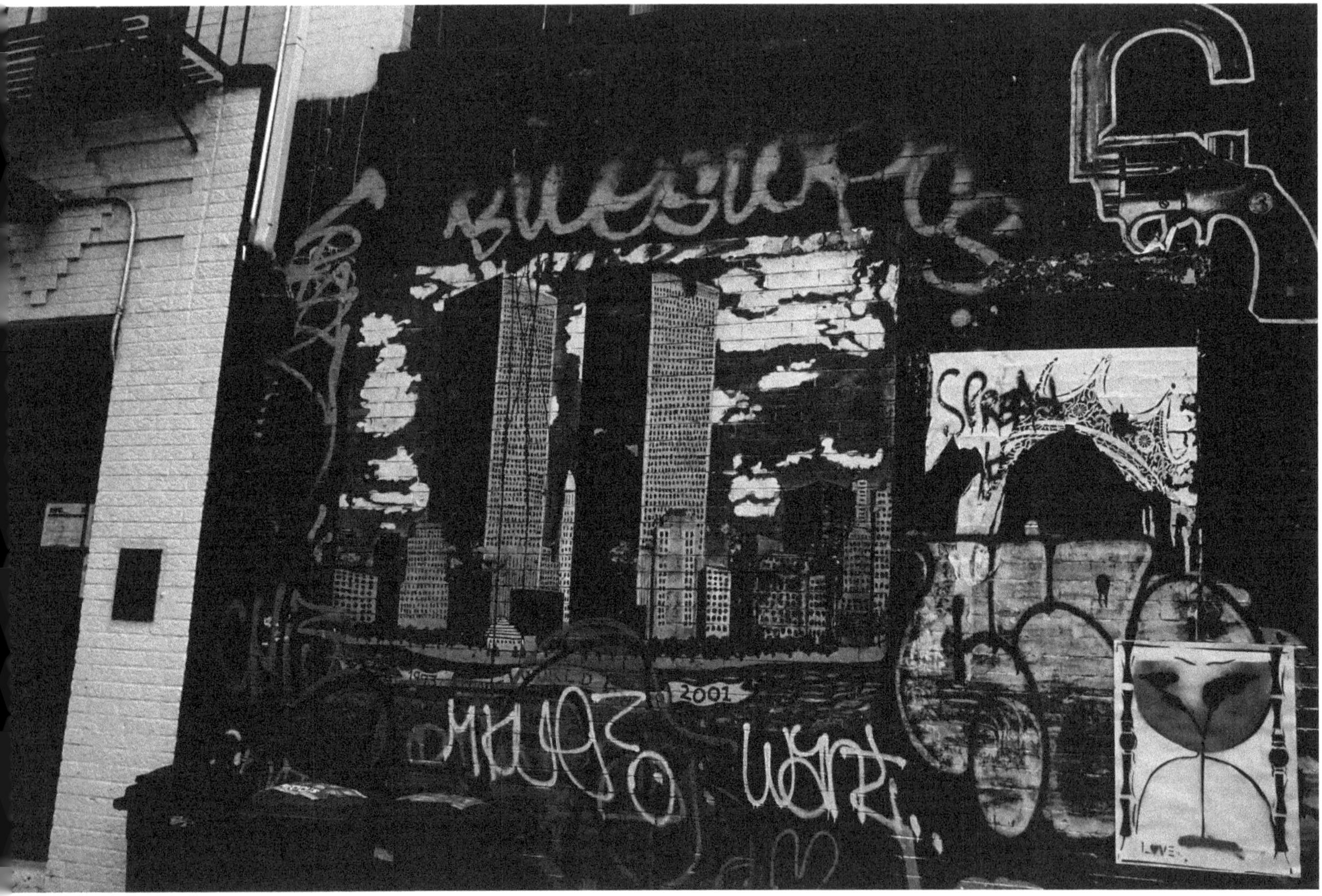

9th St. between 1st & Ave. A

Jesse Fischler, Unlok, DLove

5:27 AM

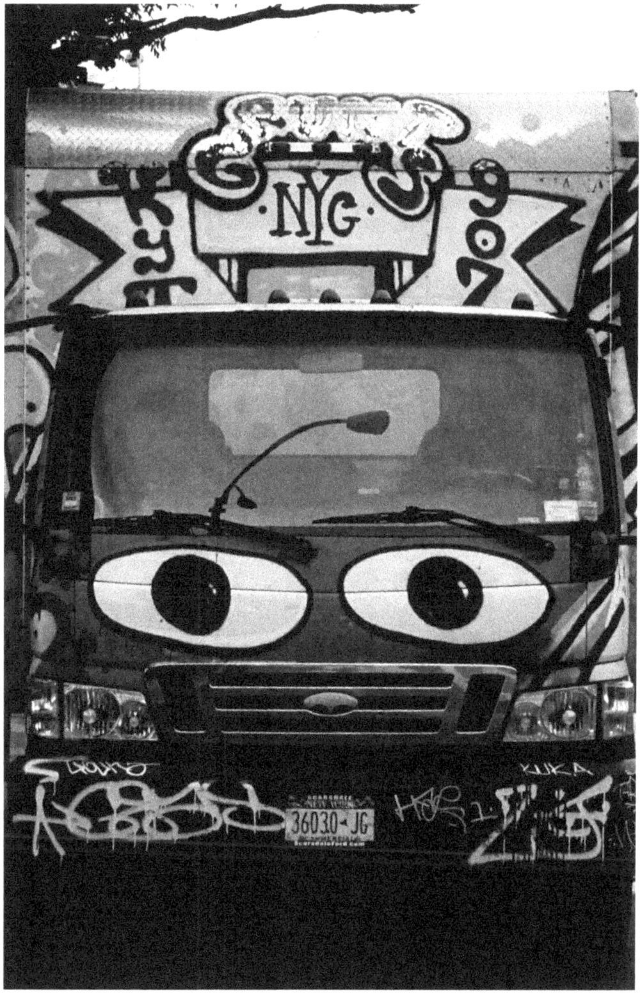

9th St. & 1st Ave.

Kyt, Grunts, 907

5:28 AM

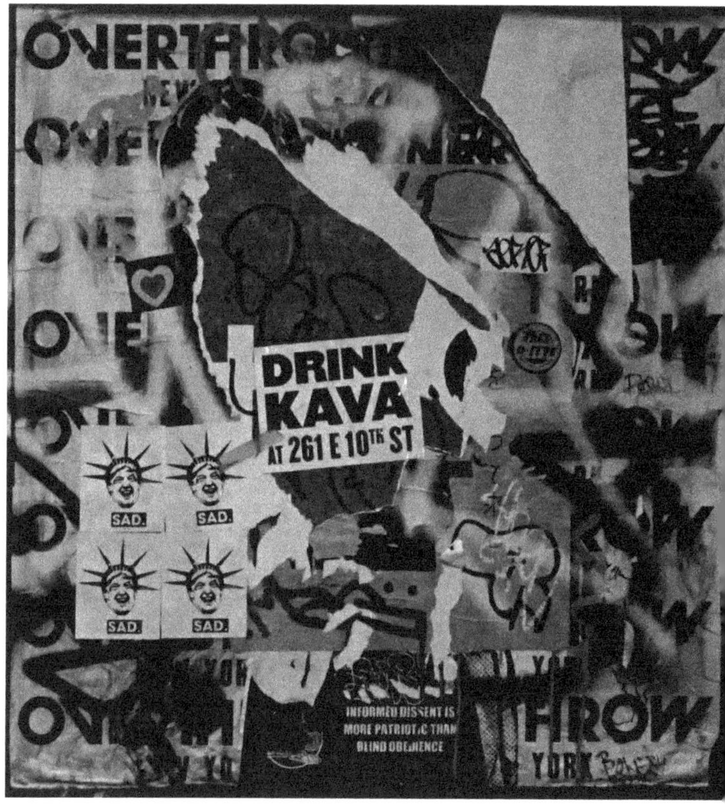

9th St. between 1st & 2nd Ave.

Unknown

5:30 AM

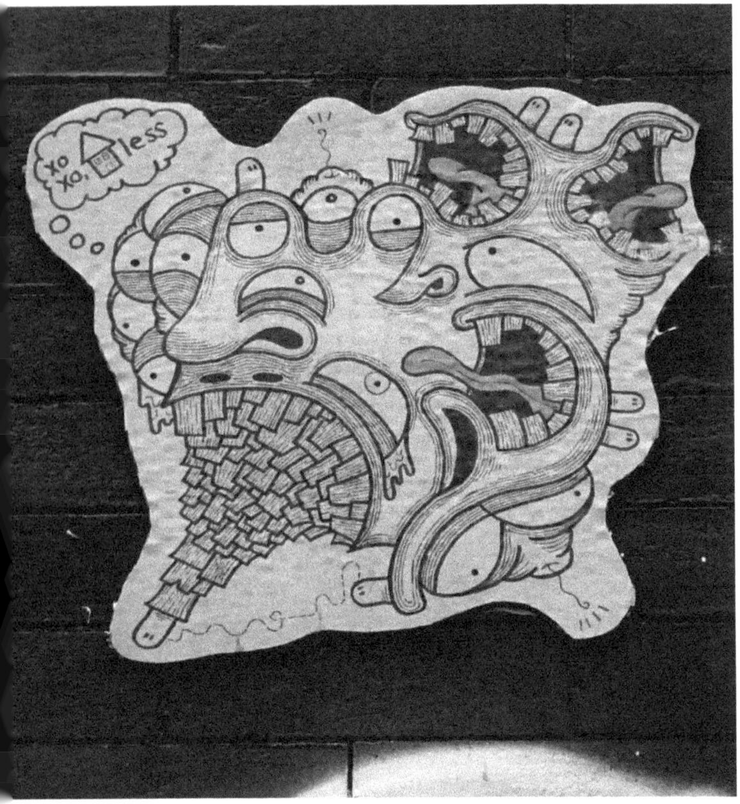

9th St. between 1st & 2nd Ave.

Homeless

5:32 AM

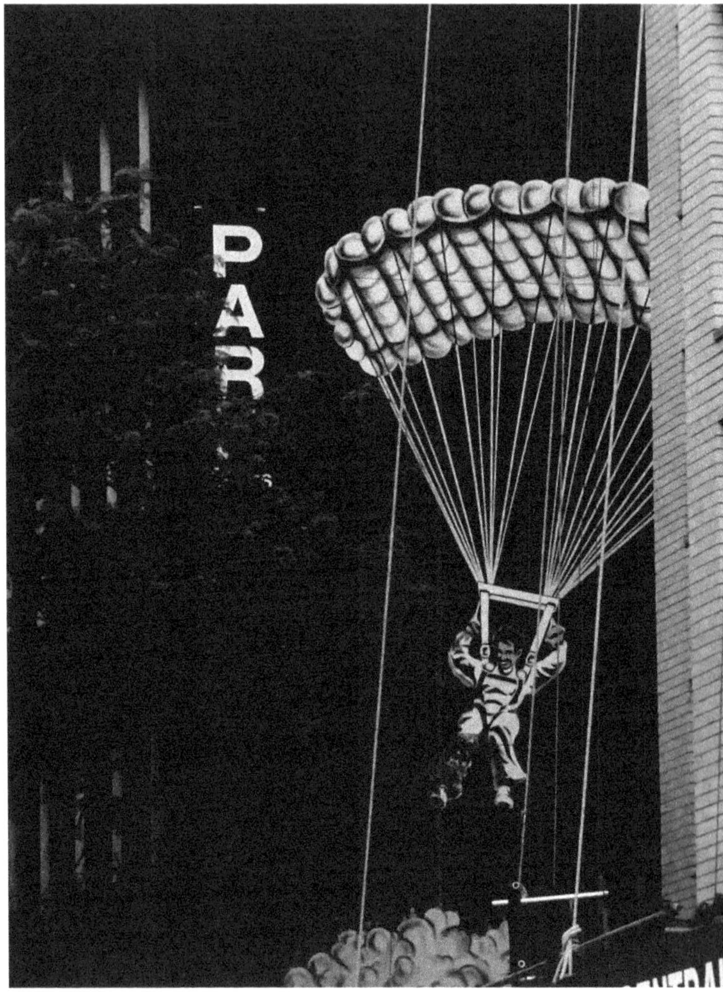

9th St. between 3rd & 4th Ave.

Tom Bob

5:35 AM

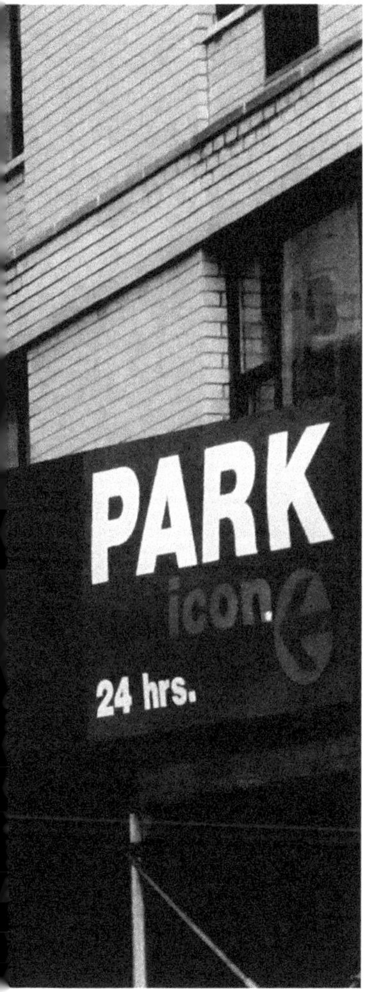

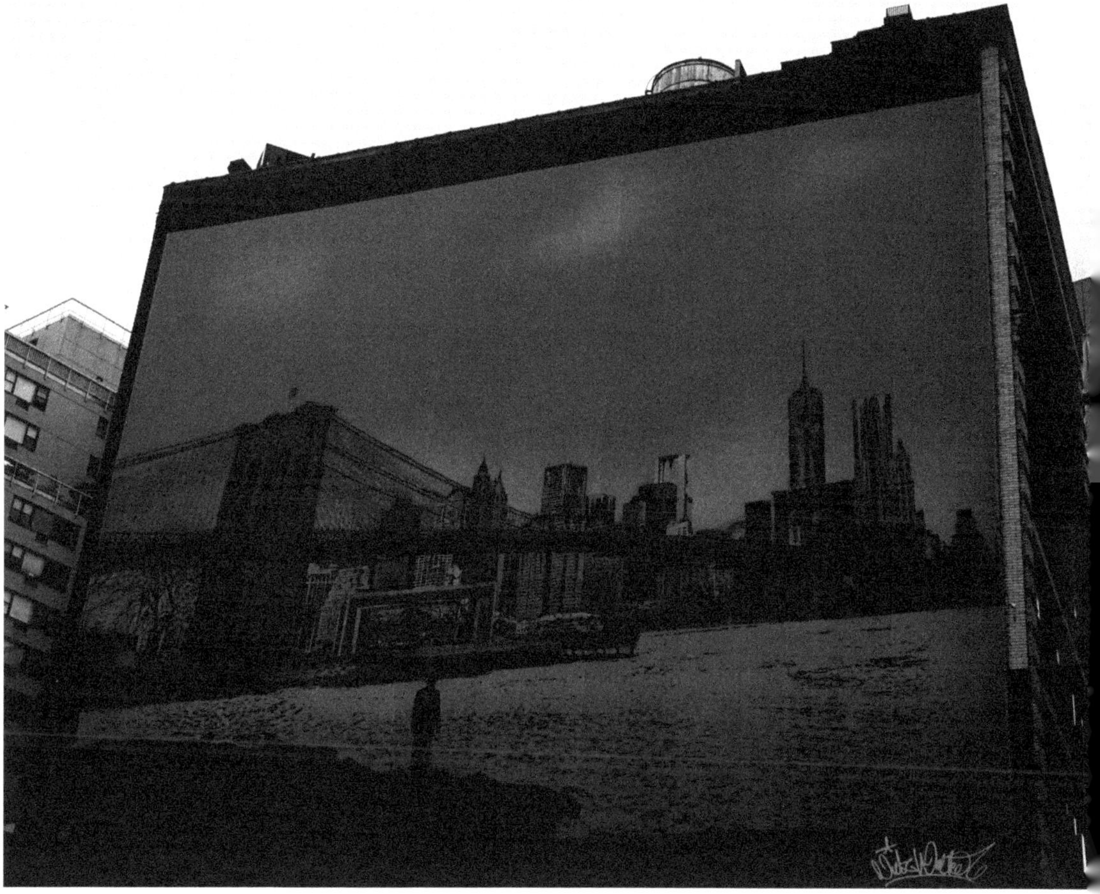

10th St. between 3rd & 4th Ave.

Nick Walker

8:44 AM

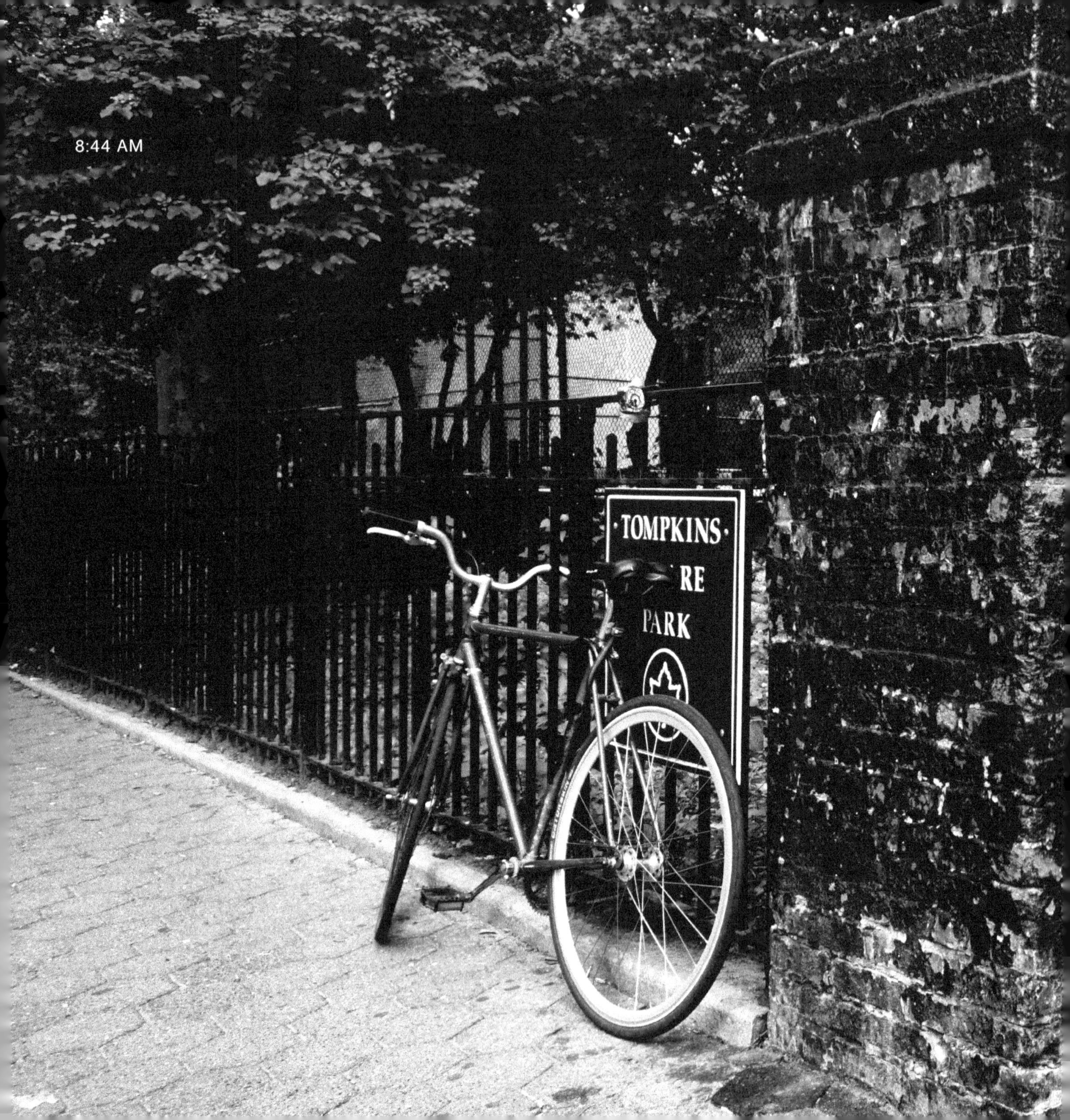

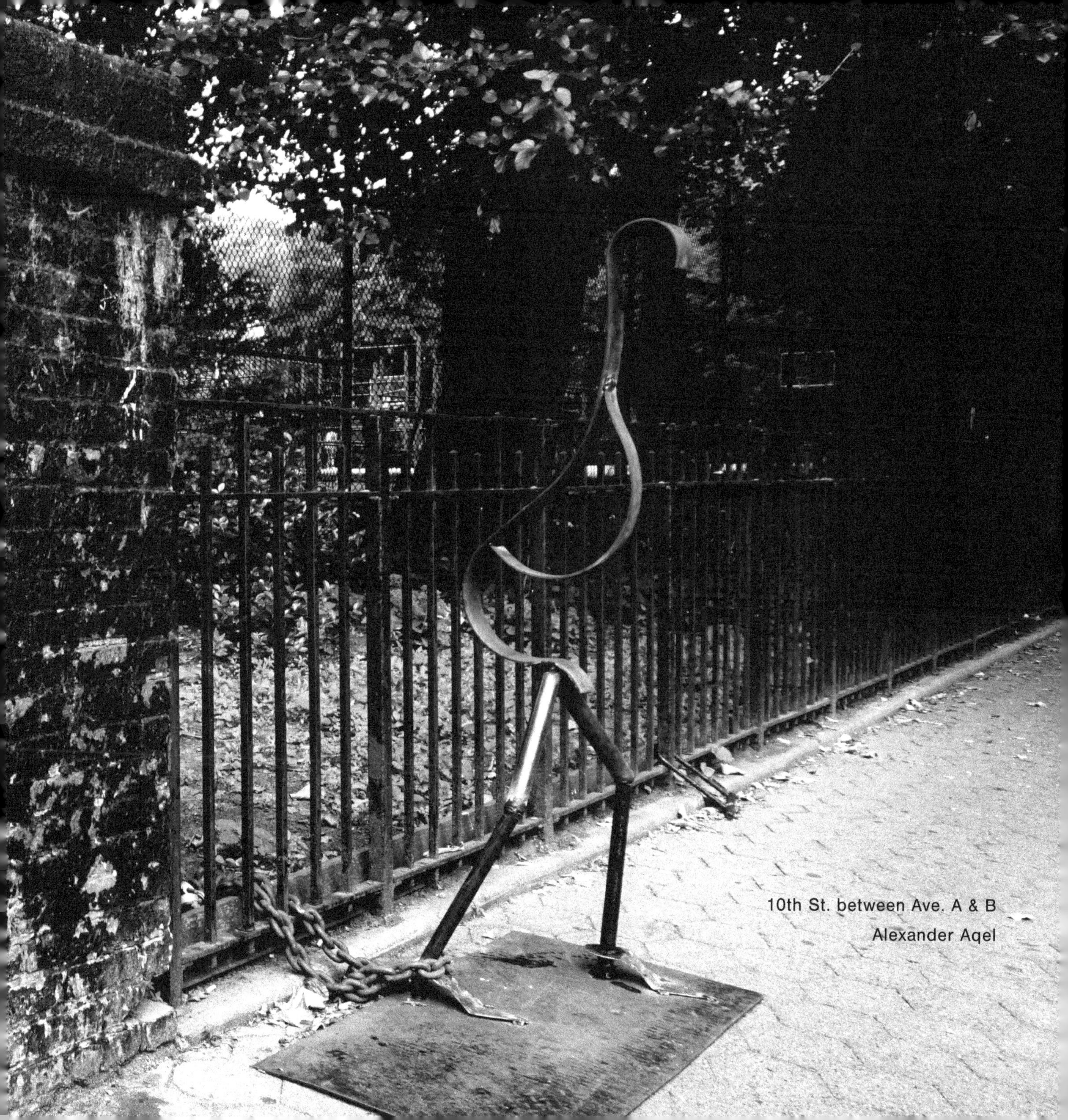

10th St. between Ave. A & B
Alexander Aqel

8:46 AM

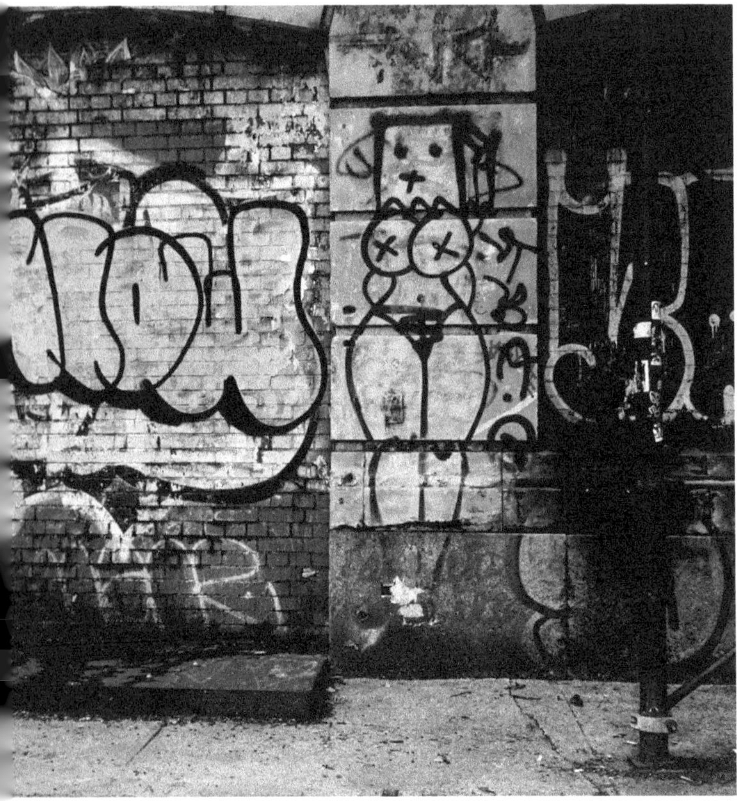

10th St. between Ave. B & C

Unknown

8:55 AM

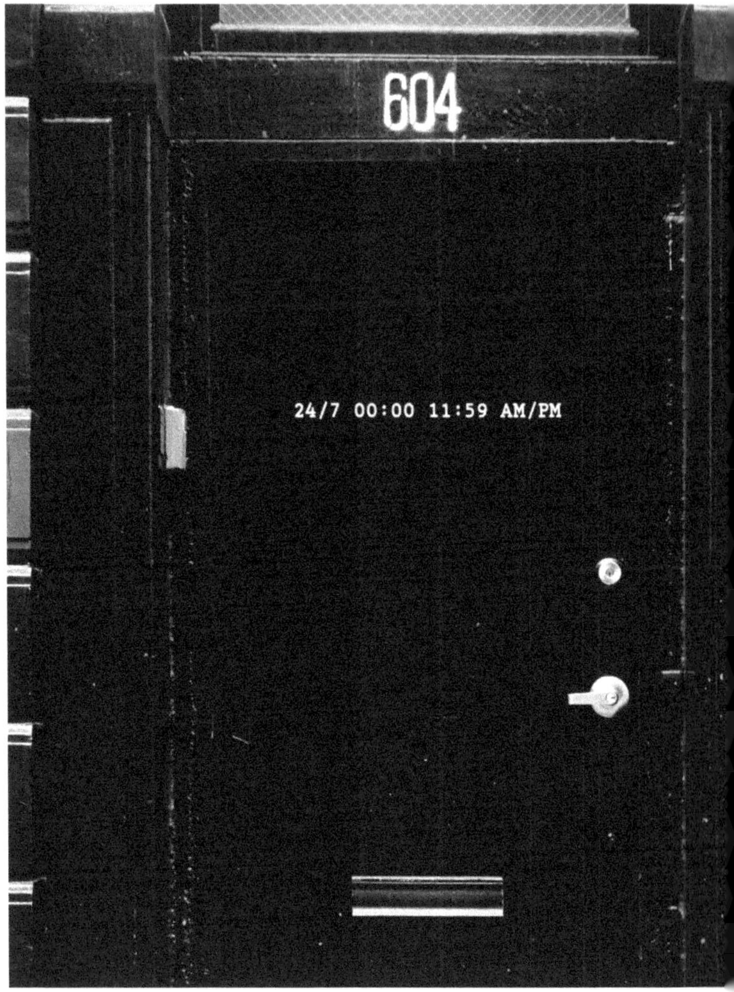

11th St. between Ave. B & C

Unknown

9:02 AM

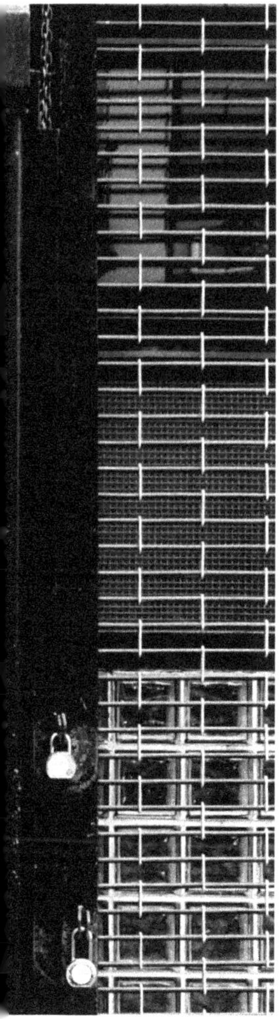

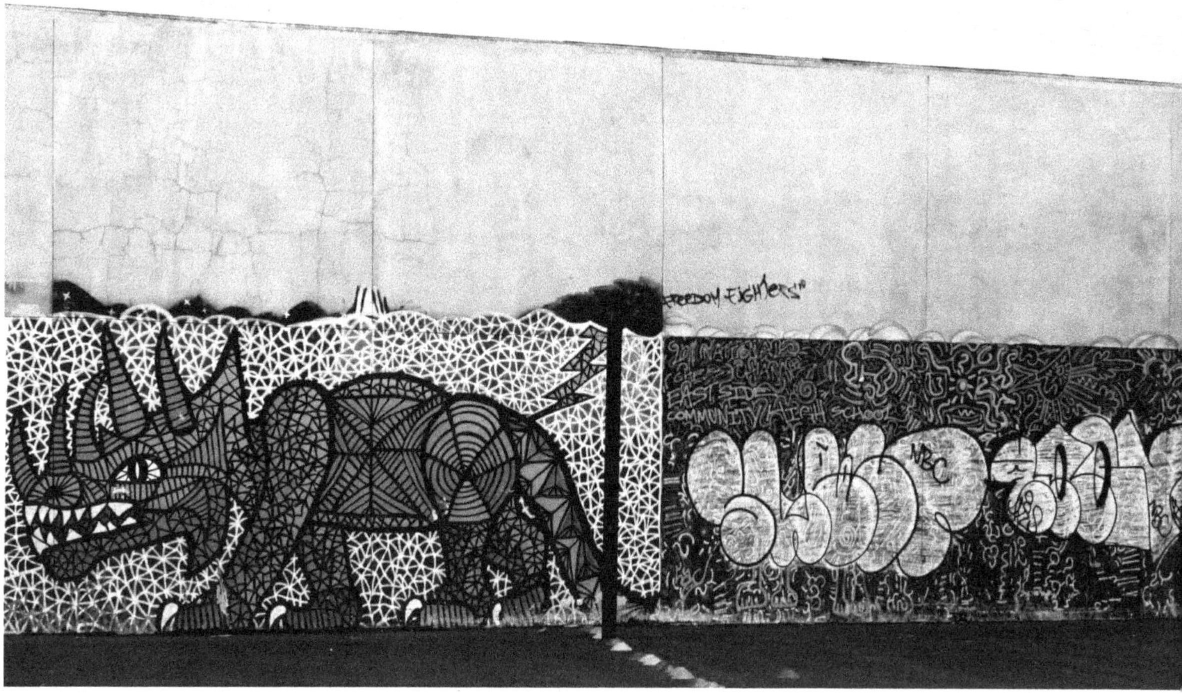

LES Playground @ 11th St. between 1st & Ave. A

Michael K., LA2

9:04 AM

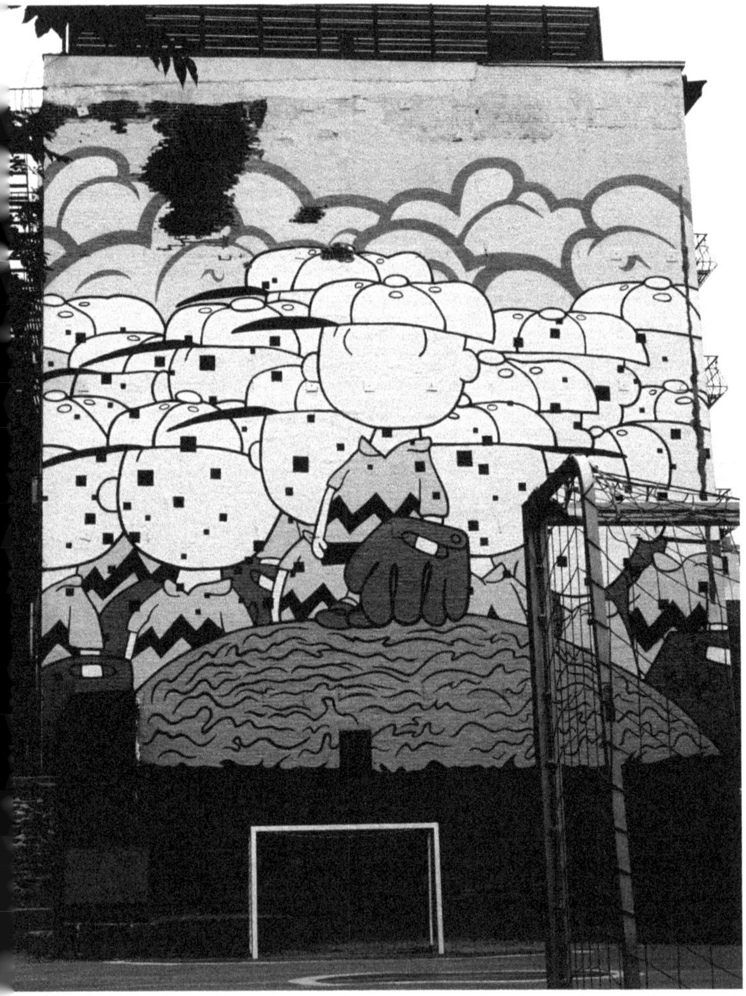

LES Playground @ 12th St. between 1st & Ave. A

Jerk Face

9:07 AM

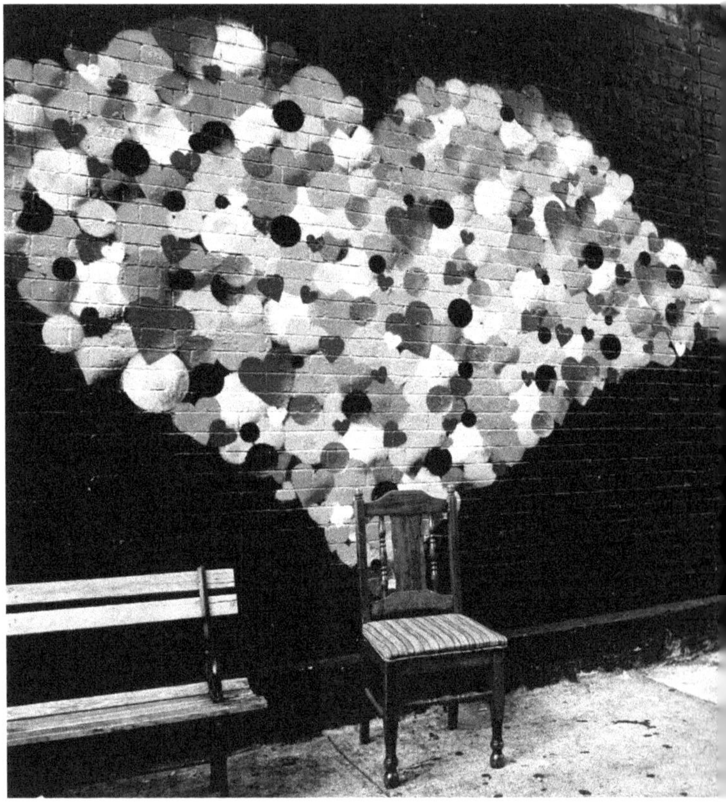

11th St. between 1st & Ave. A

Hektad

9:09 AM

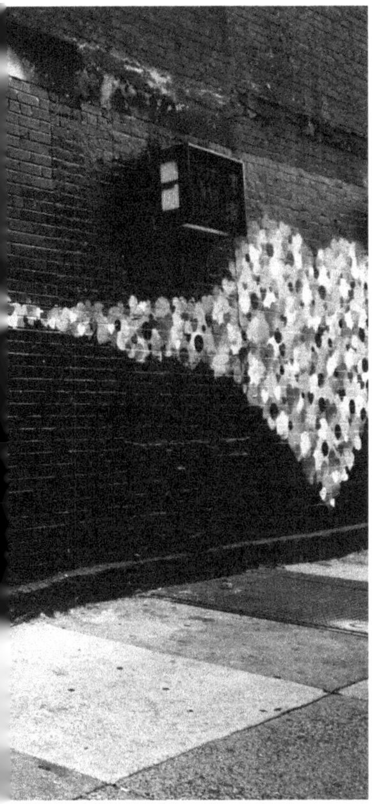

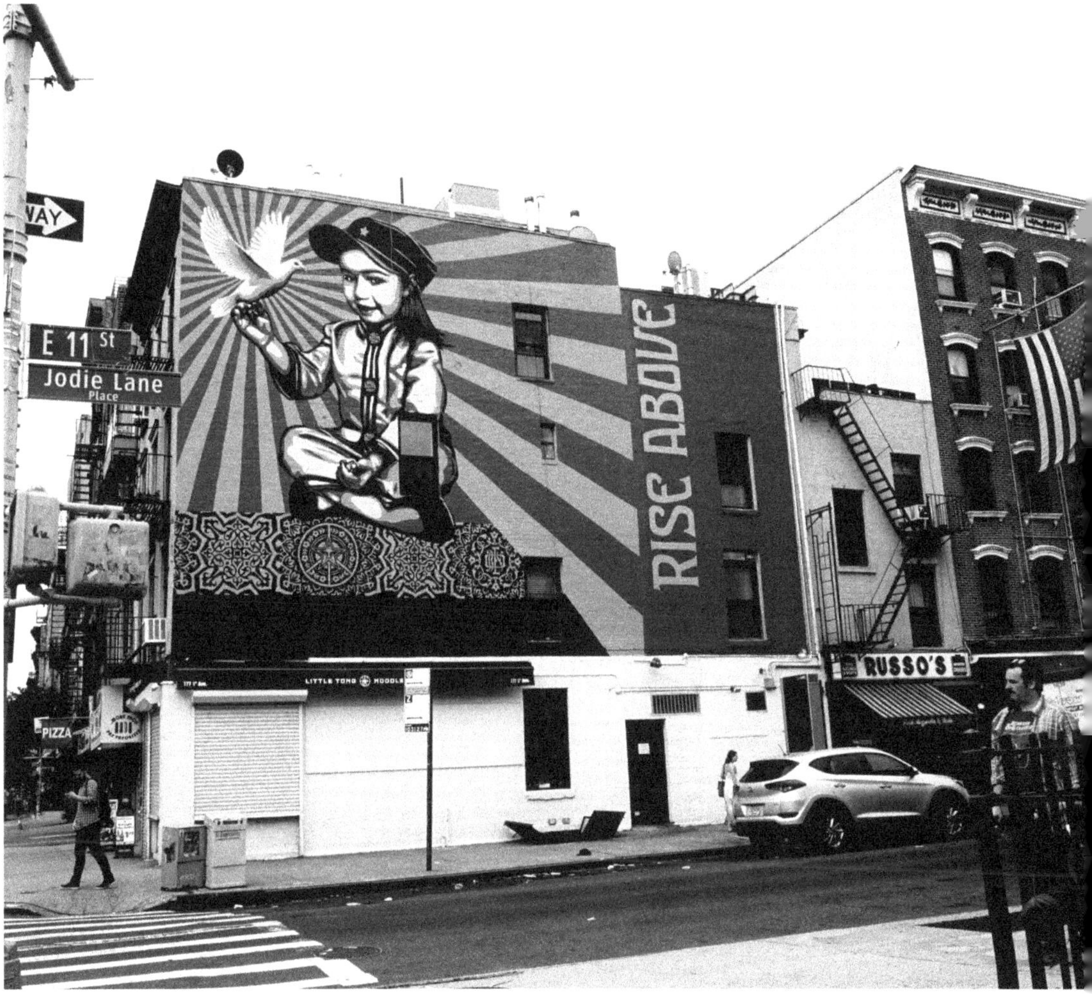

11th St. between 1st & 2nd Ave.

Shepard Fairey

9:18 AM

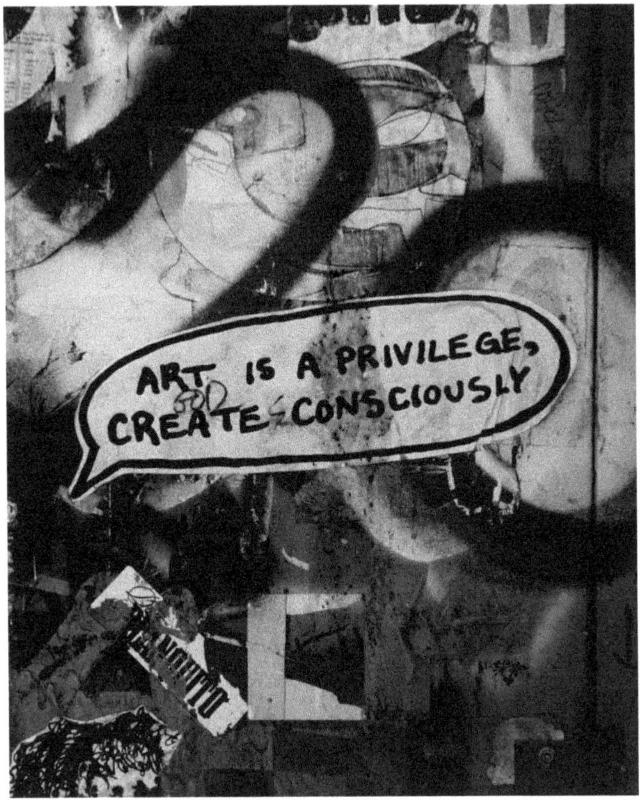

12th St. between 3rd & 4th Ave.

Unknown

9:19 AM

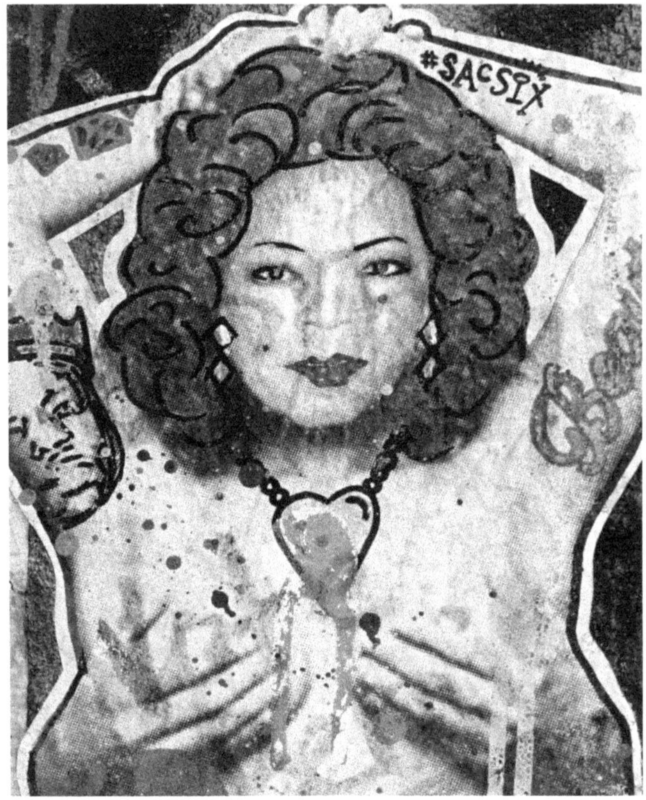

12th St. between 3rd & 4th Ave.

Sacsix

9:19 AM

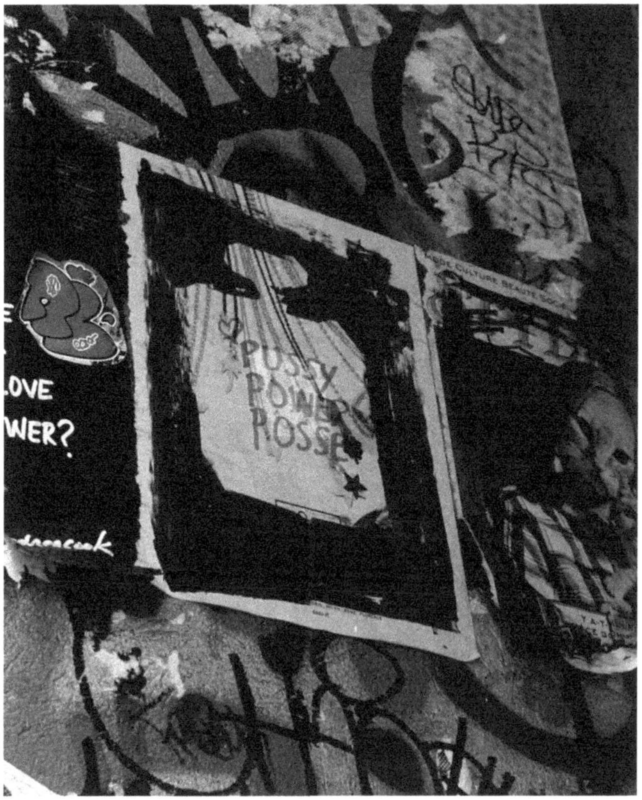

12th St. between 3rd & 4th Ave.
Andrea Cook

9:31 AM

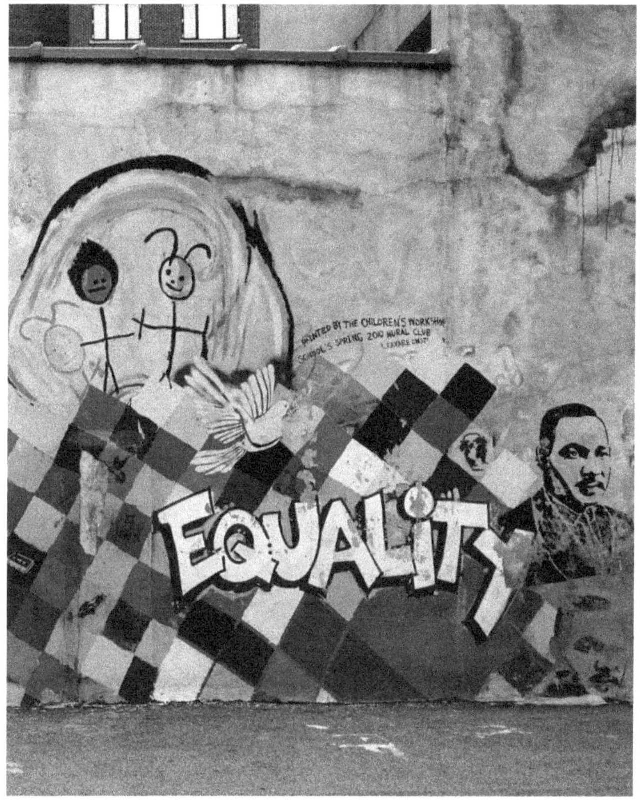

12th St. between Ave. B & C
Children's Workshop
Spring 2010 Mural Club,
Unknown

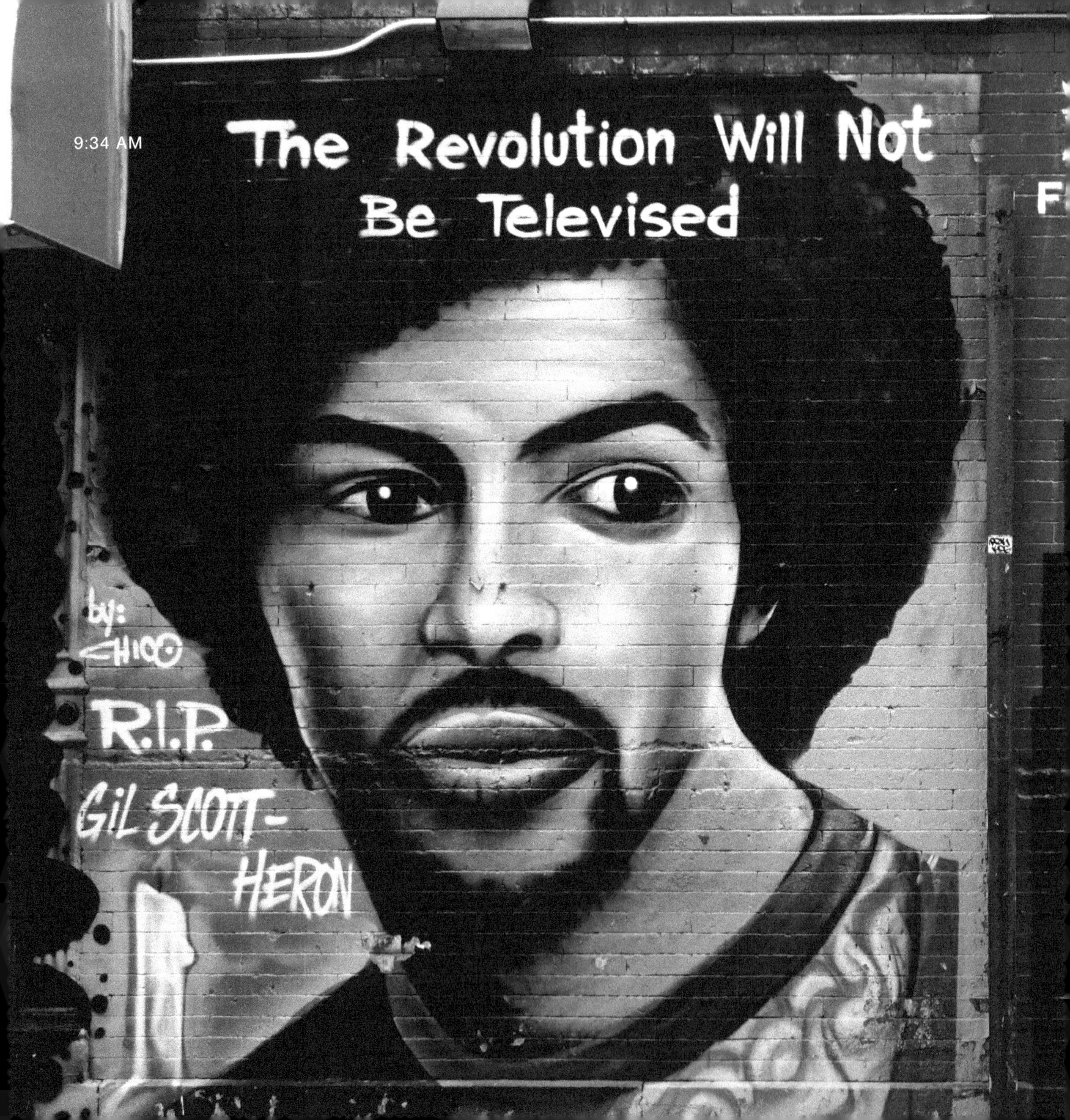
9:34 AM
The Revolution Will Not
Be Televised
by:
CHICO
R.I.P.
GIL SCOTT-
HERON

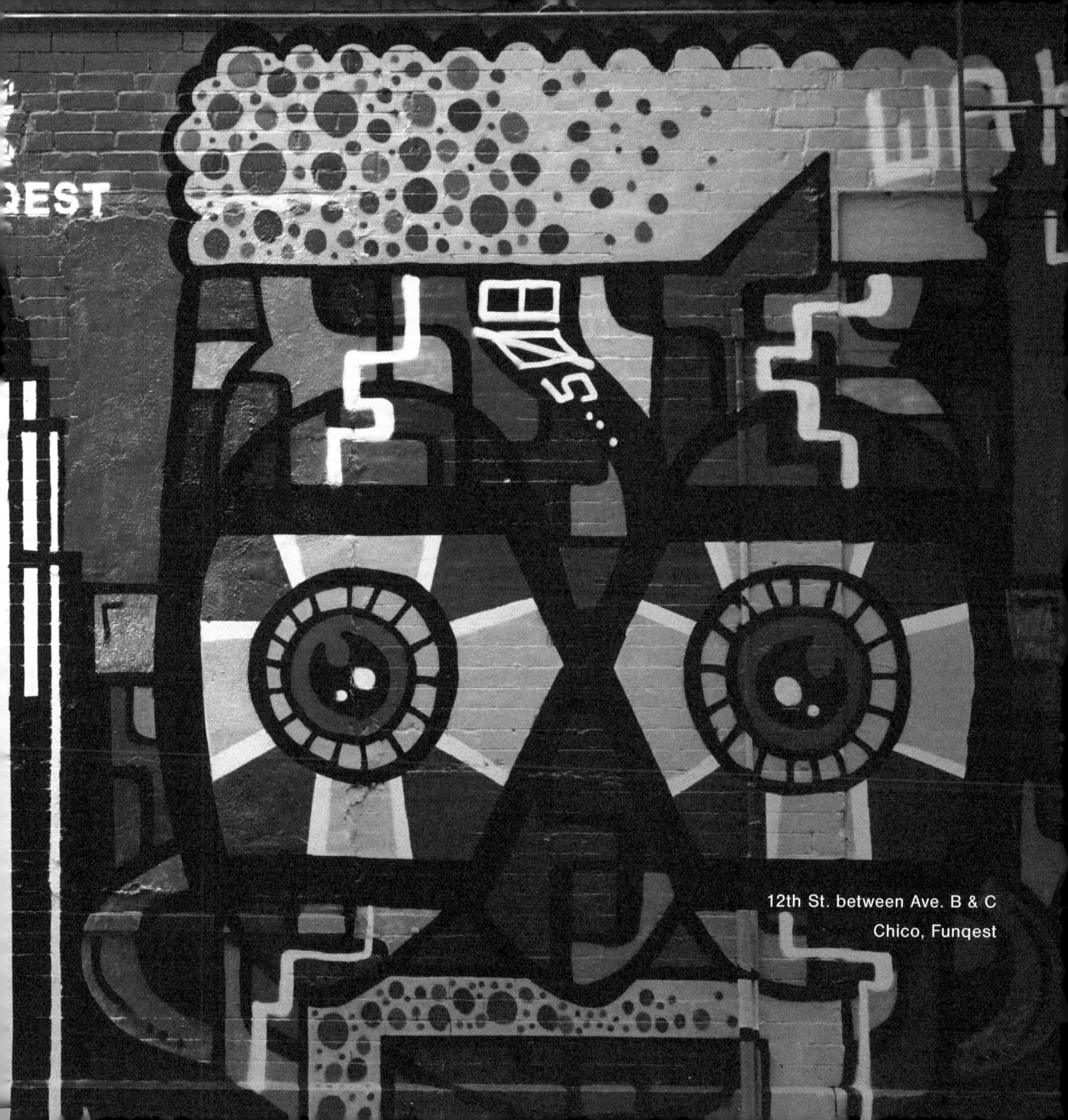

12th St. between Ave. B & C
Chico, Funqest

9:36 AM

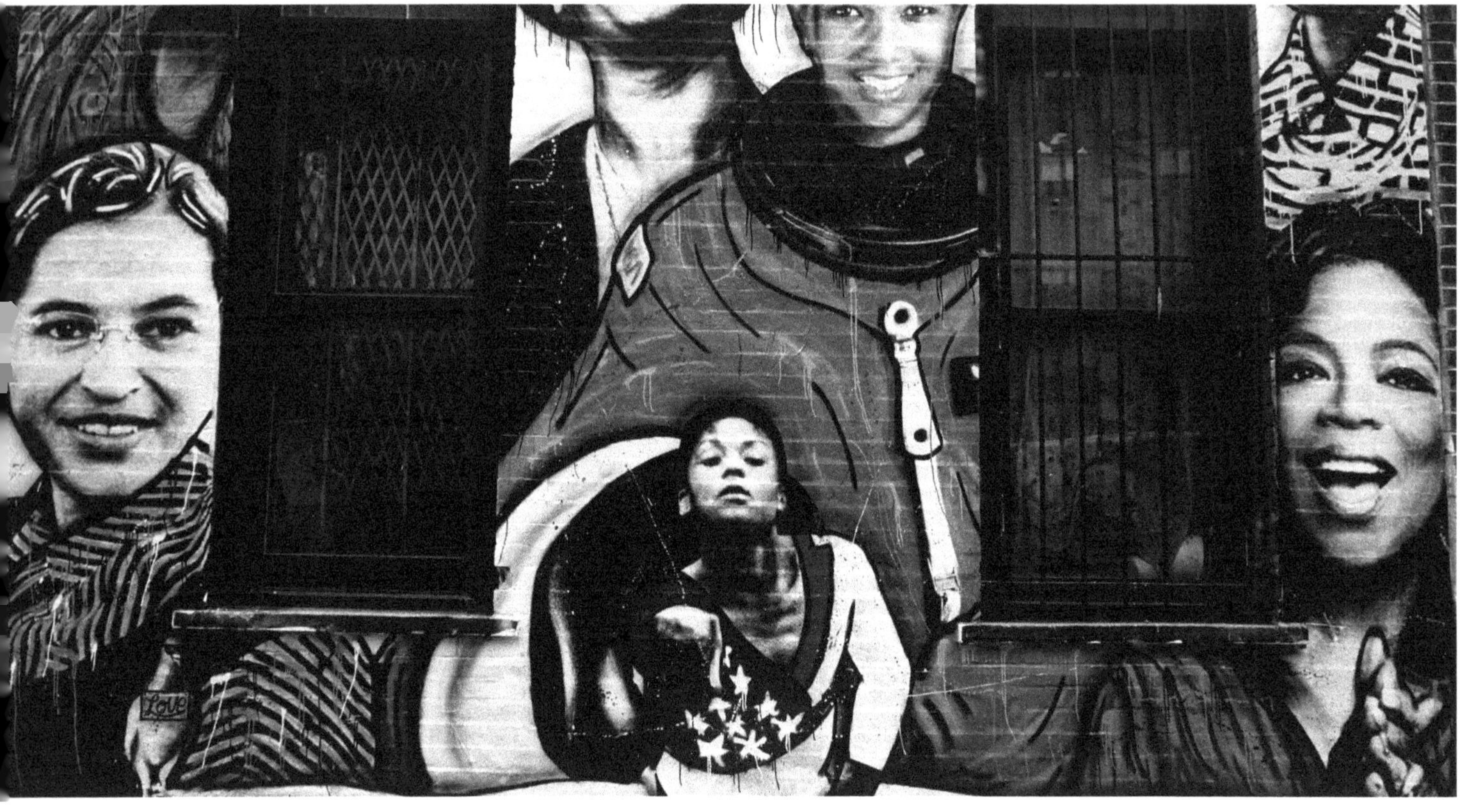

12th St. between Ave. B & C

Sacsix

9:39 AM

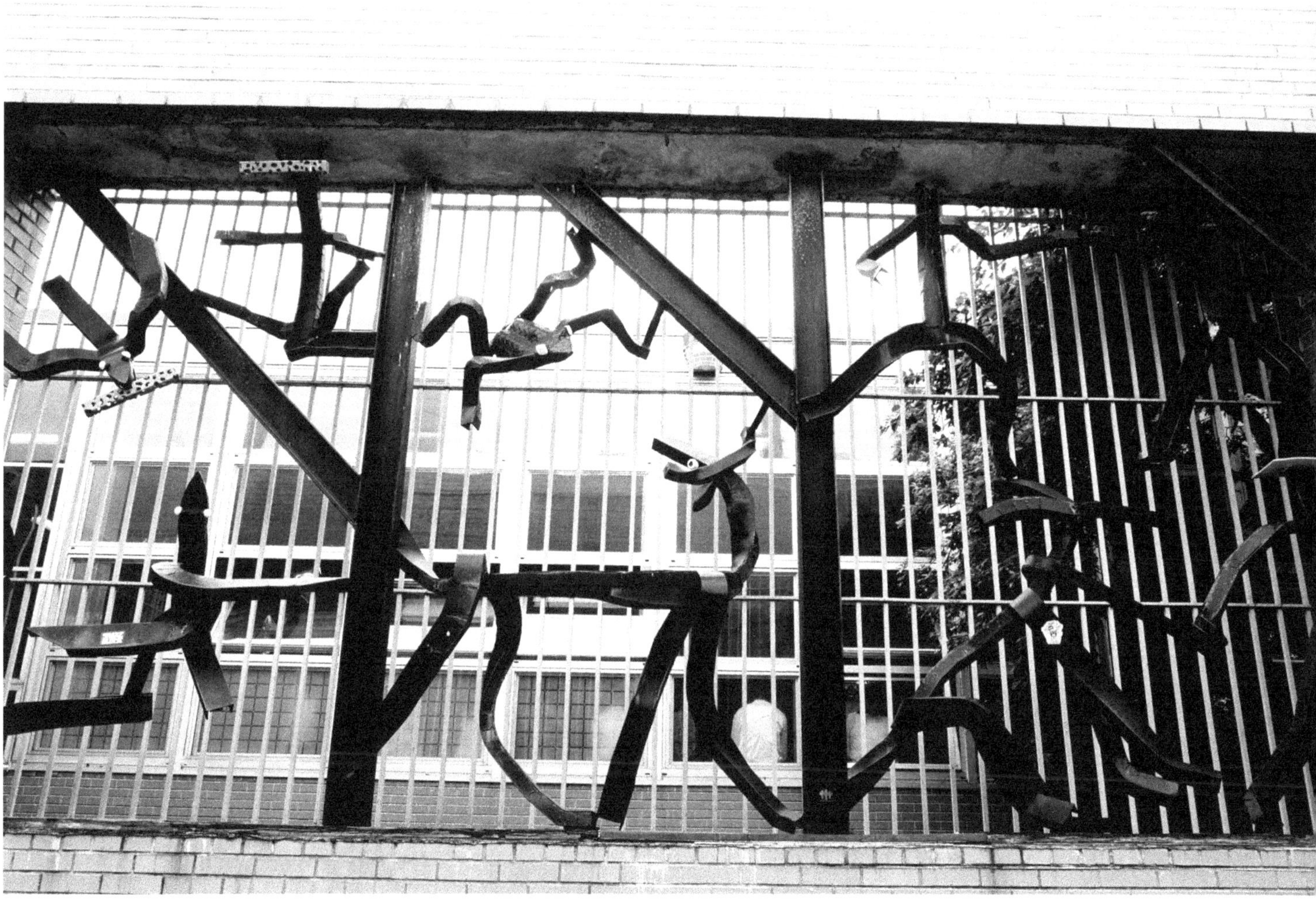

12 St. between Ave. C & D

Unknown

9:42 AM

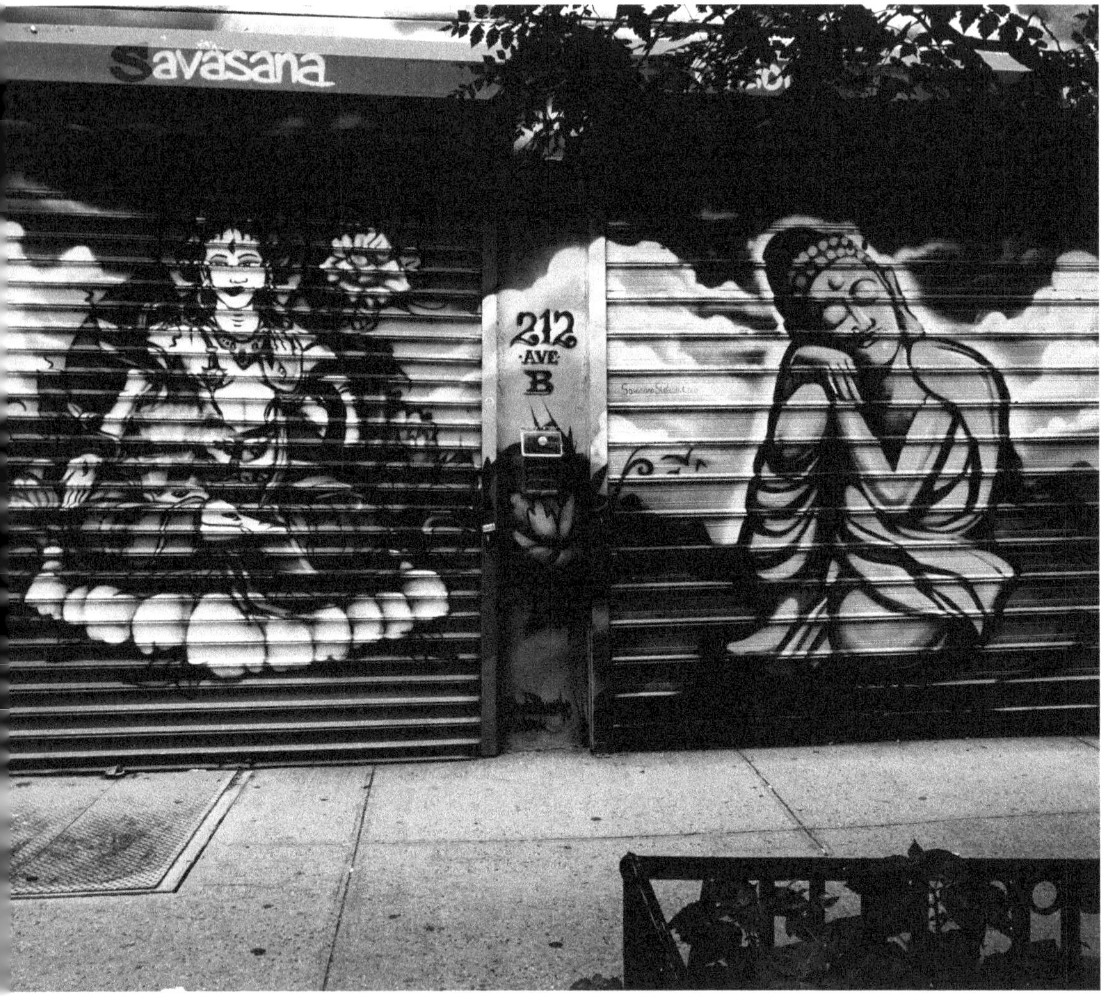

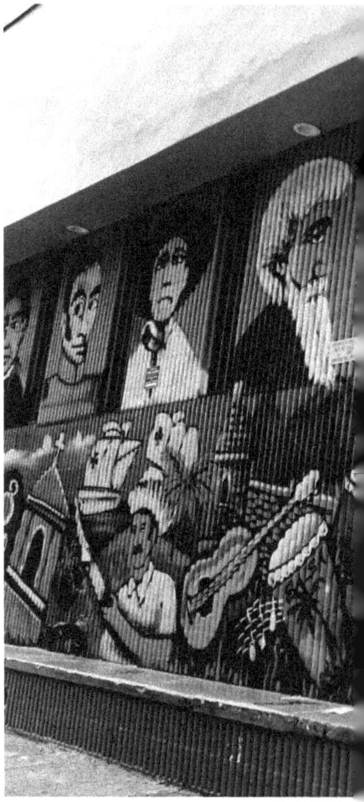

13th St. between Ave. A & B

Charlie Doves

9:47 AM

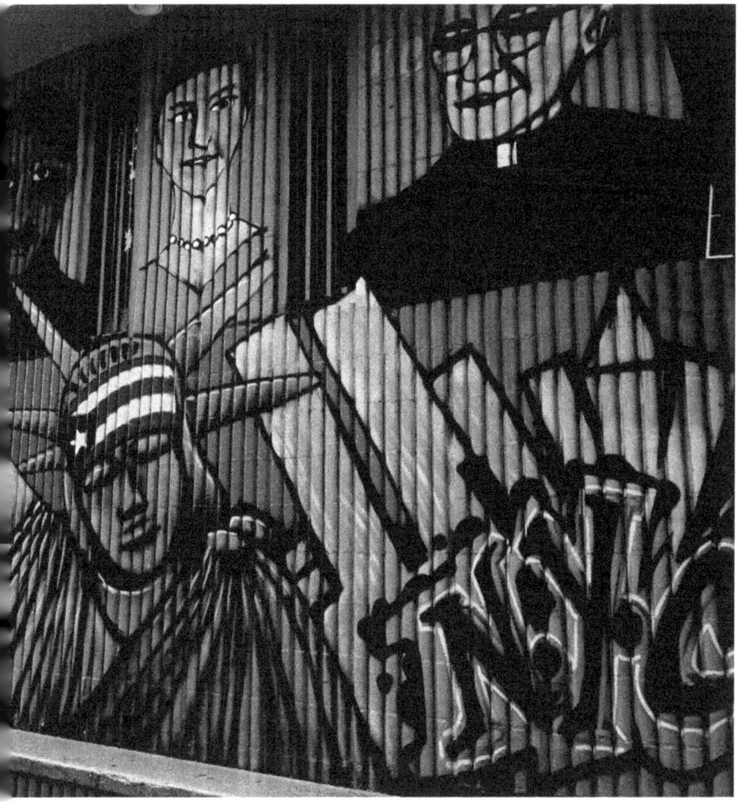

13th St. between Ave. A & B
Chico

9:49 AM

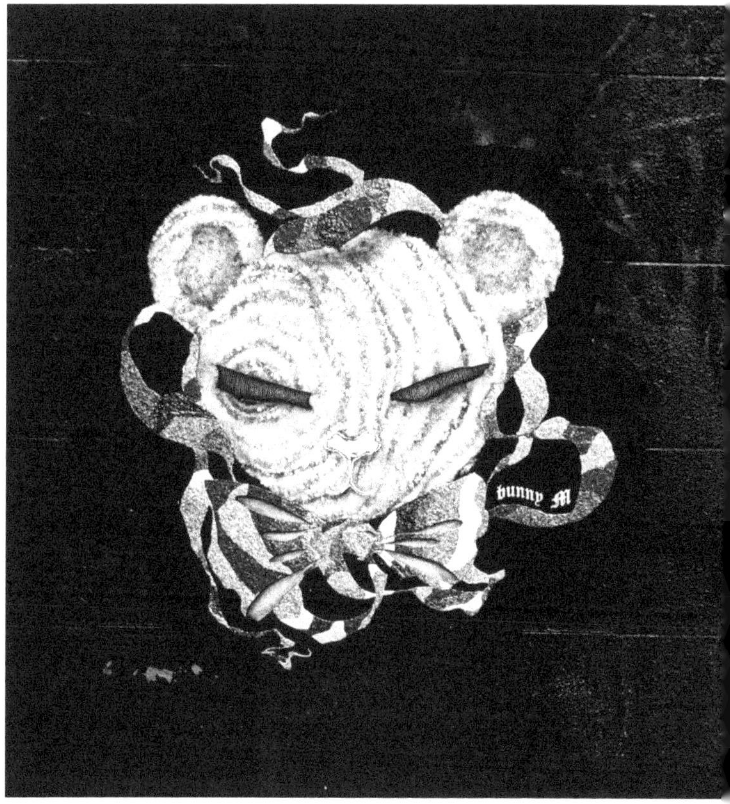

13th St. between 1st & Ave. A
Bunny M

9:53 AM

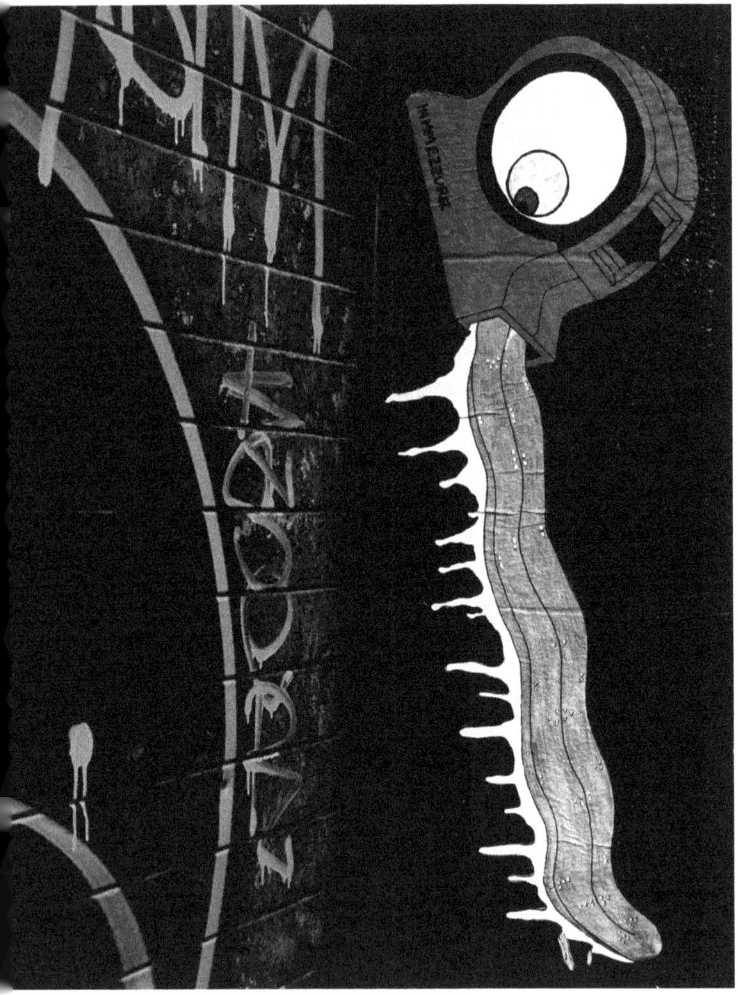

13th St. between 1st & Ave. A

Inmmezzure

9:56 AM

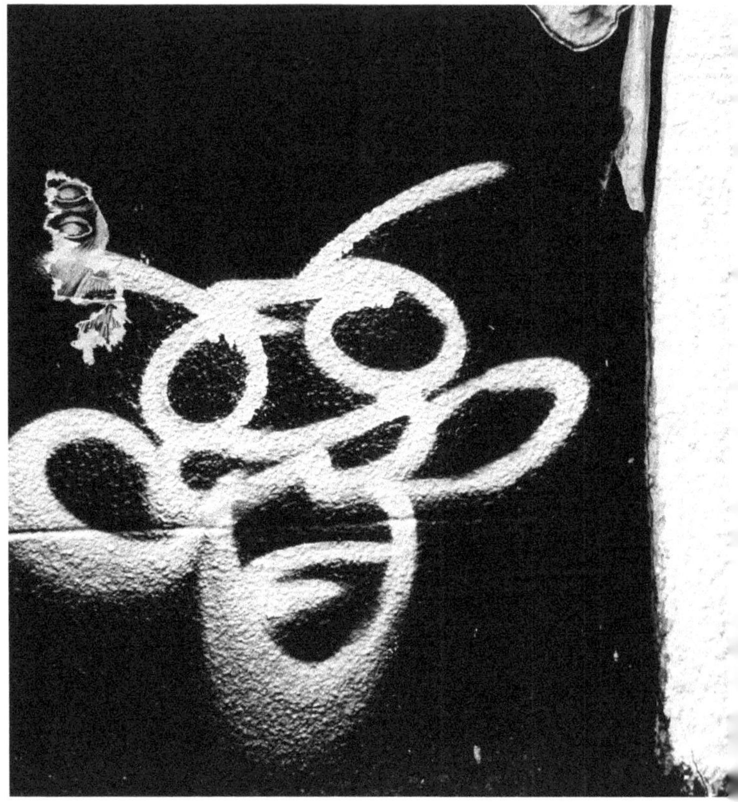

13th St. between 1st & Ave. A

Unknown, Sacsix

9:57 AM

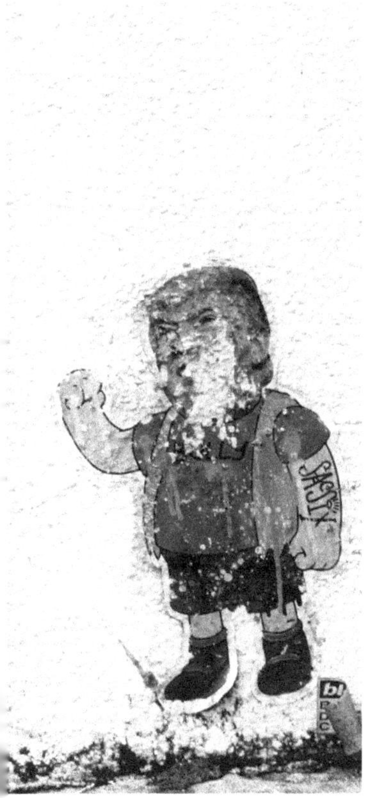

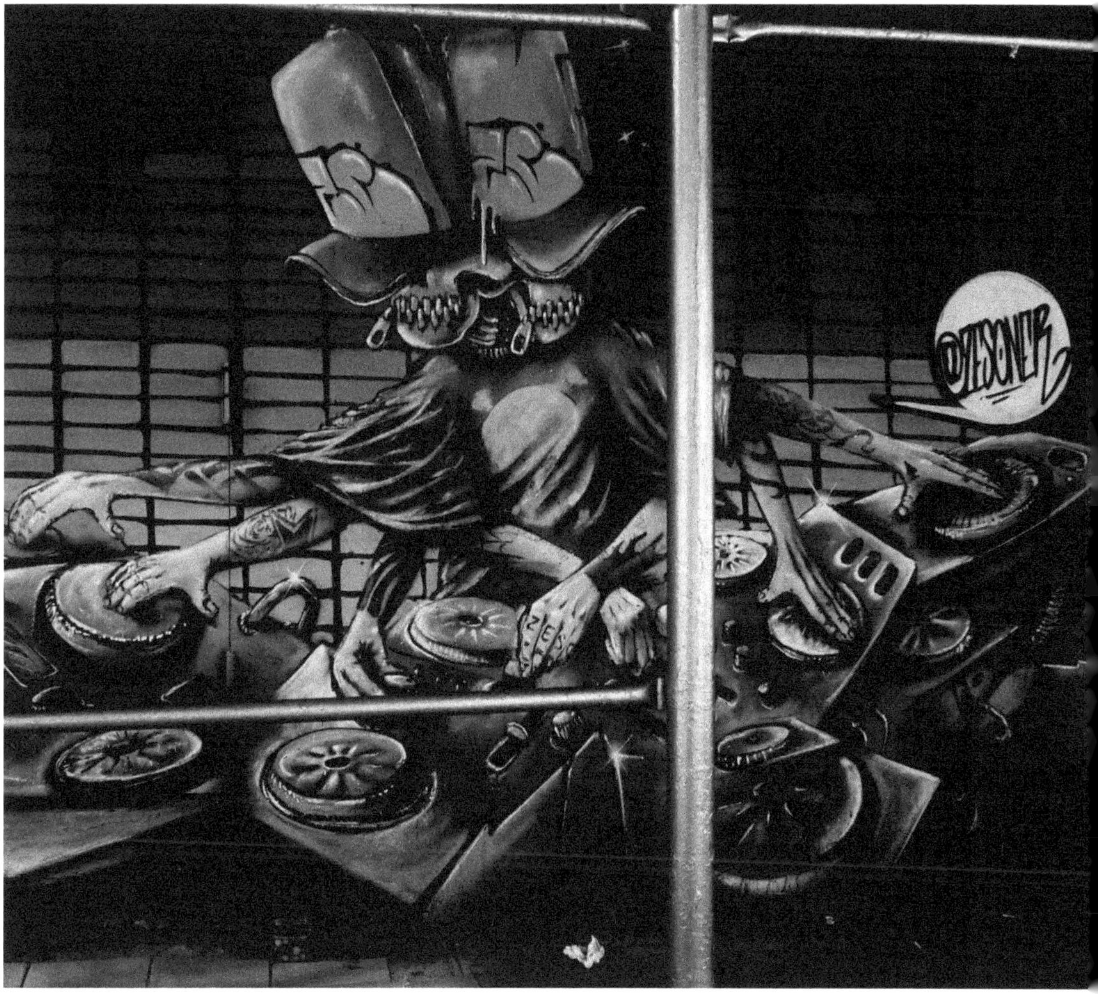

13th St. between 1st & Ave. A

Zesoner

9:59 AM

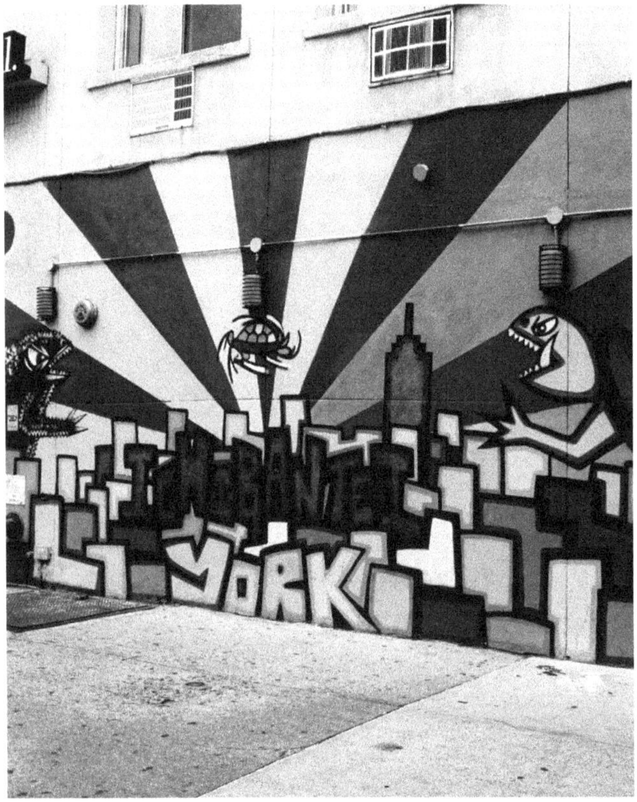

13th St. between 1st & Ave. A

Pesu

10:13 AM

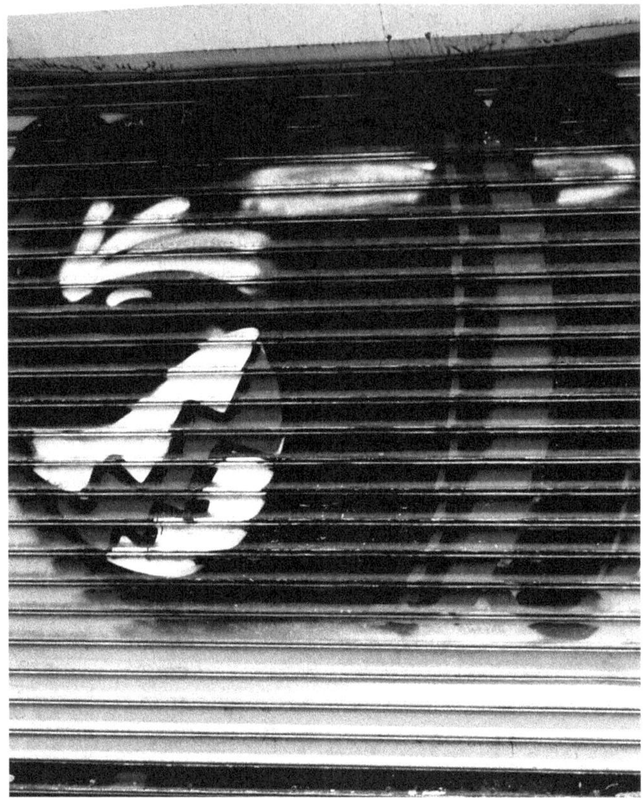

14th St. between 1st & Ave. A

Unknown

10:24 AM

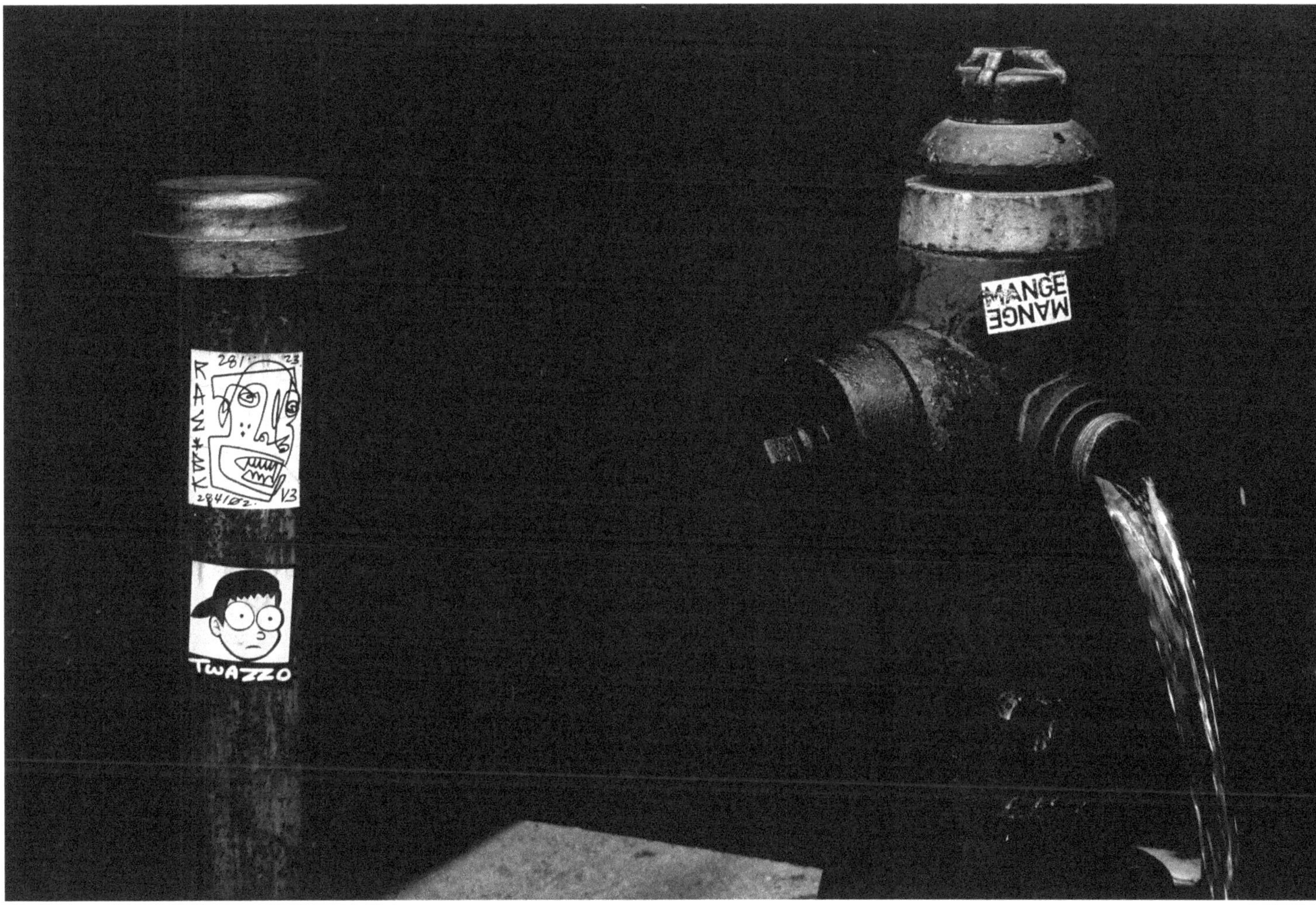

14th St. between Ave. B & C

Rae BK, Twazzo, Mange

THE AVENUES

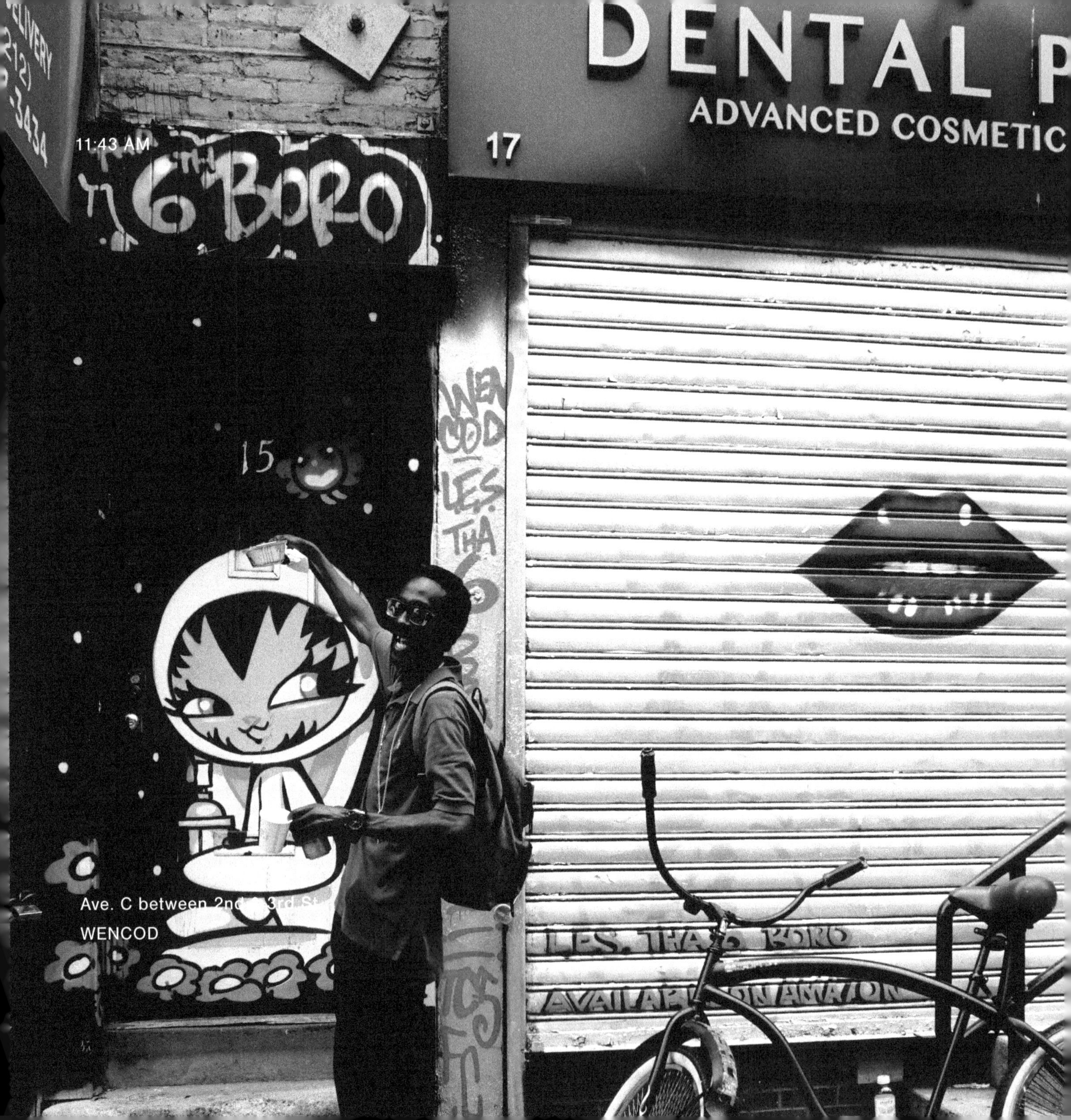

11:43 AM
Ave. C between 2nd 3rd St.
WENCOD

11:56 AM

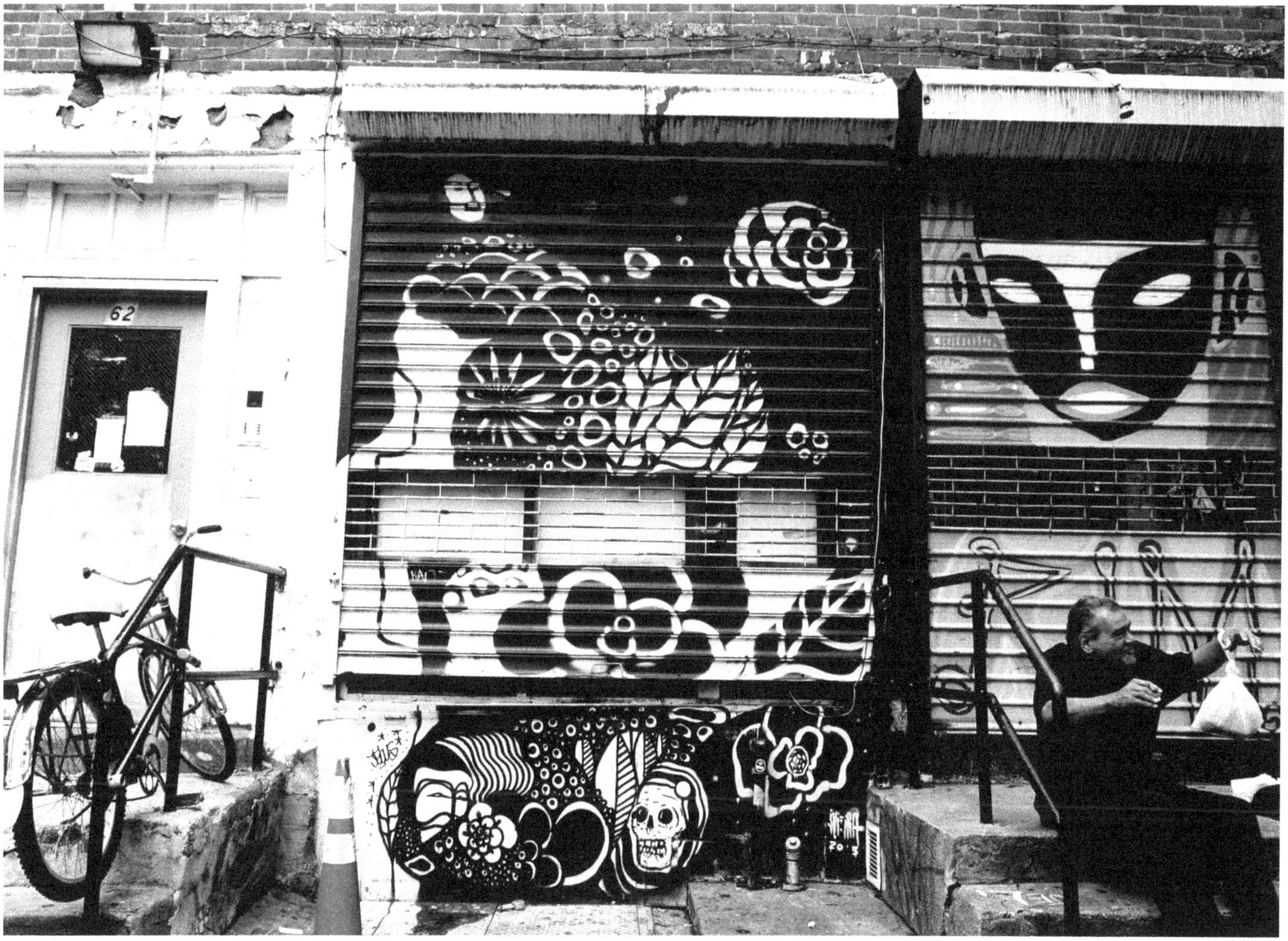

Ave. C between 4th & 5th St.

Unknown

11:58 AM

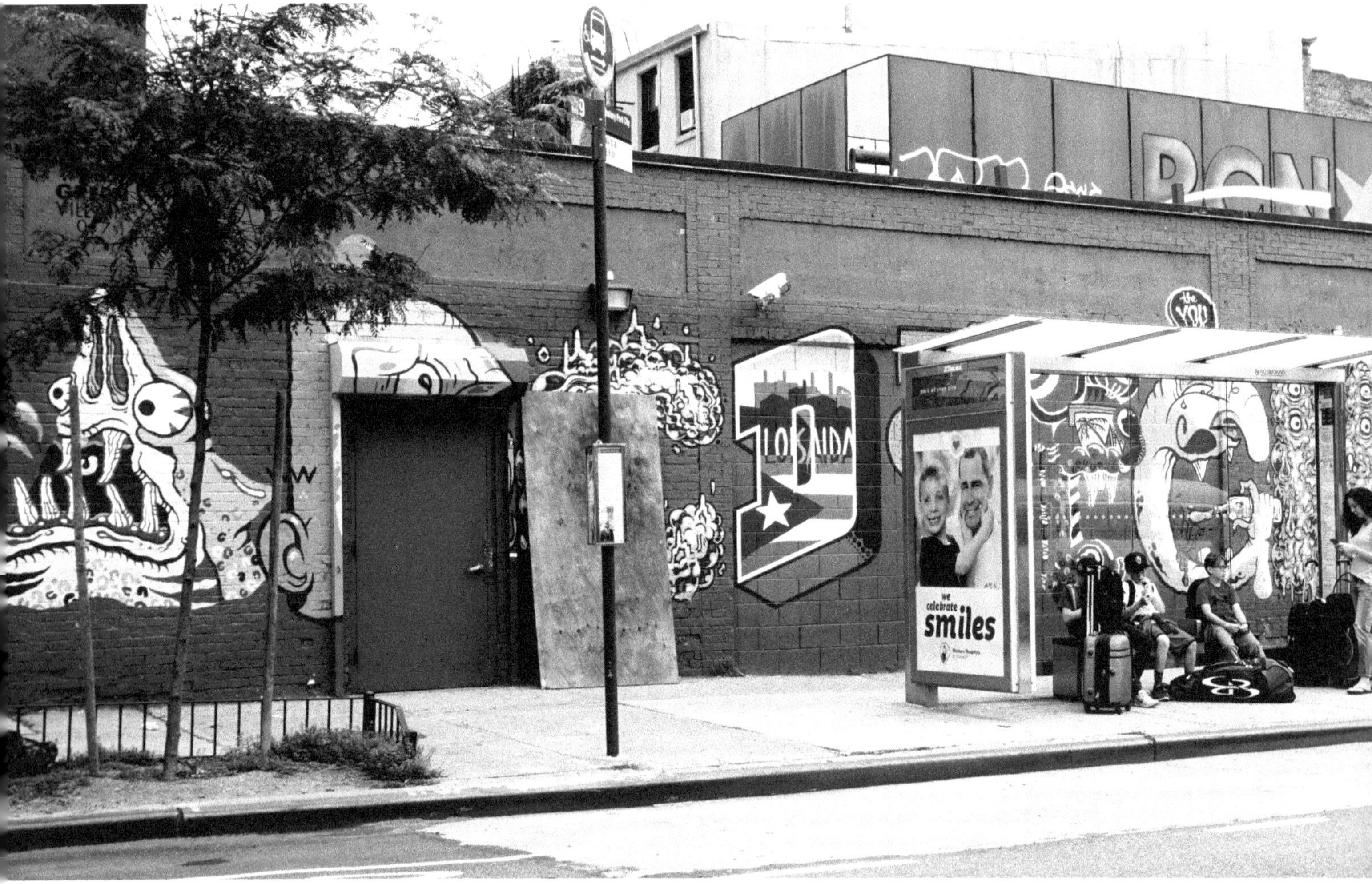

Ave. C between 5th & 6th St.

The Yok & Sheryo

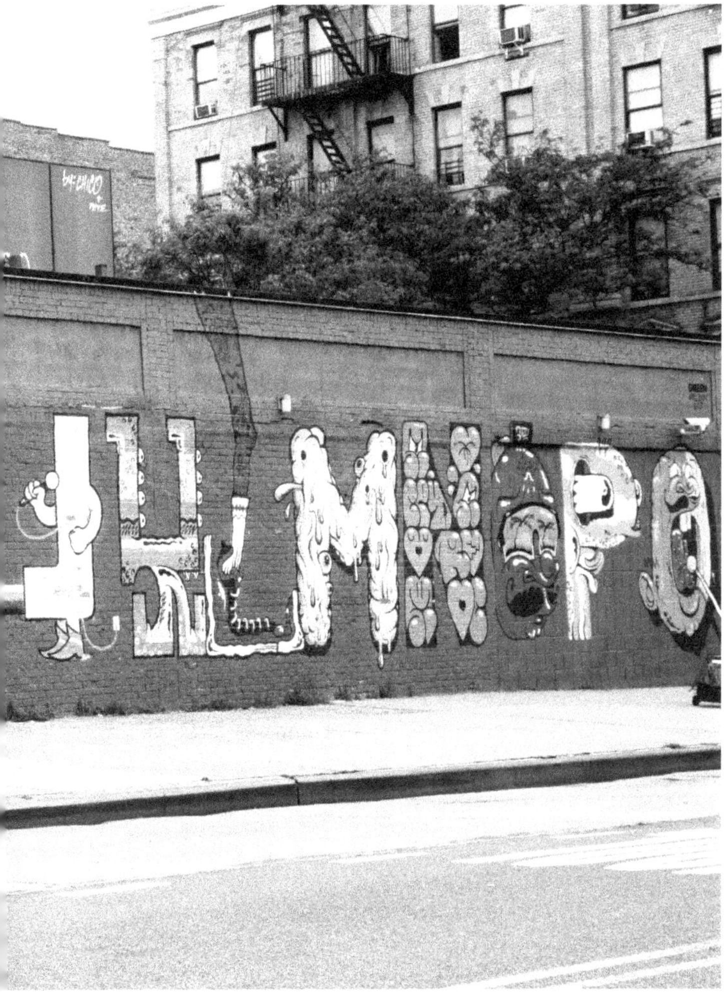

11:58 AM

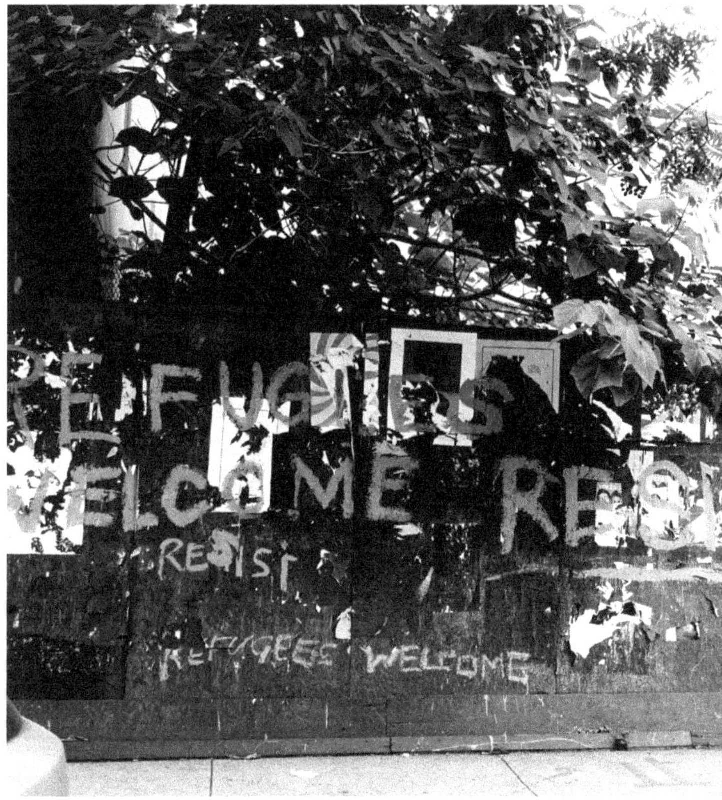

Ave. C between 6th & 7th St.

Unknown

12:00 PM

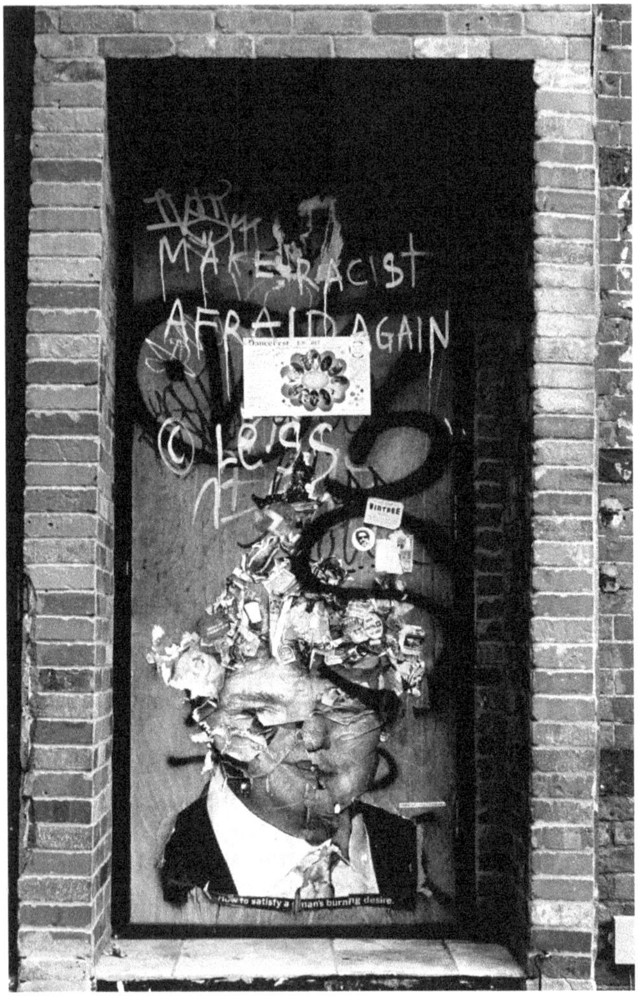

Ave. C between 6th & 7th St.

Unknown

12:02 PM

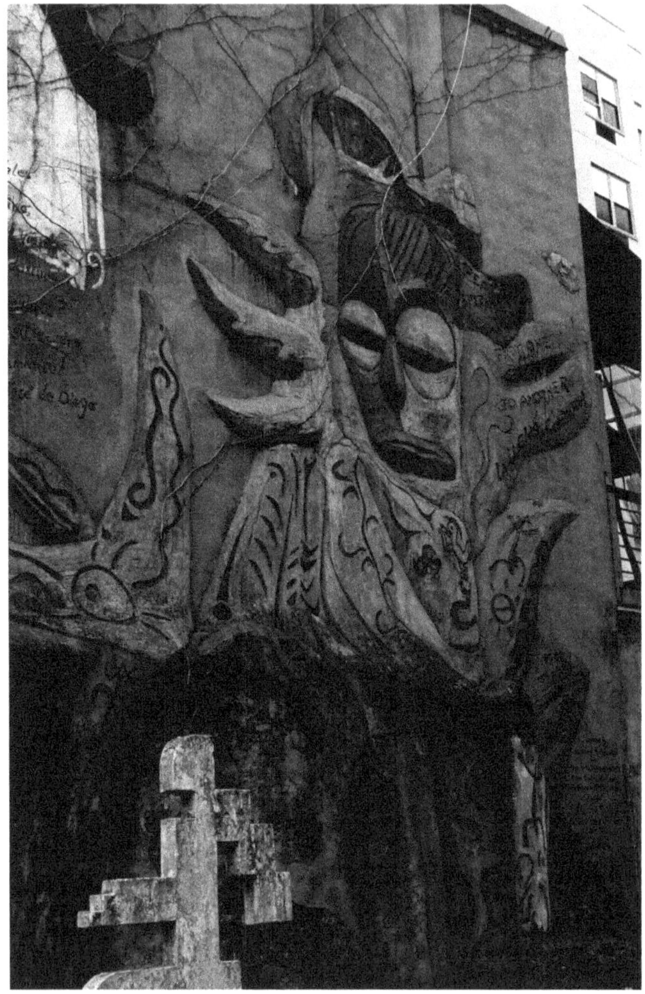

Ave. C between 6th & 7th St.

John Pitman Weber

12:05 PM

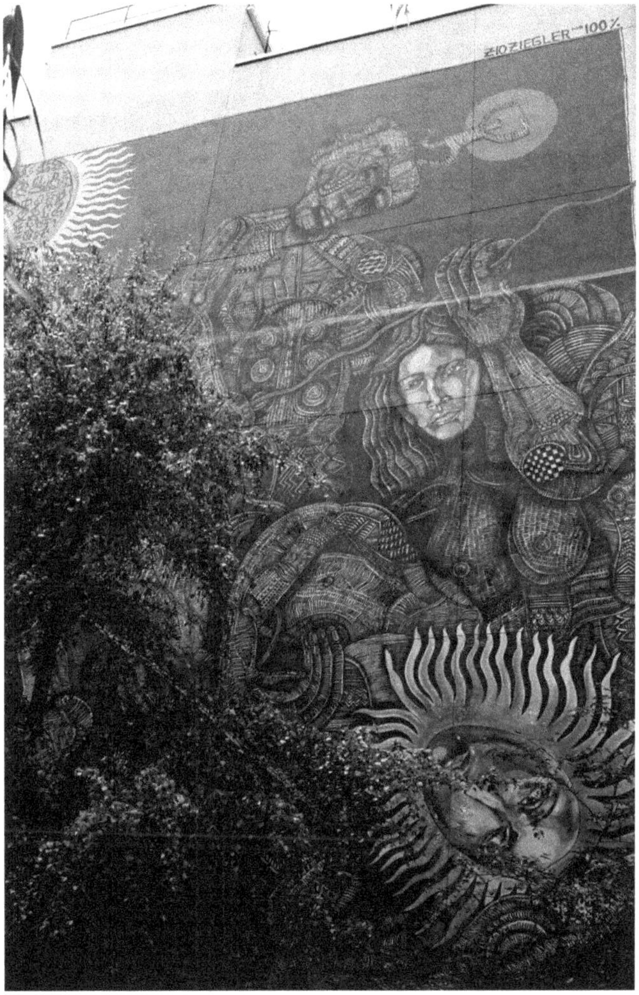

La Plaza Cultural @ Ave. C & 9th St.

Zio Ziegler

12:10 PM

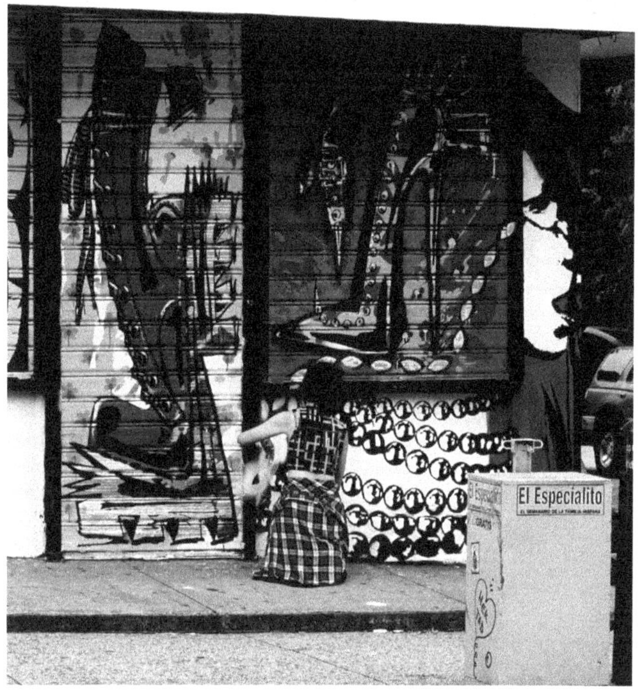

Ave. C between 11th & 12th St.

Xors

12:14 PM

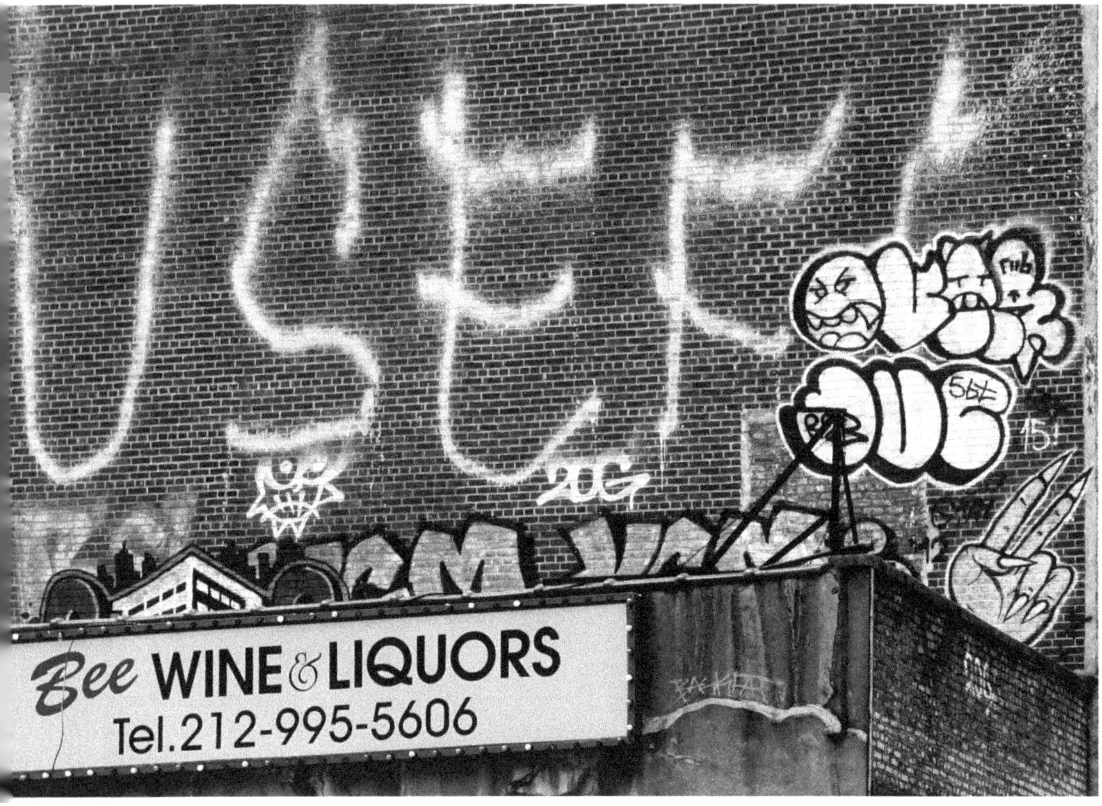

Ave. B between 13th & 14th St.

Girl

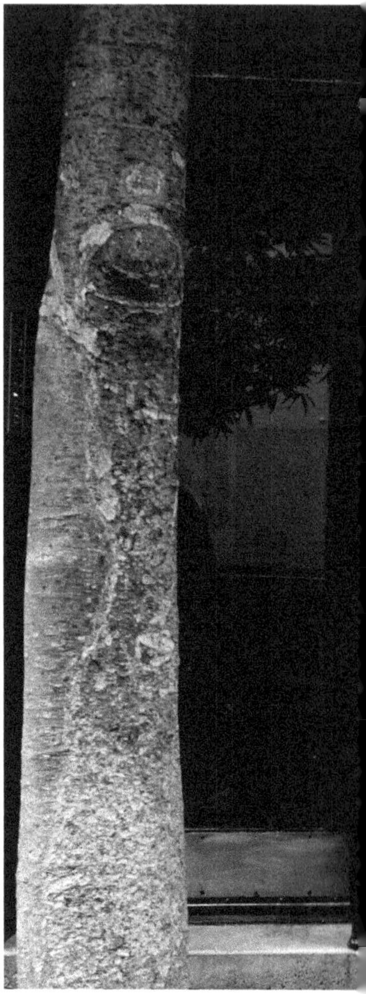

12:17 PM

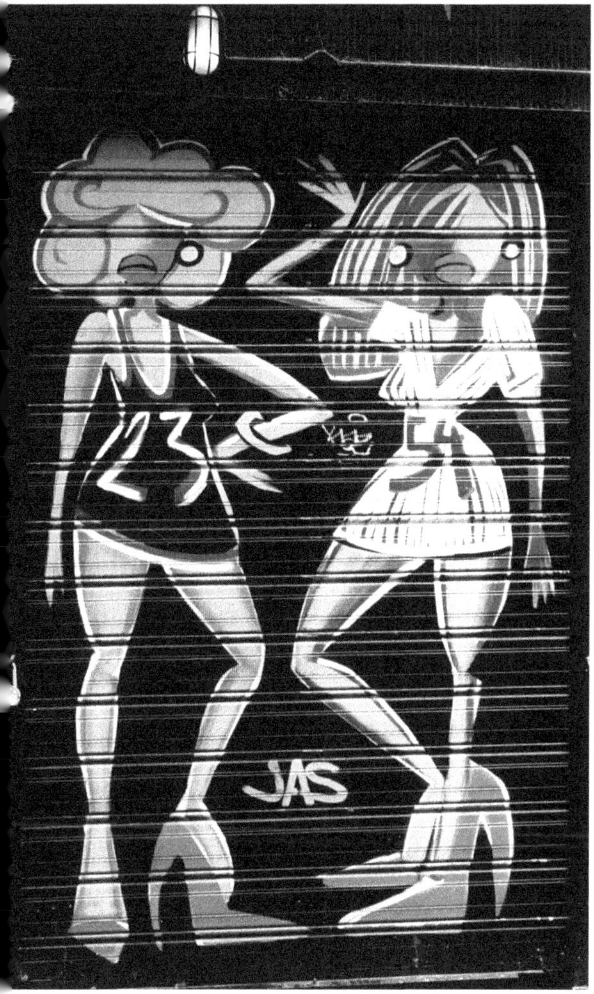

Ave. B between 11th & 12th St.

Jas

12:26 PM

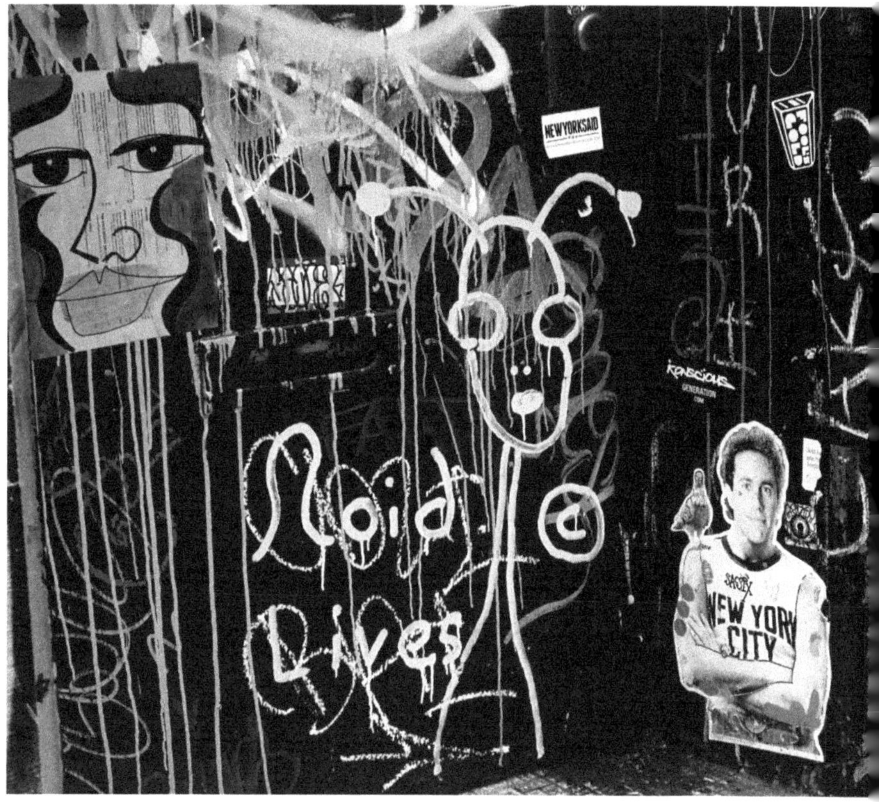

Ave. B between 6th & 7th St.

Anna Laurini, Roid, Sacsix

12:27 PM

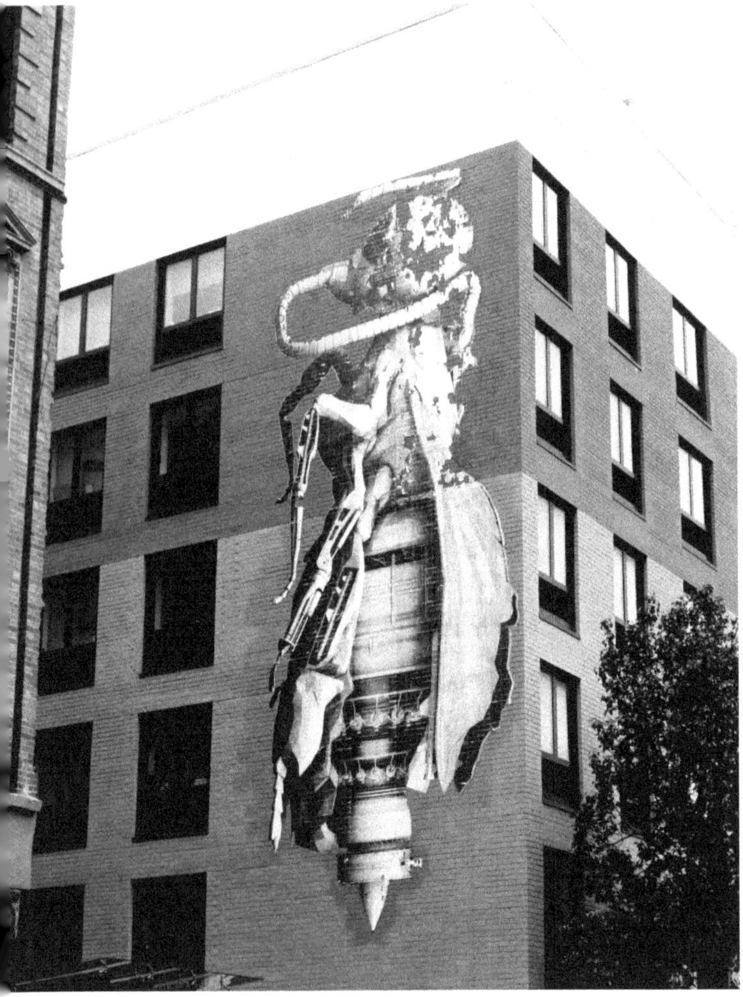

Ave. B between 4th & 5th St.

Ludo

12:31 PM

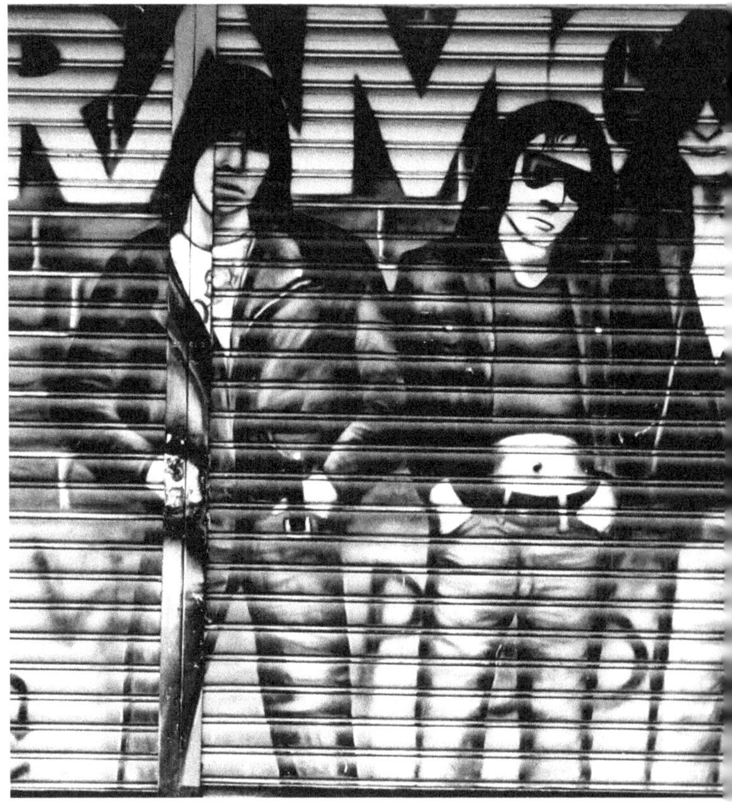

Ave. B between 2nd & 3rd St.

Chico

12:41 PM

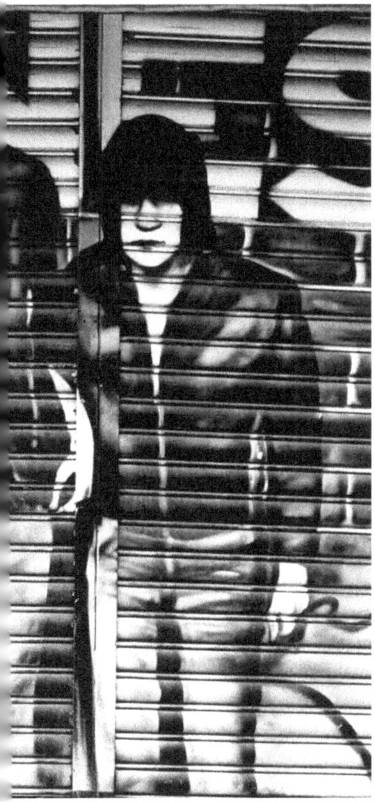

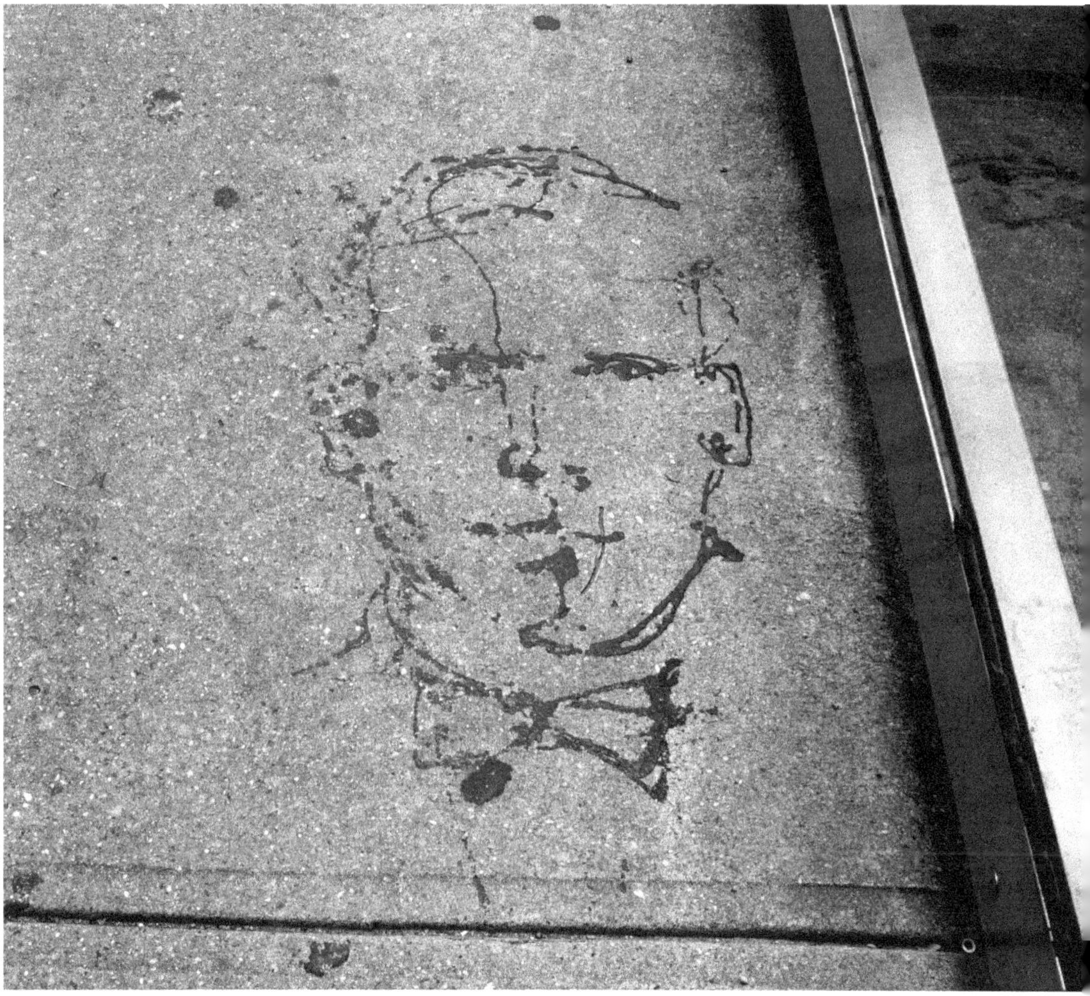

Ave. A between 5th & 6th St.

Paul Richard

12:42 PM

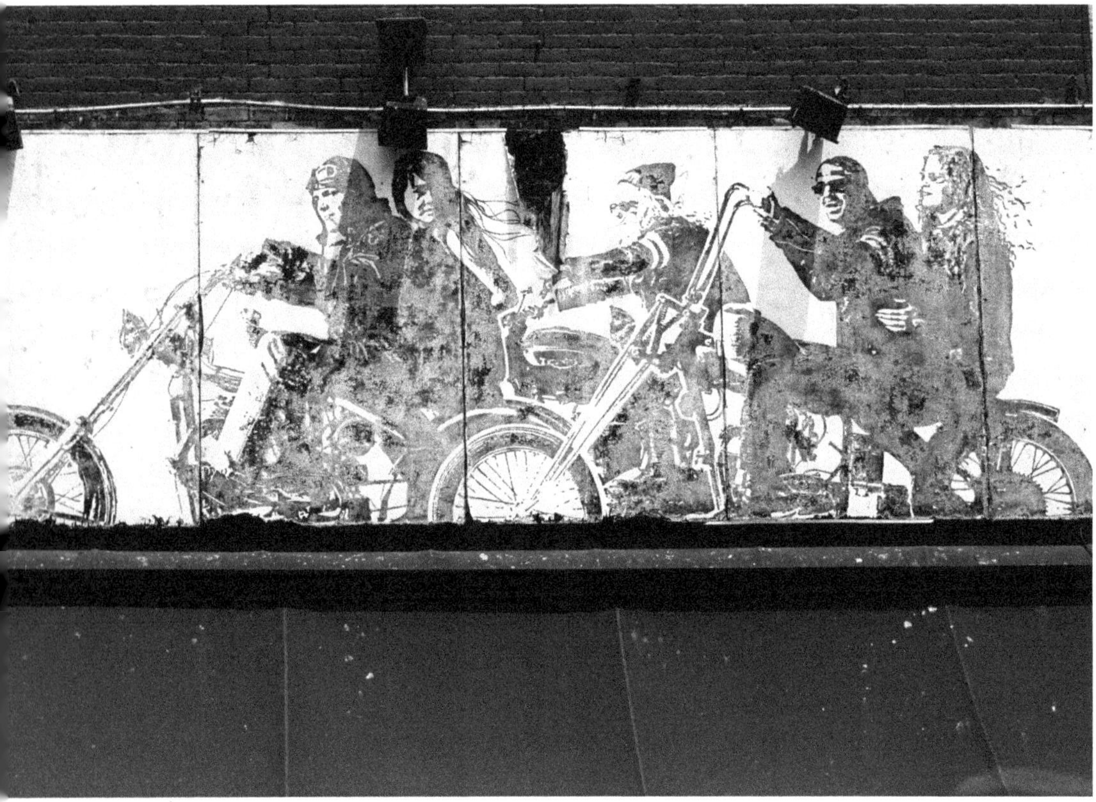

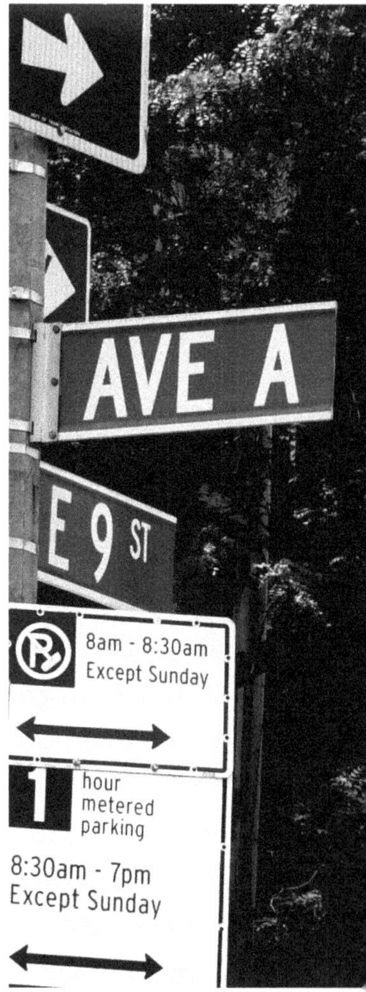

Ave. A & 6th St.

Unknown

12:46 PM

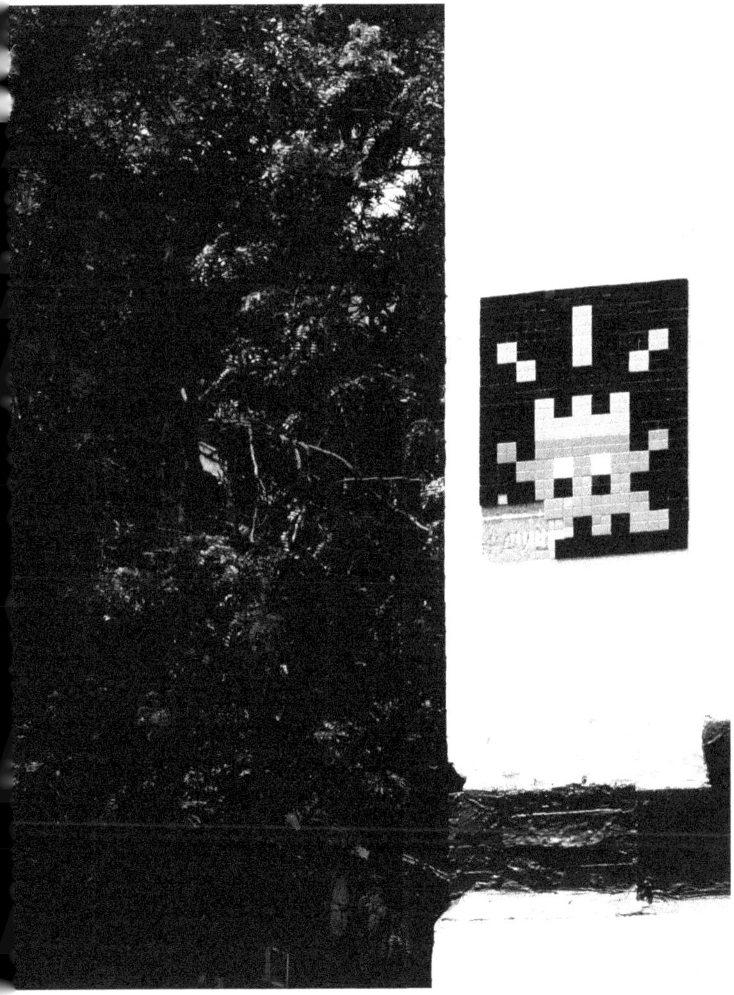

Ave. A & 9th St.

Invader

12:48 PM

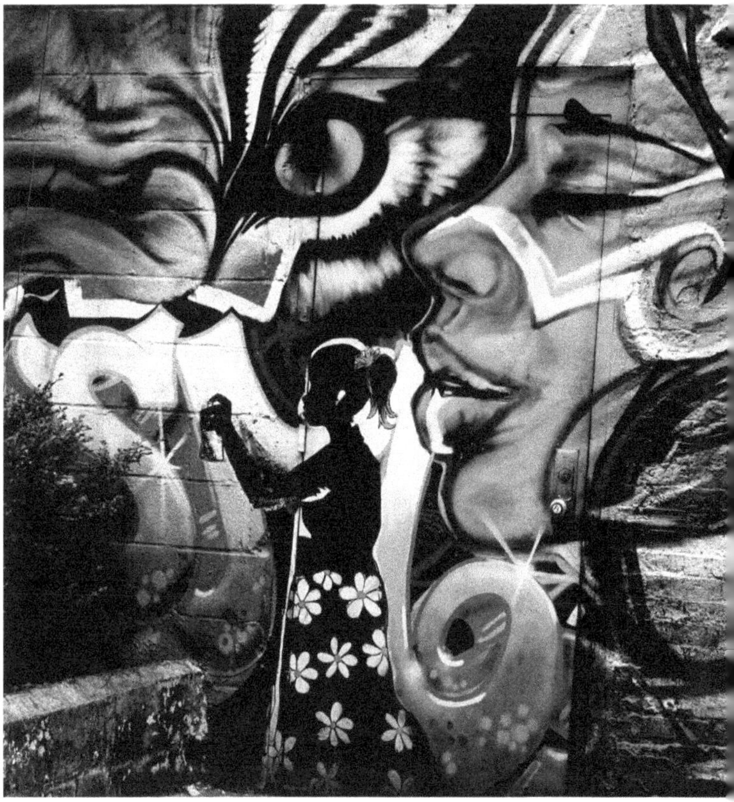

Ave. A between 10th & 11th St.

Andre Trenier, Trap, Fcee, Stella Isabella, Nicholai Khan

12:49 PM

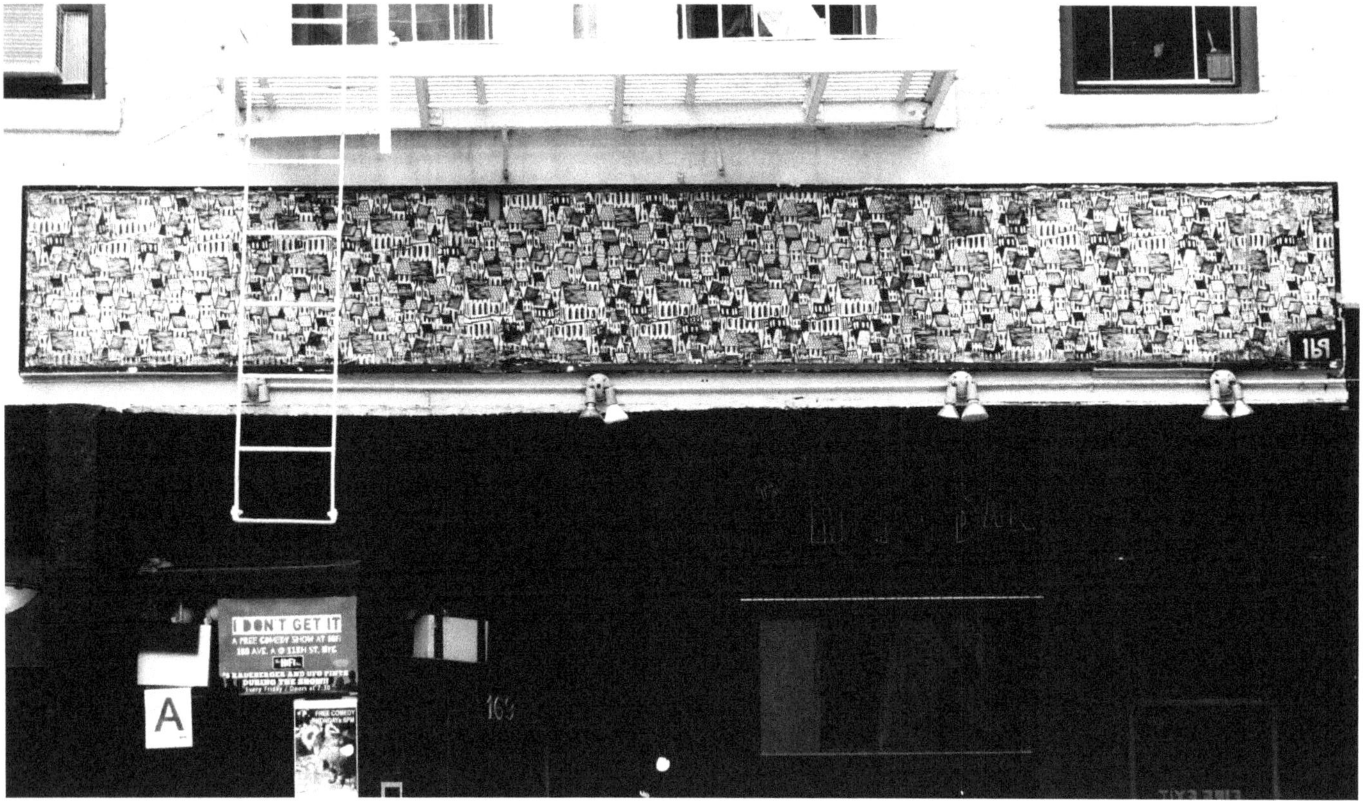

Ave. A between 10th & 11th St.

David Hochbaum

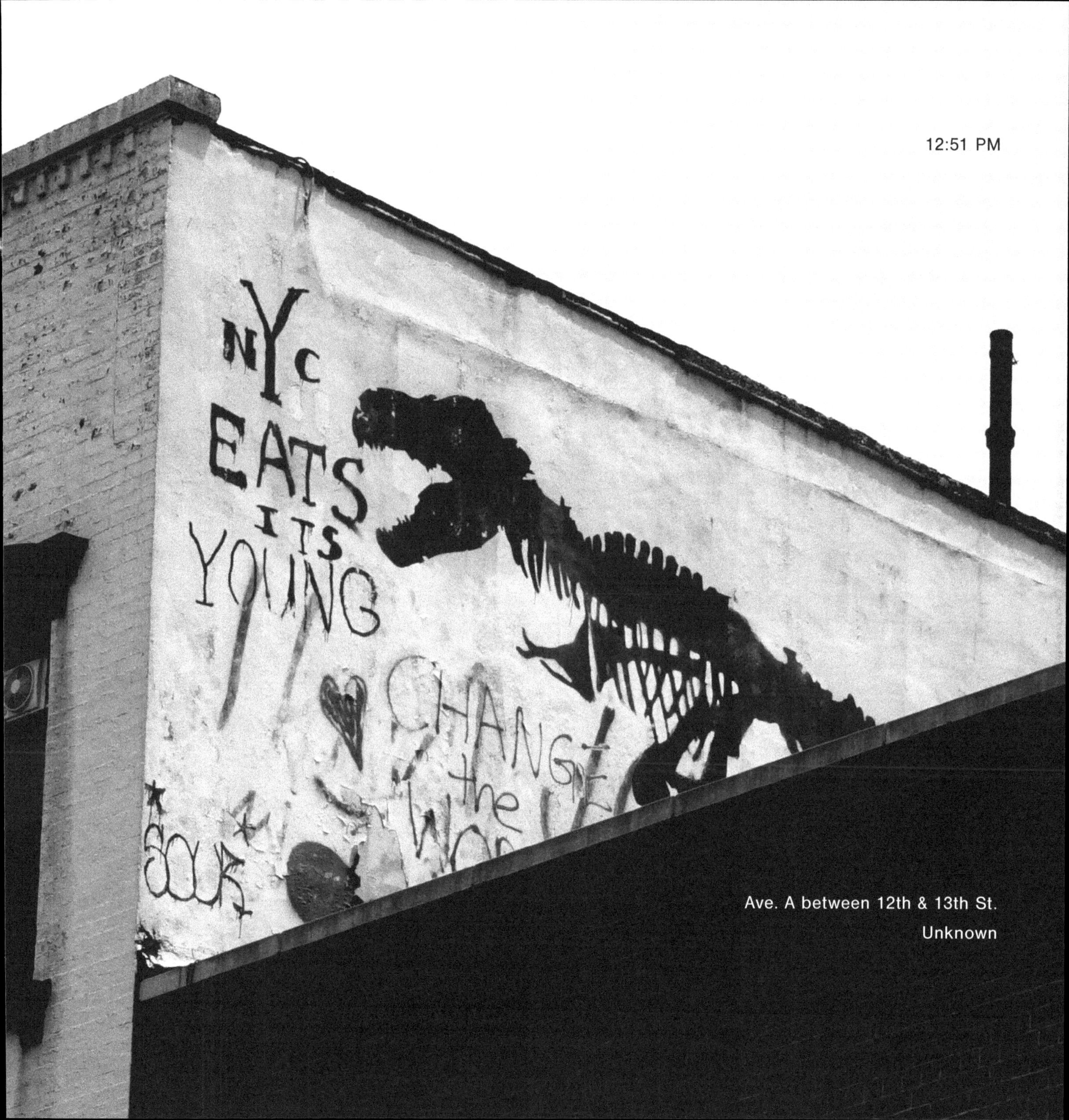

12:51 PM

Ave. A between 12th & 13th St.

Unknown

12:58 PM

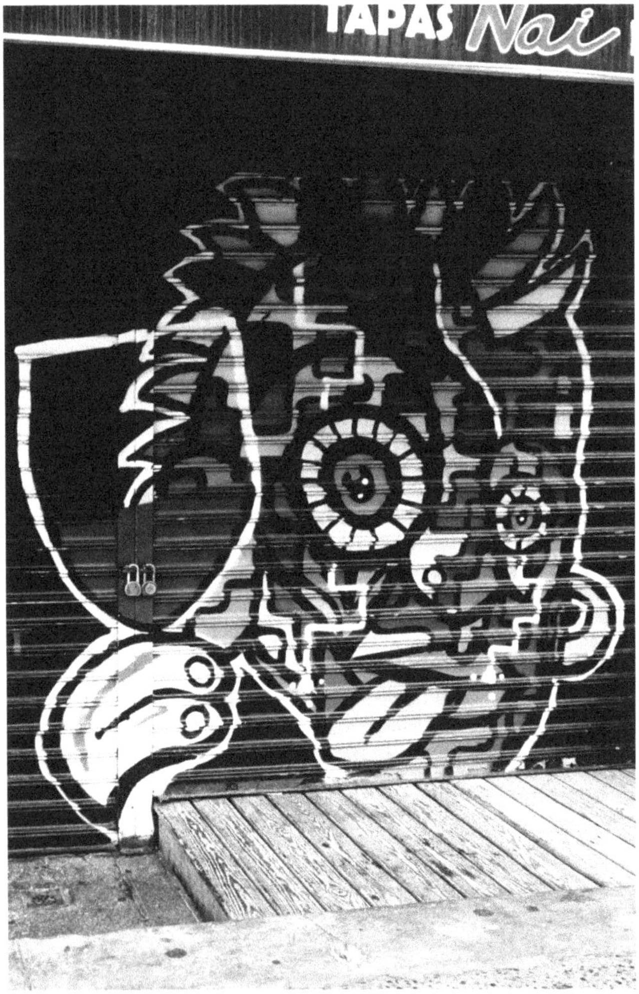

1st Ave. between 10th & 11th St.

Funqest

1:35 PM

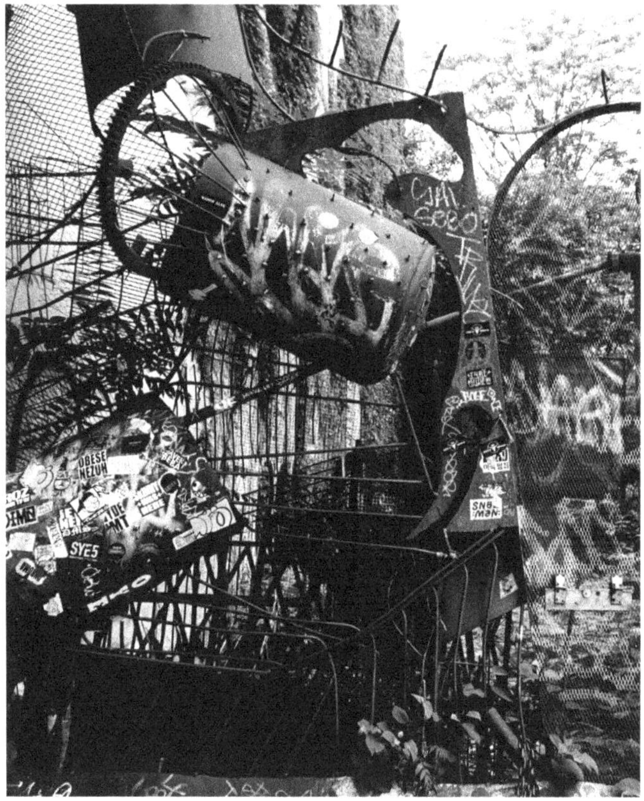

1st Ave. between 5th & 6th St.

Kalemkeris, Swing & Co.

1:50 PM

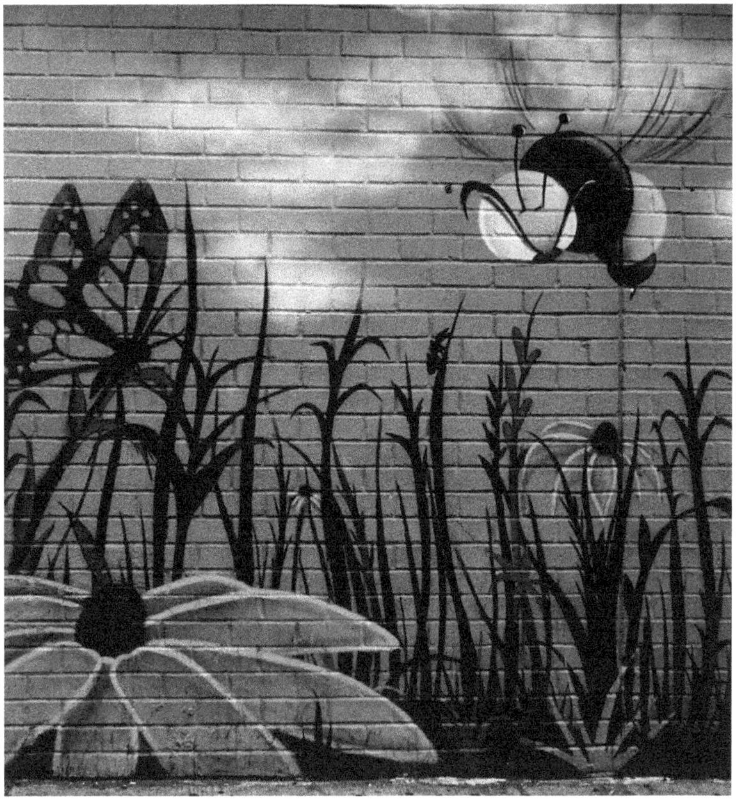

1st Ave. between 4th & 5th St.

Royal Kingbee

1:53 PM

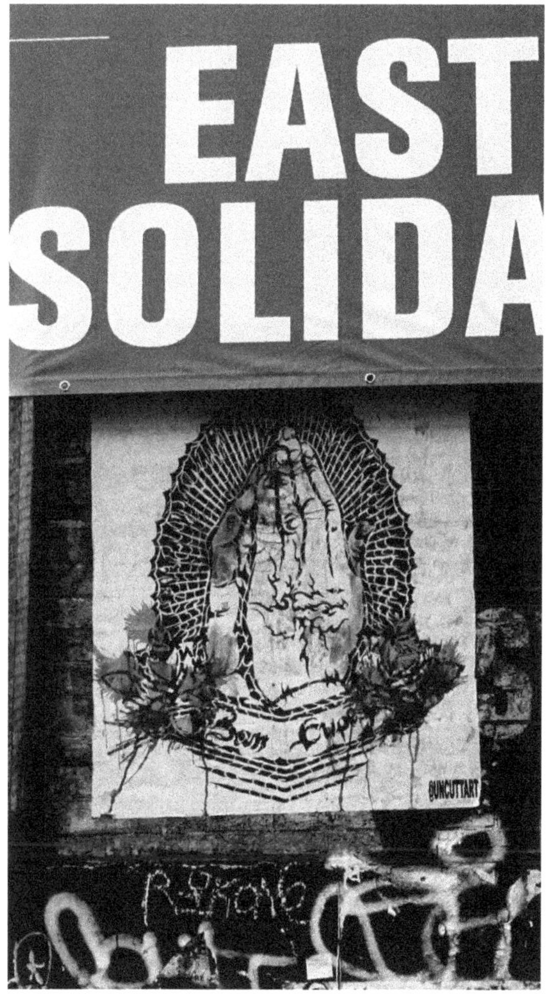

1st Ave. between 1st & 2nd St.

Uncutart

1:58 PM

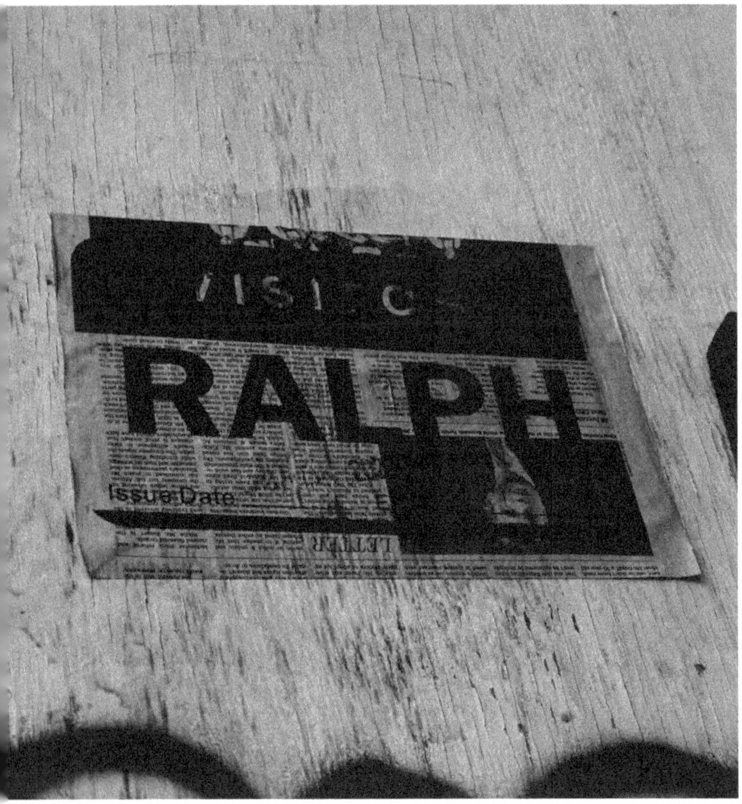

2nd Ave. between 1st & Houston St.

Visitor Ralph

2:01 PM

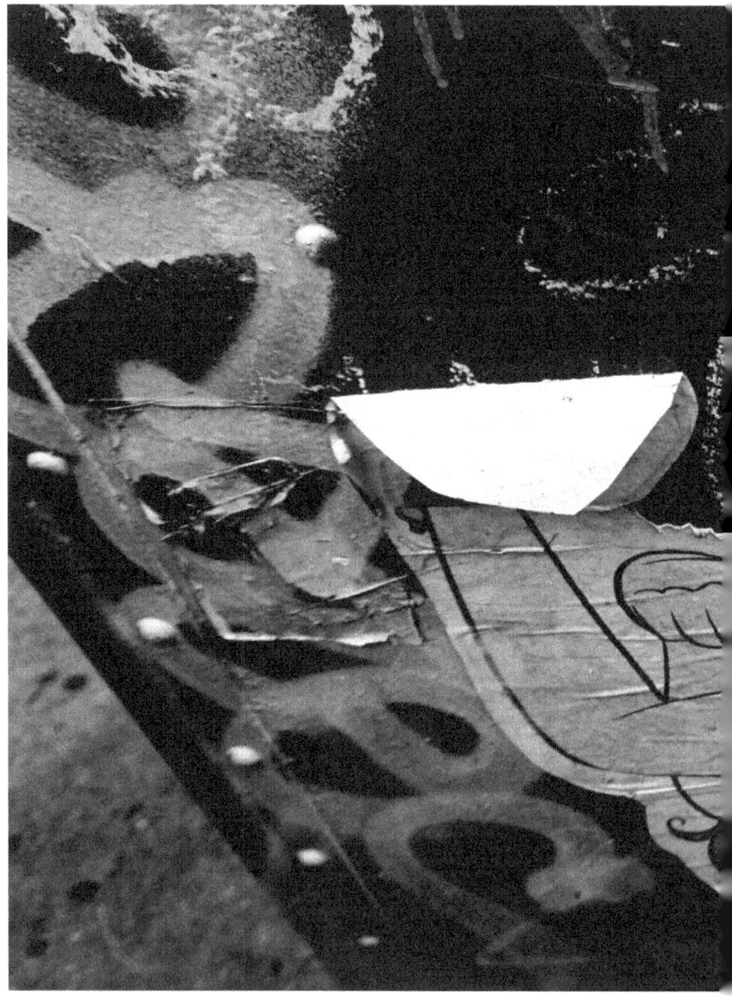

2nd Ave. between 2nd & 3rd St.

Sophie Lambda

2:08 PM

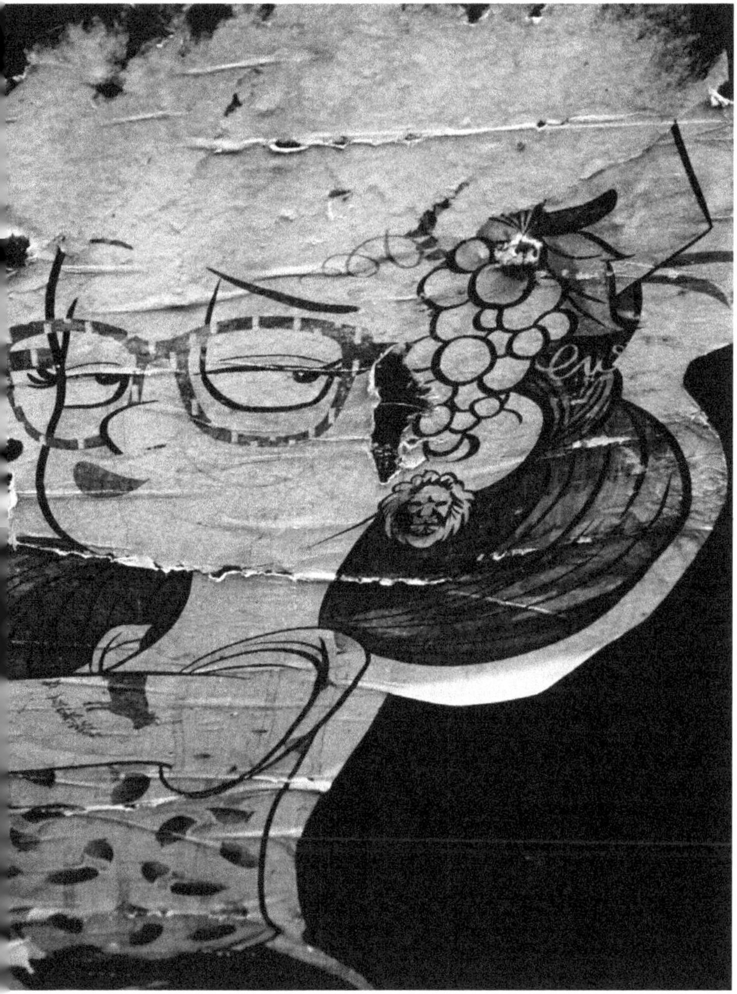

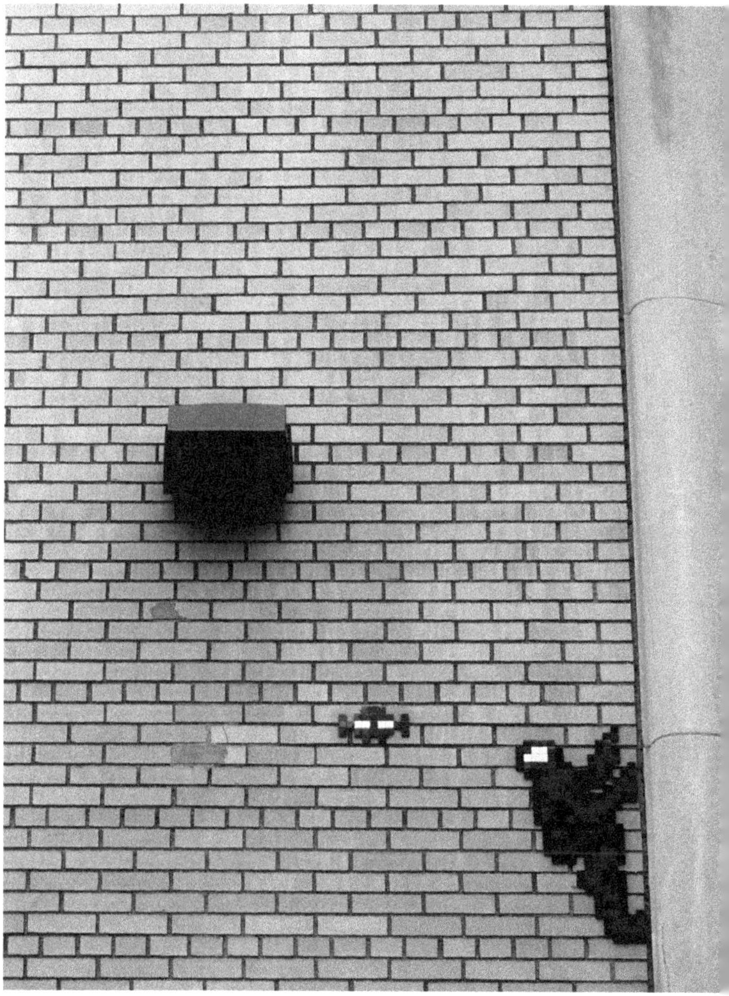

2nd Ave. between 7th St. & St. Mark's Place

Invader

2:09 PM

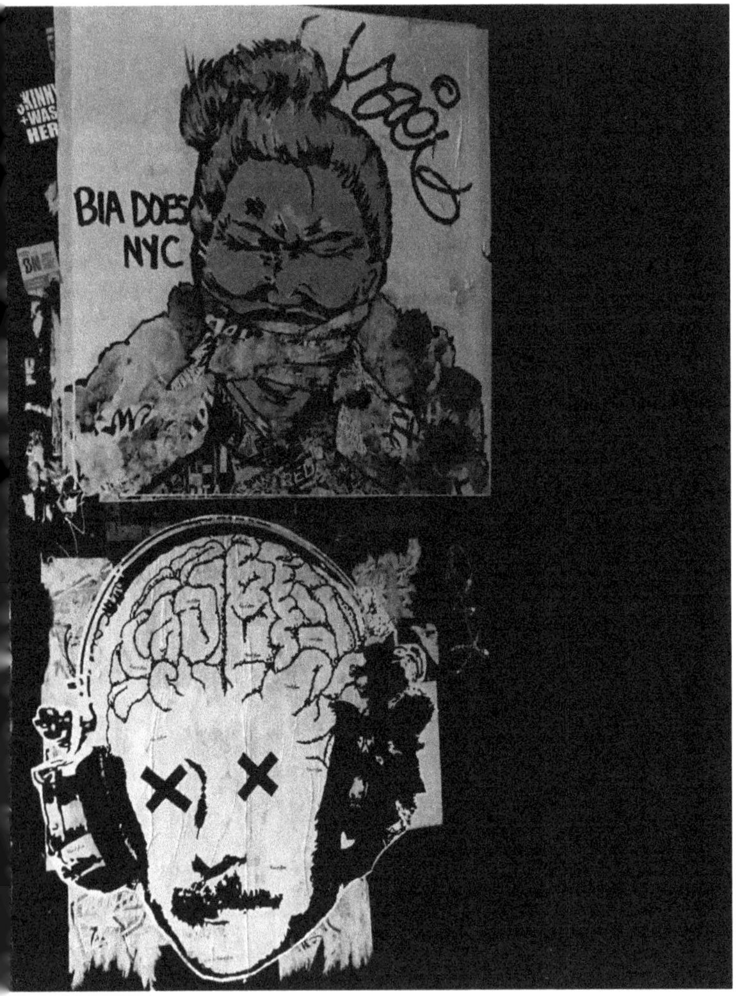

2nd Ave. between St. Mark's Place & 9th St.

Bianca Romero, Voxx Romana

2:11 PM

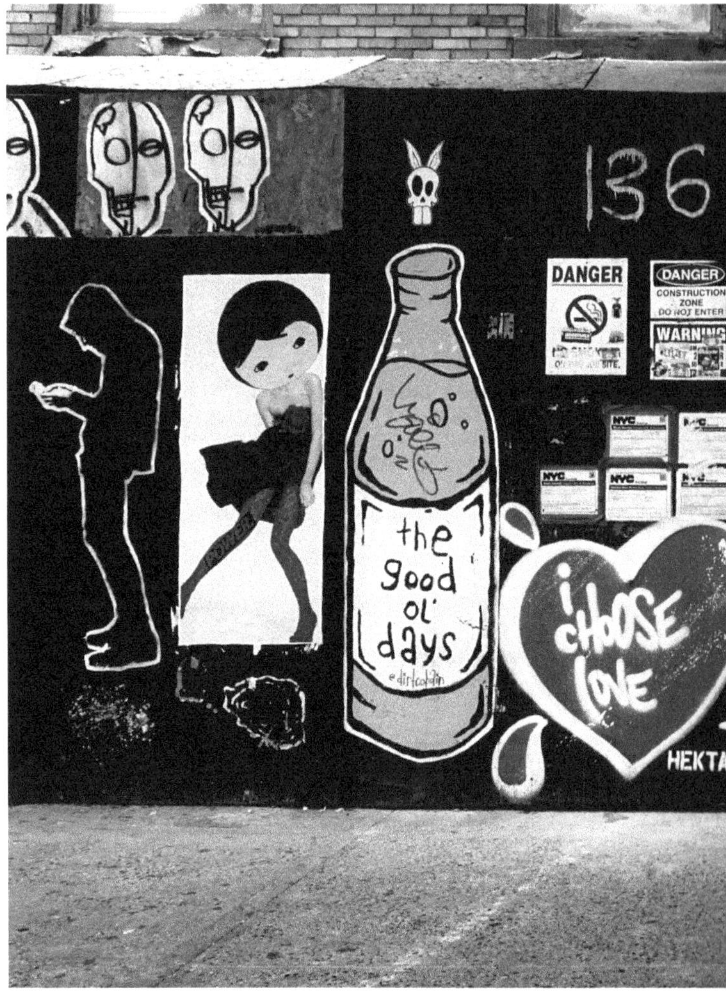

2nd Ave. between St. Mark's Place & 9th St.

Ethan Arman, Thrashbird, Libby Schoettle, Dirt Cobain, Hektad, Xors, DLove, Unknown

2:13 PM

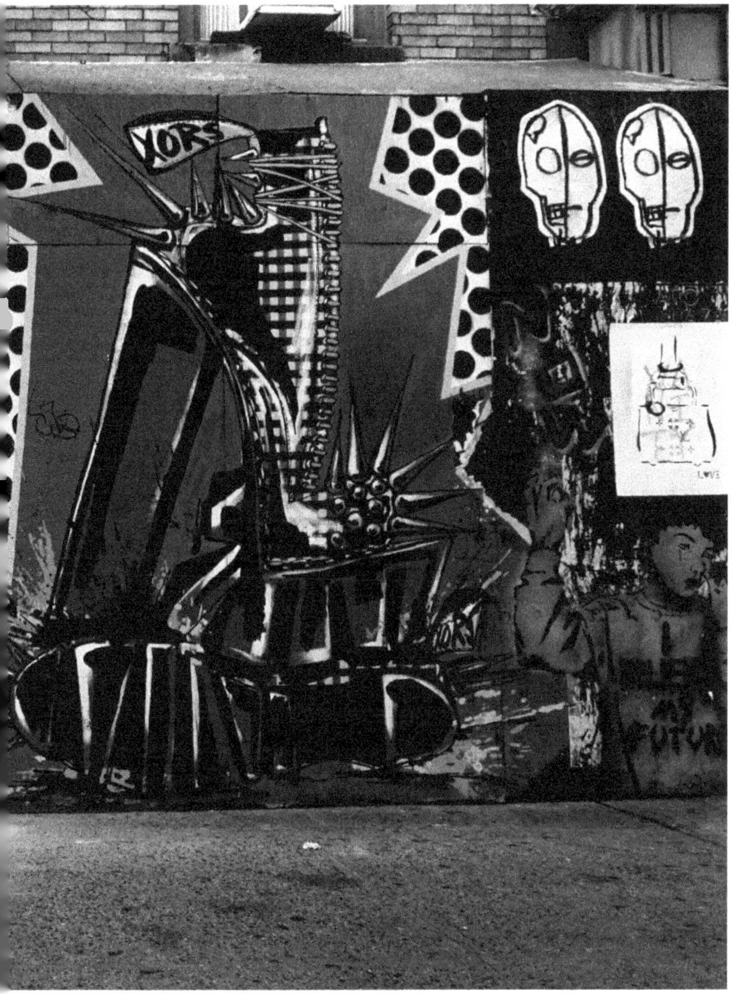

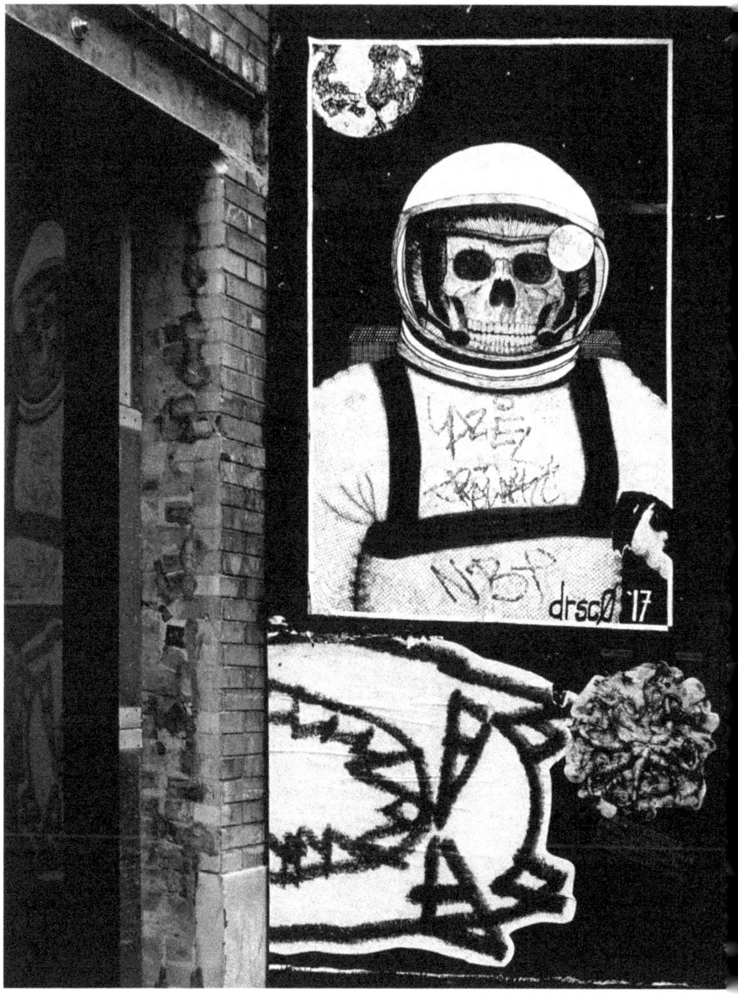

2nd Ave. between St. Mark's Place & 9th St.

Dr. Scott, Ethan Arman, AcooL55

2:16 PM

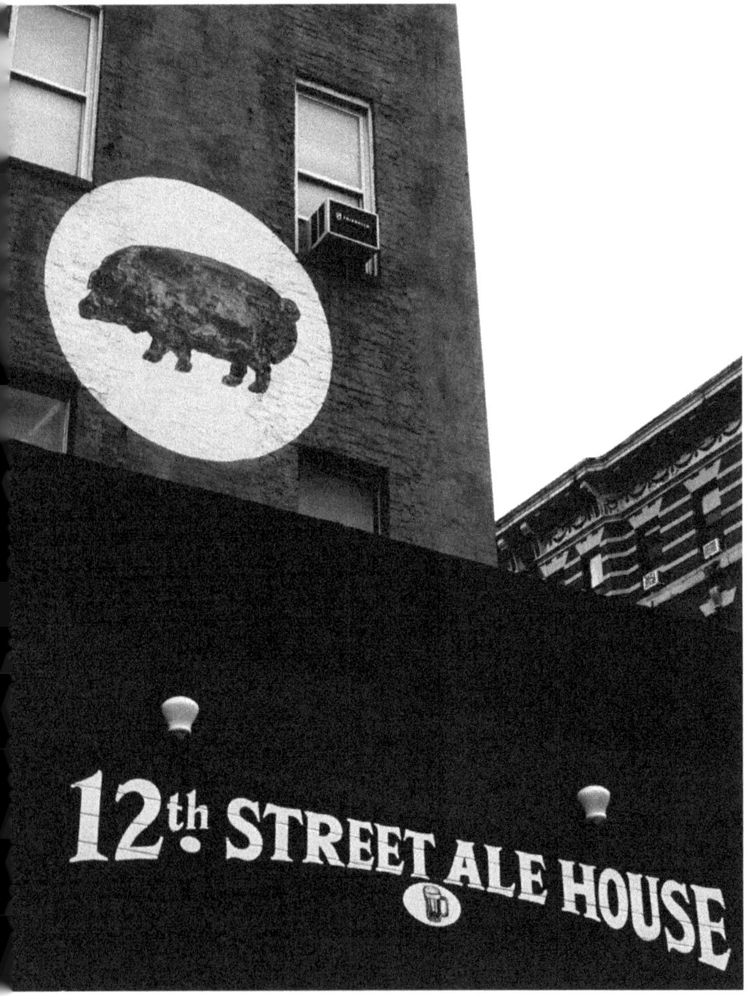

2nd Ave. between 12th & 13th St.

John S. Paul

2:24 PM

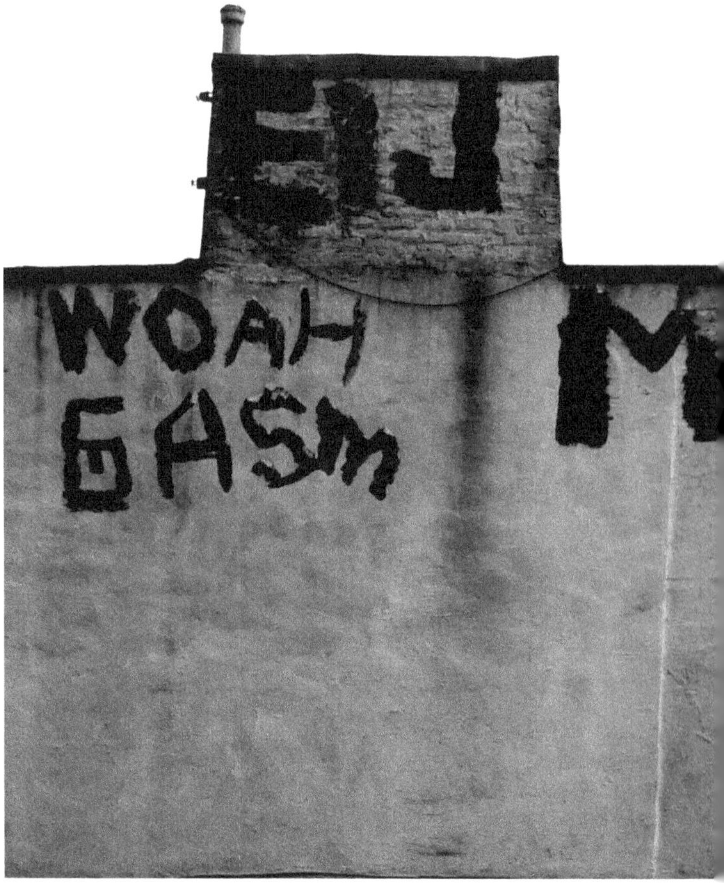

3rd Ave. between Stuyvesant St. & St. Mark's Place

Unknown

2:32 PM

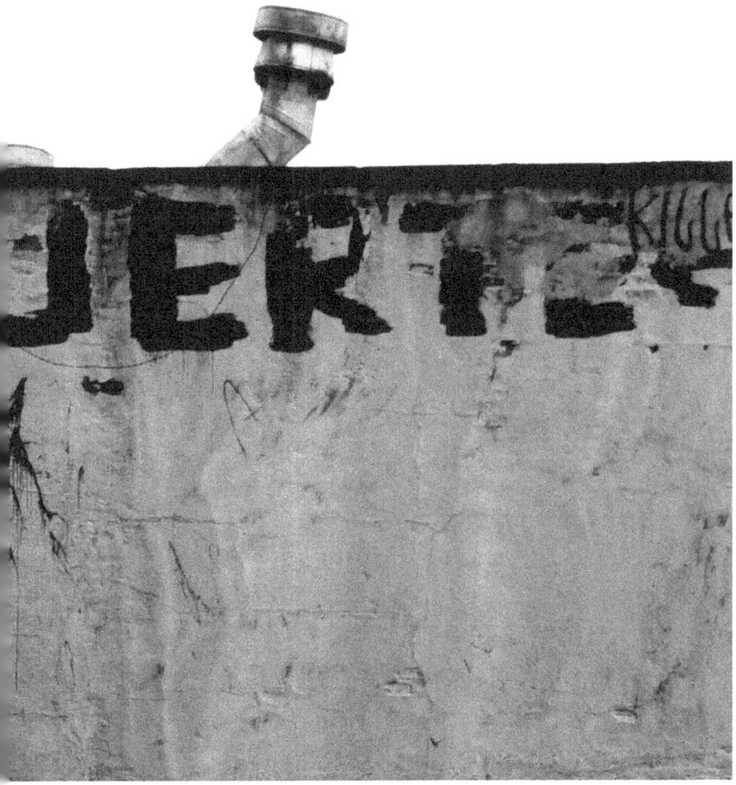

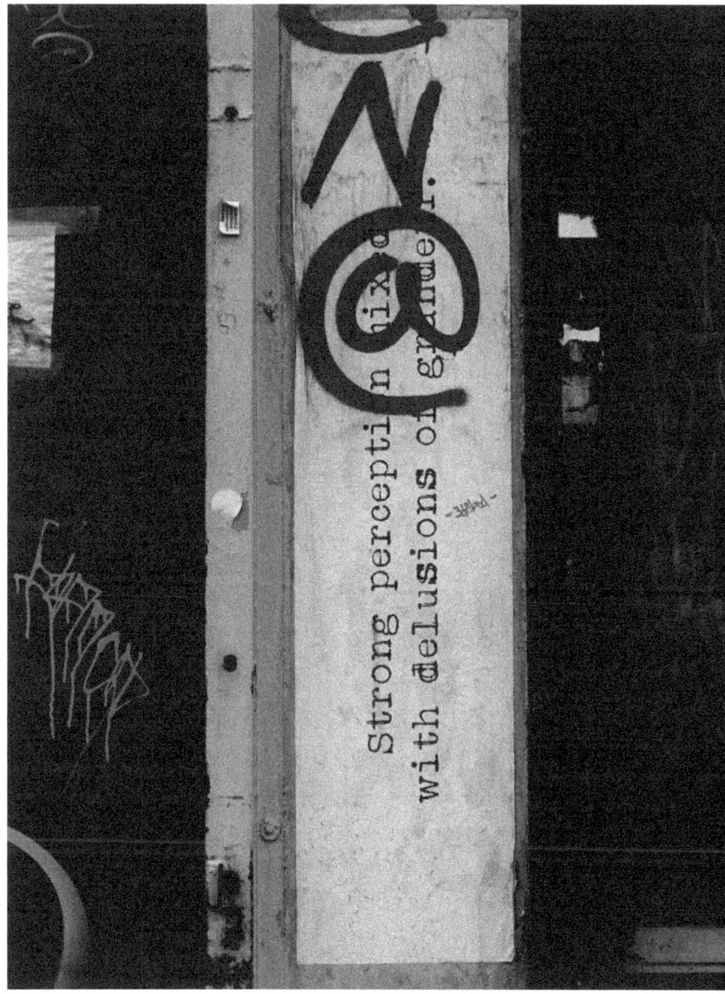

Bowery between Bond & Great Jones St.

Observerobscura

2:34 PM

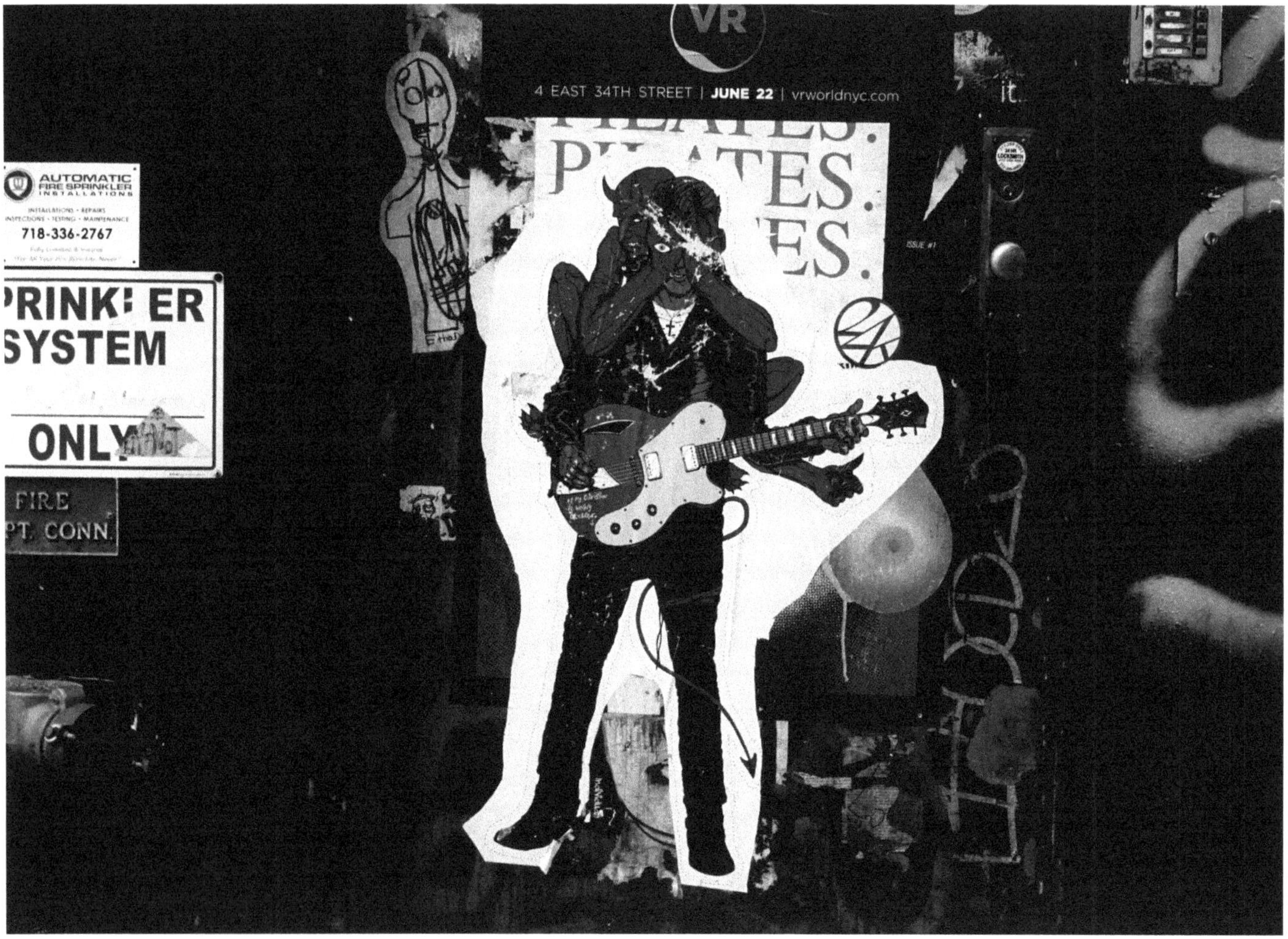

Bowery between Bond & Great Jones St.

Ethan Arman, “Boneface”

2:45 PM

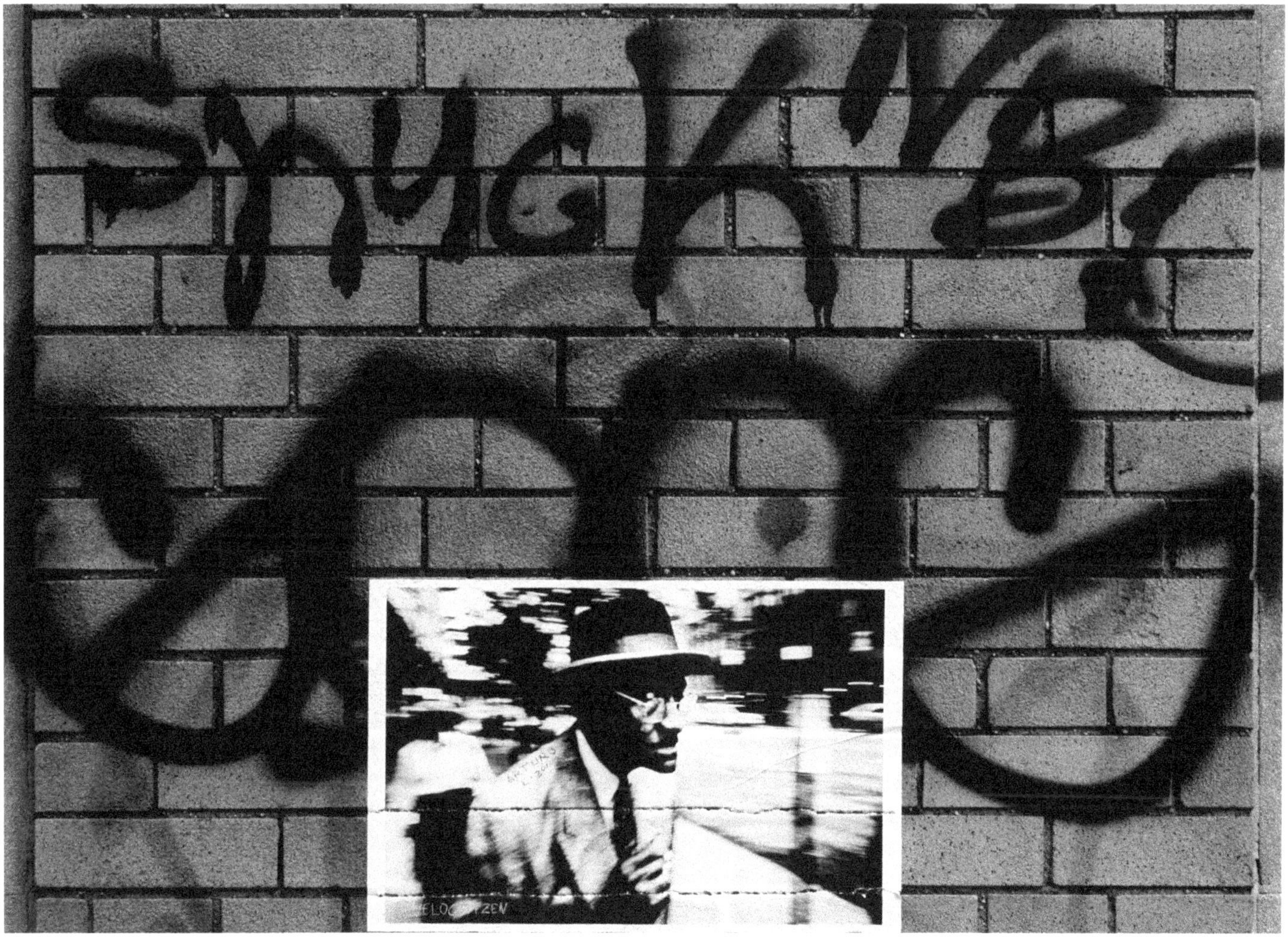

4th Ave. between 11th & 12th St.

Velocityzen

INDEX

TIME	LOCATION	ARTIST
12:00 AM	Houston St. & Bowery	Unknown
12:01 AM	Houston St. & Bowery	Unknown
12:05 AM	Houston St. & 2nd Ave.	Unknown
12:06 AM	Houston St. & 2nd Ave.	Praxis
12:07 AM	F Train Stairs @ 2nd Ave.	Dr. Scott
12:08 AM	F Train Station @ 2nd Ave.	Unknown
12:12 AM	Houston St. & 2nd Ave.	Unknown
12:23 AM	F Train Stairs @ 1st Ave.	Unknown
12:24 AM	F Train Stairs @ 1st Ave.	Unknown
12:34 AM	Houston St. between Ave. A & B	Unknown
12:46 AM	1st St. between 1st & Ave. A	JPO
12:47 AM	1st St. between 1st & Ave. A	Denton Burrows
12:48 AM	1st St. between 1st & Ave. A	Cram
12:51 AM	1st St. between 1st & Ave. A	Nicole Salgar & Chuck Berrett
12:55 AM	1st St. between 1st & 2nd Ave.	Unknown
12:56 AM	1st St. between 1st & 2nd Ave.	Hydeon
12:57 AM	1st St. between 1st & 2nd Ave.	Stickymonger
12:57 AM	1st St. between 1st & 2nd Ave.	Jenna Krypell
1:00 AM	1st St. between 1st & 2nd Ave.	Philippe Treuille
1:05 AM	1st St. between 1st & 2nd Ave.	Unlok

TIME	LOCATION	ARTIST
1:06 AM	1st St. between 1st & 2nd Ave.	Unlok, Adam Dare, Madman, Kwue Molly, Hektad
1:09 AM	1st St. between 2nd Ave. & Bowery	Hektad
1:13 AM	Extra Place	Sammy
1:16 AM	Extra Place	Unknown
1:17 AM	1st St. between 2nd Ave. & Bowery	Unknown
1:23 AM	2nd St. between 2nd Ave. & Bowery	Unknown
1:24 AM	2nd St. between 2nd Ave. & Bowery	Sam Jablon
1:29 AM	2nd St. between 1st & 2nd Ave.	Axe Colours
1:35 AM	2nd St. between 1st & 2nd Ave.	Adrian Wilson, Brandon Sines
1:38 AM	2nd St. between 1st & 2nd Ave.	Crisp
1:42 AM	2nd St. between 1st & 2nd Ave.	Himbad, Kwue Molly, Dirt Cobain
1:43 AM	2nd St. between 1st & Ave. A	Dr. Scott, "Monnica Farrel", Sacsix
1:45 AM	2nd St. between 1st & Ave. A	Unknown
1:46 AM	2nd St. between 1st & Ave. A	"Amy King"
1:48 AM	2nd St. between 1st & Ave. A	Fumero
1:49 AM	2nd St. between 1st & Ave. A	Con$umr
1:50 AM	2nd St. between 1st & Ave. A	Unknown
1:52 AM	2nd St. between Ave. A & B	Bunny M
1:59 AM	2nd St. between Ave. A & B	Coats, Michael, Mio Kunizaki, Logan, Julian, Damien Lopez, Fujii Fumiya

TIME	LOCATION	ARTIST
2:01 AM	2nd St. between Ave. A & B	Unknown
2:10 AM	2nd St. between Ave. B & C	Bradley Theodore
2:14 AM	3rd St. between Ave. C & D	Carlos Pinto
2:18 AM	3rd St. between Ave. B & C	Joe Whippler
2:21 AM	3rd St. between Ave. B & C	Linus Coraggio
2:23 AM	3rd St. between Ave. B & C	Janet Braun-Reinitz & Rochcelle Shicoff
2:29 AM	3rd St. between Ave. A & B	David Nordine
2:32 AM	3rd St. between Ave. A & B	Unknown
2:35 AM	3rd St. between 1st & Ave. A	Raemann
2:39 AM	3rd St. between 1st & 2nd Ave.	Libby Schoettle
2:40 AM	3rd St. between 1st & 2nd Ave.	Unknown
2:42 AM	3rd St. between 2nd Ave. & Bowery	Beau Stanton
2:44 AM	3rd St. between 2nd Ave. & Bowery	Alice Mizrachi
2:53 AM	4th St. between Ave. C & D	Charlie Dovest
2:56 AM	4th St. between Ave. C & D	Susan Greenstein, Marissa Perez, & 3rd grade classes of 1999-2000 at PS 15
3:03 AM	5th St. between Ave. C & D	Ema, Yeseult
3:15 AM	5th St. between 1st & 2nd Ave.	Unknown
3:20 AM	5th St. between 2nd Ave. & Bowery	Funqest
3:22 AM	5th St. between 2nd Ave. & Bowery	Urbanimal
3:29 AM	Taras Shevchenko Place	B.D. White

TIME	LOCATION	ARTIST
3:31 AM	6th St. between 2nd Ave. & Bowery	Cost
3:35 AM	6th St. between 2nd Ave. & Bowery	Paul Kostabi
3:36 AM	6th St. between 1st & 2nd Ave.	Billy the Artist
3:38 AM	6th St. between 1st & 2nd Ave.	DLove
3:39 AM	6th St. between 1st & 2nd Ave.	Unknown
3:40 AM	6th St. between 1st & 2nd Ave.	Le Fou
4:00 AM	6th St. between Ave. C & D	Unknown
4:07 AM	7th St. between Ave. B & C	Fumero
4:22 AM	7th St. between 1st & Ave. A	Anna Laurini
4:25 AM	7th St. between 1st & Ave. A	DLove
4:27 AM	7th St. between 1st & 2nd Ave.	Muckrock
4:27 AM	7th St. between 1st & 2nd Ave.	"Ilegal Mezcal"
4:29 AM	7th St. between 1st & 2nd Ave.	Cram
4:38 AM	St. Mark's Place between 3rd & 4th Ave.	The Mosaic Man
4:47 AM	St. Mark's Place between 1st & 2nd Ave.	Thomas Allen
4:49 AM	St. Mark's Place between 1st & Ave. A	Hektad
4:51 AM	St. Mark's Place between 1st & Ave. A	Daleast
4:52 AM	St. Mark's Place between 1st & Ave. A	Pixote
4:54 AM	St. Mark's Place between 1st & Ave. A	Invader
4:58 AM	St. Mark's Place between 1st & Ave. A	The Mosaic Man

TIME	LOCATION	ARTIST
4:59 AM	St. Mark's Place between 1st & Ave. A	Sir Shadow
5:06 AM	8th St. between Ave. B & C	Gary Fernandez
5:12 AM	9th St. between Ave. C & D	Jonathan Matas
5:14 AM	9th St. between Ave. B & C	Gianni Lee
5:18 AM	9th St. between Ave. B & C	Unknown
5:23 AM	9th St. between 1st & Ave. A	Stik
5:24 AM	9th St. between 1st & Ave. A	Jesse Fischler, Unlok, DLove
5:27 AM	9th St. & 1st Ave.	Kyt, Grunts, 907
5:28 AM	9th St. between 1st & 2nd Ave.	Unknown
5:30 AM	9th St. between 1st & 2nd Ave.	Homeless
5:32 AM	9th St. between 3rd & 4th Ave.	Tom Bob
5:35 AM	10th St. between 3rd & 4th Ave.	Nick Walker
8:44 AM	10th St. between Ave. A & B	Alexander Aqel
8:46 AM	10th St. between Ave. B & C	Unknown
8:55 AM	11th St. between Ave. B & C	Unknown
9:02 AM	LES Playground @ 11th St. between 1st & Ave. A	Michael K., LA2
9:04 AM	LES Playground @ 12th St. between 1st & Ave. A	Jerk Face
9:07 AM	11th St. between 1st & Ave. A	Hektad
9:09 AM	11th St. between 1st & 2nd Ave.	Shepard Fairey

TIME	LOCATION	ARTIST
9:18 AM	12th St. between 3rd & 4th Ave.	Unknown
9:19 AM	12th St. between 3rd & 4th Ave.	Sacsix
9:19 AM	12th St. between 3rd & 4th Ave.	Andrea Cook
9:31 AM	12th St. between Ave. B & C	Children's Workshop Spring 2010 Mural Club, Unknown
9:34 AM	12th St. between Ave. B & C	Chico, Funqest
9:36 AM	12th St. between Ave. B & C	Sacsix
9:39 AM	12th St. between Ave. C & D	Unknown
9:42 AM	13th St. between Ave. A & B	Charlie Doves
9:47 AM	13th St. between Ave. A & B	Chico
9:49 AM	13th St. between 1st & Ave. A	Bunny M
9:53 AM	13th St. between 1st & Ave. A	Inmmezzure
9:56 AM	13th St. between 1st & Ave. A	Unknown, Sacsix
9:57 AM	13th St. between 1st & Ave. A	Zesoner
9:59 AM	13th St. between 1st & Ave. A	Pesu
10:13 AM	14th St. between 1st & Ave. A	Unknown
10:24 AM	14th St. between Ave. B & C	Rae BK, Twazzo, Mange
11:43 AM	Ave. C between 2nd & 3rd St.	WENCOD
11:56 AM	Ave. C between 4th & 5th St.	Unknown
11:58 AM	Ave. C between 5th & 6th St.	The Yok & Sheryo
11:58 AM	Ave. C between 6th & 7th St.	Unknown

TIME	LOCATION	ARTIST
12:00 PM	Ave. C between 6th & 7th St.	Unknown
12:02 PM	Ave. C between 6th & 7th St.	John Pitman Weber
12:05 PM	La Plaza Cultural @ Ave. C & 9th St.	Zio Ziegler
12:10 PM	Ave. C between 11th & 12th St.	Xors
12:14 PM	Ave. B between 13 & 14th St.	Girl
12:17 PM	Ave. B between 11th & 12th St.	Jas
12:26 PM	Ave. B between 6th & 7th St.	Anna Laurini, Roid, Sacsix
12:27 PM	Ave. B between 4th & 5th St.	Ludo
12:31 PM	Ave. B between 2nd & 3rd St.	Chico
12:41 PM	Ave. A between 5th & 6th St.	Paul Richard
12:42 PM	Ave. A & 6th St.	Unknown
12:46 PM	Ave. A & 9th St.	Invader
12:48 PM	Ave. A between 10th & 11th St.	Andre Trenier, Trap, Fcee, Stella Isabella, Nicholai Khan
12:49 PM	Ave. A between 10th & 11th St.	David Hochbaum
12:51 PM	Ave. A between 12th & 13th St.	Unknown
12:58 PM	1st Ave. between 10th &11th St.	Funqest
1:35 PM	1st Ave. between 5th & 6th St.	Kalemkeris, Swing & Co.
1:50 PM	1st Ave. between 4th & 5th St.	Royal Kingbee
1:53 PM	1st Ave. between 1st & 2nd St.	Uncutart
1:58 PM	2nd Ave. between 1st & Houston St.	Visitor Ralph

TIME	LOCATION	ARTIST
2:01 PM	2nd Ave. between 2nd & 3rd St.	Sophie Lambda
2:08 PM	2nd Ave. between 7th St. & St. Mark's Place	Invader
2:09 PM	2nd Ave. between St. Mark's Place & 9th St.	Bianca Romero, Voxx Romana
2:11 PM	2nd Ave. between St. Mark's Place & 9th St.	Ethan Arman, Thrashbird, Libby Schoettle, Dirt Cobain, Hektad, Xors, DLove, Unknown
2:13 PM	2nd Ave. between St. Mark's Place & 9th St.	Dr. Scott, Ethan Arman, AcooL55
2:16 PM	2nd Ave. between 12th & 13th St.	John S. Paul
2:24 PM	3rd Ave. between Stuyvesant St. & St. Mark's Place	Unknown
2:32 PM	Bowery between Bond & Great Jones St.	Observerobscura
2:34 PM	Bowery between Bond & Great Jones St.	Ethan Arman, "Boneface"
2:45 PM	4th Ave. between 11th & 12th St.	Velocityzen

MoSA Books. An imprint of 12a Press.

Created by Benjamin Stein

Designed by Frank Guia

Library of Congress Control Number: 2018900511

ISBN: 978-0-692-05512-0

Contact mosa@museumofstreetart.org to purchase photography
or for wholesale book orders.

First Edition: October 2018

www.ingramcontent.com/pod-product-compliance
Ingram Content Group UK Ltd.
Pitfield, Milton Keynes, MK11 3LW, UK
UKHW062156030826
14089UKWH00028B/91

9 780692 055120